THE MAKING OF
ECONOMIC SOCIETY

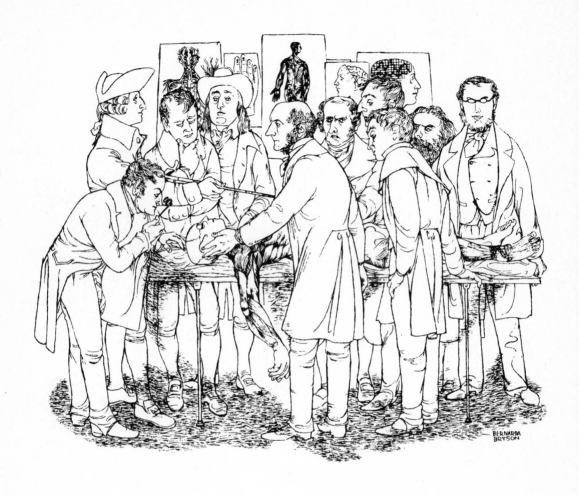

Colloquy on Economic Man

Present at the colloquy (left to right): Adam Smith, Thomas Malthus, David Ricardo, Jeremy Bentham, John Stuart Mill, François Marie Charles Fourier, Claude Henri Saint-Simon, Auguste Comte, Karl Marx, and Pierre Joseph Proudhon.

Carrying on the Anatomical Studies

Left to right: Thorstein Veblen, Joseph Schumpeter, John Maynard Keynes, and Alfred Marshall.

6th edition

THE MAKING OF ECONOMIC SOCIETY

REVISED FOR THE 1980s

Robert L. Heilbroner

PRENTICE-HALL, INC., *Englewood Cliffs, N.J. 07632*

Library of Congress Cataloging in Publication Data

HEILBRONER, ROBERT L.
   The making of economic society.

   Includes bibliographical references and index.
   1. Economic history.   I. Title.
HC51.H44 1980   330.9   79–17106
ISBN   0–13–545830–7

Editorial/production supervision
and interior design by Esther S. Koehn
Manufacturing buyer: Edmund W. Leone

*Certain parts of this text have been freely adapted
from* The Economic Problem, *5th edition, by
Robert L. Heilbroner and Lester C. Thurow*

Printed in the United States of America

10   9   8   7   6   5   4   3   2

Prentice-Hall International, Inc., *London*
Prentice-Hall of Australia Pty. Limited, *Sydney*
Prentice-Hall of Canada, Ltd., *Toronto*
Prentice-Hall of India Private Limited, *New Delhi*
Prentice-Hall of Japan, Inc., *Tokyo*
Prentice-Hall of Southeast Asia Pte. Ltd., *Singapore*
Whitehall Books Limited, *Wellington, New Zealand*

Contents

6   *The Change in Market Structure*   *112*

7   *The Great Depression*   *139*

8   *The Evolution of Guided Capitalism*   *153*

II   THE CHALLENGE TO
THE MARKET SYSTEM   *197*

THE MAKING OF
ECONOMIC SOCIETY

Introduction

No one has to tell a student who is about to tackle his first economics course in the 1980s that the subject is of vital importance. Economics is no longer a mysterious aspect of the world, confined to the back sections of newspapers and newsmagazines—the sections we used to skip because they were so dull. It has become part of the headline fare of our day. Not since the Great Depression have economic problems been so insistent, so worrisome, so much a part of our everyday conversation. Inflation, unemployment, the stock market, the high price and short supplies of oil, the worrisome food situation—all these concerns have brought economics into the center of our lives. If there was ever a time when students actually *wanted* to learn about economic problems, it is today.

Nevertheless, as I write these words, caution plucks at my sleeve. Not so many years ago, when a preceding edition of this text was being written, the opening chapter began in a very different vein—"We Americans tend to think of ourselves as members of the richest society on earth"—after which the text went on to point out some of the seamier sides of American life, to which we paid too little attention. In those opening pages there was no mention of a ravaging inflation or a fear of oncoming deep recession, a stock market collapse, or a shortage of oil. *None of the pressing issues of our time were acute only a few years ago!*

This makes me wonder if the problems that will be in the headlines a few years from now will be those that seem most important as I write these pages. Perhaps three years hence we will be worrying about the economic plight of our cities more than we will be fretting about inflation. Perhaps we will be talking about automation rather than recession as the cause of unemployment. It is possible that the stock market may be dangerously high, or that oil will be coming out of our ears. Maybe we will even be so lucky as to have economics as a whole once again relegated to the back pages of the papers, to the immense satisfaction of everyone but economics professors.

It is perhaps disconcerting for a student to be told right off that the ability of economists to forecast the emergence of new problems is very poor. Yet our experience tells us that the economic crystal ball is very clouded and that the wisest thing to expect in the economy is the unexpected. I bring up this somewhat embarrassing state of affairs not to run down my profession, but to explain what our objectives should be in taking up the subject of economics. Of course we want to learn about the critical problems of the moment, and a student should emerge from his first course with a clearer understanding of some of our present problems than before he began. But a moment's reflection on the unforeseen twists and turns of the past tells us that we want something more than information about a specific set of issues. *What we want is a general understanding of the economic system in which we live*—an understanding that will throw light across a large enough range of matters to illumine the unexpected problems we will encounter tomorrow, as well as those we face at the moment.

How can we obtain such a lantern? One way is through the study of *economic theory*—that is, by learning about the problems of the day from a very generalized and abstract point of view. Economic theory is a powerful intellectual tool, and its mastery is indispensable for anyone who aspires to become an economist. Yet I am inclined to think that theory is best reserved for—and best understood by—those who have already gained a grasp of economics that smells more of the real world than the diagrams and equations we find in a standard economics text.

Then why not plunge directly into a study of the real world, learning about the main elements of economic life—giant corporations, labor unions, government? There is much to be said for a study of economic institutions as the first step to a thorough mastery of economics, but here too, I think something is missing without which the knowledge we gain will be less useful and flexible than we want.

The missing ingredient is a familiarity with the *history* of our economic society, a sense of how our dominant institutions came into being in the first place. Only from a standpoint of history can we see our institutions, and the problems they create, as part of the ongoing process of our economic life. Only from a point of view that places our present concerns as the outgrowth of the past can we hope to gain a perspective on the problems of the future that will emerge from those of today.

Hence we are off to a study of the present that necessarily begins in the past. For the next several chapters, we will be tracing the growh of our present-day society from its distant beginnings—not merely to rediscover our past, but to see our present-day economic structure in a new, and I hope revealing, light.

Only after we have learned something about the "making" of our economic society will we turn to a consideration of the issues that trouble us so much. But by that time, I think, we will already see that the study of economics does not stop at the present, nor at our shores. Our perspective on the evolution of economic systems and the succession of problems to which economics gives rise will lead us first to place America's problems in the context of the world's economic problems, and thereafter to try to place them in the context of the sweep of history itself.

But I have said enough by way of introduction. The merit and the interest of a historical approach to our economic problems will have to prove themselves in the pages to come. I do not promise that you will be expert economists when you are done, but I hope you will want to be.

Concepts, Words, and Questions

All the following chapters end with summaries of key concepts, to help you focus on the important propositions in that chapter; key words, to add to your vocabulary; and a few questions, to make you think out for yourself some of the main points at issue. This brief introductory chapter has no need for such a section, but this short note will alert you to the summary sections that you will be encountering in the work to come.

I

THE EMERGENCE
OF MODERN
ECONOMIC SOCIETY

1 *The Economic Problem*

Now that we have decided on our course of exploration, it would be convenient if we could immediately begin to examine our economic past. But not quite yet. Before we can retrace economic history, we need to know what economic history *is*. And that, in turn, requires us to take a moment to clarify what we mean by economics and by the economic problem itself.

The answer is not a complicated one. Economics is essentially the study of a process we find in all human societies—"the" economic problem is simply *the process of providing for the material well-being of society.* In its simplest terms, economics is the study of how man earns his daily bread.

This hardly seems like a particularly exciting subject for historical scrutiny. Indeed, when we look back over the pageant of what is usually called "history," the humble matter of bread hardly strikes the eye at all. Power and glory, faith and fanaticism, ideas and ideologies are the aspects of the human chronicle that crowd the pages of history books. If the simple quest for bread is a moving force in human destiny, it is well concealed behind what one philosopher historian has called "that history of international crime and mass murder which has been advertised as the history of mankind." [1]

Yet, if mankind does not live by bread alone, it is obvious that it cannot live without bread. Like every other living thing, the human being must eat—the imperious first rule of continued existence. And this first prerequisite is less to be taken for granted than at first appears, for the human organism is not, in itself, a highly efficient mechanism for survival. From each hundred calories of food it consumes, it can deliver only about twenty calories of mechanical energy. On a decent diet, man can produce just about one horsepower-hour of work daily, and with that he must replenish his exhausted body. With what is left over, he is free to build a civilization.

As a result, in many countries, the sheer continuity of human existence is far from assured. In the vast continents of Asia and Africa, in the Near

[1] Karl Popper, *The Open Society and Its Enemies*, 3rd ed. (London: Routledge, 1957), II, 270.

East, even in some countries of South America, brute survival is the problem that stares humanity in the face. Millions of human beings have died of starvation or malnutrition in our present era, as countless hundreds of millions have died over the long past. Whole nations are acutely aware of what it means to face hunger as a condition of ordinary life; it has been said, for example, that a peasant in Bangladesh, from the day he is born to the day he dies, never knows what it is to have a full stomach. In many of the so-called underdeveloped nations, the life span of the average person is less than half of ours. Not many years ago, an Indian demographer made the chilling calculation that of one hundred Asian and one hundred American infants, more Americans would be alive at age sixty-five than Indians at age *five!* The statistics, not of life but of premature death throughout most of the world, are overwhelming and crushing.

THE INDIVIDUAL AND SOCIETY

Thus we can see that economic history must focus on the central problem of survival and on how man has solved that problem. For most Americans, this may make economics seem very remote. Few of us are conscious of anything resembling a life-or-death struggle for existence. That it might be possible for us to experience severe want, that we might ever know in our own bodies the pangs of hunger experienced by an Indian villager or a Bolivian peon is a thought nearly impossible for most of us to entertain seriously.

Short of a catastrophic war, it is highly unlikely that most of us ever will know the full meaning of the struggle for existence. Nonetheless, even in our prosperous and secure society, there remains, however unnoticed, an aspect of life's precariousness, a reminder of the underlying problem of survival. *This is our helplessness as economic individuals.*

For it is a curious fact that as we leave the most impoverished peoples of the world, where the human being with his too few calories scratches out for himself a bare subsistence, we find the economic insecurity of the individual many times multiplied. The solitary Eskimo, Bushman, Indonesian, Nigerian, left to his own devices, will survive a considerable time. Living close to the soil or to his animal prey, such an individual can sustain his own life, at least for a while, singlehandedly. With a community numbering only a few hundred, he can live indefinitely. Indeed, a considerable percentage of the human race today lives in precisely such fashion—in small, virtually self-contained peasant communities that provide for their own survival with a minimum of contact with the outside world. This large portion of mankind suffers great poverty, but it also knows a certain economic independence. If it did not, it would have been wiped out centuries ago.

When we turn to the New Yorker or the Chicagoan, on the other hand, we are struck by exactly the opposite condition, by a prevailing ease of material life coupled with an extreme *dependence* on others. We can no longer envisage the solitary individual or the small community surviving unaided in the great metropolitan areas where most Americans live, unless they loot warehouses or stores for food and necessities. The overwhelming majority of Americans have never grown food, caught game, raised meat, ground grain into flour, or even fashioned flour into bread. Faced with the challenge of clothing themselves or building their own homes, they would be hopelessly untrained and unprepared. Even to make minor repairs in the machines that surround them, they must call on other members of the community whose business it is to fix cars or repair plumbing or whatever. Paradoxically, perhaps, the richer the nation, the more apparent is this inability of its average inhabitant to survive unaided and alone.

division of labor   There is, of course, an answer to the paradox. We survive in rich nations because the tasks we cannot do ourselves are done for us by an army of others on whom we can call for help. If we cannot grow food, we can buy it; if we cannot provide for our needs ourselves, we can hire the services of someone who can. This enormous *division of labor* enhances our capacity a thousandfold, for it enables us to benefit from other men's skills as well as our own. In our next chapter it will play a central role.

Along with this invaluable gain, however, comes a certain risk. It is a sobering thought, for example, that we depend on the services of only about 100,000 men, out of a national labor force of over 100 million, to provide us with that basic commodity, coal. An even smaller number of workers are responsible for running the locomotives that haul all the nation's rail freight. A still small number—roughly 50,000—makes up our total airline pilot crew. Failure of any one of these very small groups to perform its functions would cripple us: in the case of airline pilots, slightly; in the case of locomotive engineers, badly; in the case of coal miners, perhaps disastrously. As we know, when from time to time we face a bad strike, our entire economic machine may falter because a strategic group ceases to perform its accustomed tasks.

Thus, along with the abundance of material existence as we know it goes a hidden vulnerability: Our abundance is assured only insofar as the organized cooperation of huge armies of people is to be counted upon. Indeed, our continuing existence as a rich nation hinges on the tacit precondition that the mechanism of social organization will continue to function effectively. *We are rich, not as individuals, but as members of a rich society, and our easy assumption of material sufficiency is actually only as reliable as the bonds that forge us into a social whole.*

economics and scarcity Strangely enough, then, we find that man, not nature, is the source of most of our economic problems, at least above the level of subsistence. To be sure, the economic problem itself—that is, the need to struggle for existence —derives ultimately from the *scarcity* of nature. If there were no scarcity, goods would be as free as air, and economics—at least in one sense of the word—would cease to exist as a social preoccupation.

And yet if the scarcity of nature sets the stage for the economic problem, it does not impose the only strictures against which men must struggle. For scarcity, as a felt condition, is not solely the fault of nature. If Americans today, for instance, were content to live at the level of Mexican peasants, all our material wants could be fully satisfied with but an hour or two of daily labor. We would experience little or no scarcity, and our economic problems would virtually disappear. Instead, we find in America—and indeed in all industrial societies—that as the ability to increase nature's yield has risen, so has the reach of human wants. In fact, in societies such as ours, where relative social status is importantly connected with the possession of material goods, we often find that "scarcity" as a psychological experience and good becomes more pronounced as we grow wealthier: Our desires to possess the fruits of nature race out ahead of our mounting ability to produce goods.

Thus the "wants" that nature must satisfy are by no means fixed. But, for that matter, nature's yield itself is not a constant. It varies over a wide range, depending on the social application of human energy and skill. Scarcity is therefore not attributable to nature alone but to "human nature" as well; and economics is ultimately concerned not merely with the stinginess of the physical environment, but equally with the appetite of the human being and the productive capability of the community.

the tasks of economic society Hence we must begin a systematic analysis of economics by singling out the functions that social organization must perform to bring human nature into social harness. And when we turn our attention to this fundamental problem, we can quickly see that it involves the solution of two related and yet separate elemental tasks. A society must:

1. organize a system to assure the production of enough goods and services for its own survival, and
2. arrange the distribution of the fruits of its production so that more production can take place.

These two tasks of economic continuity are, at first look, very simple. But it is a deceptive simplicity. Much of economic history is concerned with the manner in which various societies have sought to cope with these elementary problems; and what strikes us in surveying their attempts is that most of them were partial failures. (They could not have been *total* failures, or society would not have survived.) So we had better look more carefully into the two main economic tasks, to see what hidden difficulties they may conceal.

mobilizing effort

PRODUCTION AND DISTRIBUTION

What obstacles does a society encounter in organizing a system to produce the goods and services it needs?

Since nature is usually stingy, it seems that the production problem must be essentially one of applying engineering or technical skills to the resources at hand, of avoiding waste and utilizing social effort as efficaciously as possible.

This is indeed an important task for any society, and a great deal of formal economic thought, as the word itself suggests, is devoted to economizing. Yet this it not the core of the production problem. Long before a society can even concern itself about using its energies "economically," it must first marshal the energies to carry out the productive process itself. That is, *the basic problem of production is to devise social institutions that will mobilize human energy for productive purposes.*

This basic requirement is not always so easily accomplished. For example, in the United States in 1933, the energies of nearly one-quarter of our work force were somehow prevented from engaging in the production process. Although millions of unemployed men and women were eager to work, although empty factories were available for them to work in, despite the existence of pressing wants, a terrible and mystifying breakdown short-circuited the production process, with the result that an entire third of our previous annual output of goods and services simply disappeared.

We are by no means the only nation that has, on occasion, failed to find work for large numbers of willing workers. In the very poorest nations, where production is most desperately needed, we frequently find that mass unemployment is a chronic condition. The streets of many Asian cities are thronged with people who cannot find work. But this, too, is not a condition imposed by the scarcity of nature. There is, after all, an endless amount of work to be done, if only in cleaning the filthy streets or patching up the homes of the poor, building roads, or digging ditches. What is lacking is a social mechanism to mobilize human energy for production purposes. And this is the case just as much when the unemployed are only a small fraction of the work force as when they constitute a veritable army.

These examples point out to us that the production problem is not solely a physical and technical struggle with nature. On these "scarcity" aspects of the problem will depend the ease with which a nation may forge ahead and the level of well-being it can reach with a given effort. But the original mobilization of productive effort itself is a challenge to its *social organization,* and on the success or failure of that social organization will depend the volume of the human effort that can be directed to nature.

allocating effort

But putting men and women to work is only the first step in the solution of the production problem. They must not only be put to work; they must be put to work *in the right places* to produce the goods and services that society needs. Thus, *in addition to assuring a large enough quantity of social effort, the economic institutions of society must also assure a viable allocation of that social effort.*

In a nation such as India or Bolivia, where the great majority of the population is born in peasant villages and grows up to be peasant cultivators, the solution to this problem offers little to vex our understanding. The basic needs of society—food and fiber—are precisely the goods that its peasant population "naturally" produces. But in an industrial society, the proper allocation of effort becomes an enormously complicated task. People in the United States demand much more than bread and cotton. They need, for instance, such things as automobiles. Yet no one "naturally" produces an automobile. On the contrary, in order to produce one, an extraordinary spectrum of special tasks must be performed. Some people must make steel; others must make rubber. Still others must coordinate the assembly process itself. And this is but a tiny sampling of the far from "natural" tasks that must be performed if an automobile is to be produced.

As with the mobilization of its total production effort, society does not always succeed in the proper allocation of its effort. It may, for instance, turn out too many cars or too few. Of greater importance, it may devote its energies to the production of luxuries while large numbers of its people are starving. Or it may even court disaster by an inability to channel its productive effort into areas of critical importance.

Such allocative failures may affect the production problem quite as seriously as a failure to mobilize an adequate quantity of effort, for a viable society must produce not only goods, but the *right* goods. And the allocative question alerts us to a still broader conclusion. It shows us that the act of production, in and of itself, does not fully answer the requirements for survival. Having produced enough of the right goods, society must now *distribute* those goods so that the production process can go on.

distributing output

Once again, in the case of the peasant who feeds himself and his family from his own crop, this requirement of adequate distribution may seem simple enough. But when we go beyond the most primitive society, the problem is not always so readily solved. In many of the poorest nations of the East and South, urban workers have often been unable to deliver their daily horsepower-hour of work because they have not been given enough of society's output to run their human engines to capacity. Worse yet, they have often languished on the job while granaries bulged with grain and the well-to-do complained of the ineradicable laziness of the masses. At the other side of the picture, the distribution mechanism may fail because the rewards it hands out do not succeed in persuading people to perform their necessary tasks. Shortly after the Russian Revolution, some factories were organized into communes in which managers and janitors pooled their pay, and from which all drew equal allotments. The result was a rash of absenteeism among the previously better-paid workers and a threatened breakdown in industrial production. Not until the old unequal wage payments were reinstituted did production resume its former course.

As was the case with failures in the production process, distributive failures need not entail a total economic collapse. Societies can exist—and most do exist—with badly distorted productive and distributive efforts. Only rarely, as in the instances above, does maldistribution actively interfere with the actual ability of a society to staff its production posts. More frequently, an inadequate solution to the distribution problem reveals itself in social and political unrest, or even in revolution.

Yet this, too, is an aspect of the total economic problem. For if society is to insure its steady material replenishment, it must parcel out its production in a fashion that will maintain not only the capacity but the willingness to go on working. And thus again we find the focus of economic inquiry directed to the study of human institutions. For a viable economic society, we can now see, must not only overcome the stringencies of nature, but also contain and control the intransigence of human nature.

THREE SOLUTIONS TO THE ECONOMIC PROBLEM

Thus, to the economist, society presents itself in what is to us an unaccustomed aspect. Underneath the problems of poverty or pollution or inflation, he sees a process at work that he must understand before he can turn his attention to the issues of the day, no matter how pressing. That process is society's basic *mechanism for survival*, a mechanism for accomplishing the complicated tasks of production and distribution necessary for its own continuity.

But the economist sees something else as well, something that at first seems quite astonishing. Looking over the diversity of contemporary societies, and back over the sweep of all history, he sees that mankind has succeeded in solving the production and distribution problems in but three ways. That is, within the enormous diversity of the actual social institutions that guide and shape the economic process, the economist divines but three overarching *types* of systems that separately or in combination enable humankind to solve its economic challenge. These great systemic types can be called economies run by *Tradition*, economies run by *Command*, and economies run by the *Market*. Let us briefly see what is characteristic of each.

tradition   Perhaps the oldest and, until a very few years ago, by far the most generally prevalent way of solving the economic challenge has been that of tradition. It has been a mode of social organization in which both production and distribution were based on procedures devised in the distant past, rigidified by a long process of historic trial and error, and maintained by heavy sanctions of law, custom, and belief.

Societies based on tradition solve the economic problems very manageably. First, they deal with the production problem—the problem of assuring that the needful tasks will be done—by assigning the jobs of fathers to their sons. Thus, a hereditary chain assures that skills will be passed along and jobs will be staffed from generation to generation. In ancient Egypt, wrote Adam Smith, the first great economist, "every man was bound by a principle of religion to follow the occupation of his father and was supposed to commit the most horrible sacrilege if he changed it for another." [2] And it was not merely in antiquity that tradition preserved a productive orderliness within society. In our own Western culture, until the fifteenth or sixteenth century, the hereditary allocation of tasks was also the main stabilizing force within society. Although there was some movement from country to town and from occupation to occupation, birth usually determined one's role in life. One was born to the soil or to a trade; and on the soil or within the trade, one followed in the footsteps of one's forebears.

Thus, tradition has been the stabilizing and impelling force behind a great repetitive cycle of society, assuring that society's work would be done each day very much as it had been done in the past. Even today, among the less-industrialized nations of the world, tradition continues to play this immense organizing role. In India, for example, until very recently, one was born to a caste that had its own occupation. "Better thine own work is, though done with fault," preached the Bhagavad-Gita, the great philosophic moral poem of India, "than doing others' work, even excellently."

Tradition not only provides a solution to the production problem of society, but it also regulates the distribution problem. Take, for example, the Bushmen of the Kalahari Desert in South Africa, who depend for their livelihood on their hunting prowess. Elizabeth Marshall Thomas, a sensitive observer of these peoples, reports on the manner in which tradition solves the problem of distributing their kill.

[2] *The Wealth of Nations* (New York: Modern Library, 1937), p. 62.

The gemsbok has vanished. . . . Gai owned two hind legs and a front leg, Tsetchwe had meat from the back, Ukwane had the other front leg, his wife had one of the feet and the stomach, the young boys had lengths of intestine. Twikwe had received the head and Dasina the udder.

It seems very unequal when you watch Bushmen divide the kill, yet it is their system, and in the end no person eats more than any other. That day Ukwane gave Gai still another piece because Gai was his relation, Gai gave meat to Dasina because she was his wife's mother. . . . No one, of course, contested Gai's large share, because he had been the hunter and by their law that much belonged to him. No one doubted that he would share his large amount with others, and they were not wrong, of course; he did.[3]

The manner in which tradition can divide a social product may be, as the illustration shows, very subtle and ingenious. It may also be very crude and, by our standards, harsh. Tradition has often allocated to women, in nonindustrial societies, the most meager portion of the social product. But however much the end product of tradition may accord with, or depart from, our accustomed moral views, we must see that it is a workable *method* of dividing society's production.

the cost of tradition   Traditional solutions to the economic problems of production and distribution are most commonly encountered in primitive agrarian or nonindustrial societies where, in addition to serving an economic function, the unquestioning acceptance of the past provides the necessary perseverance and endurance to comfort harsh destinies. Yet even in our own society, tradition continues to play a part in solving the economic problem. It plays its smallest role in determining the distribution of our own social output, although the persistence of such traditional payments as tips to waiters, allowances to minors, or bonuses based on length of service are all vestiges of old traditional ways of distributing goods, as is the differential between men's and women's pay for equal work.

More important is the continued reliance on tradition, even in America, as a means of solving the production problem—that is, in allocating the performance of tasks. Much of the actual process of selecting in employment in our society is heavily influenced by tradition. We are all familiar with families in which sons follow their fathers into a profession or a business. On a somewhat broader scale, tradition also dissuades us from certain employments. Children of American middle-class families, for example, do not usually seek factory work, even though factory jobs may pay better than office jobs, because blue-collar employment is not in the middle-class tradition.

Thus, even in our society—clearly not a "traditional" one—custom provides an important mechanism for solving the economic problem. But

[3] *The Harmless People* (New York: Knopf, 1959), pp. 49–50.

now we must note one very important consequence of the mechanism of tradition. *Its solution to the problems of production and distribution is a static one.* A society that follows the path of tradition in its regulation of economic affairs does so at the expense of large-scale, rapid social and economic change.

Thus, the economy of a Bedouin tribe or a Burmese village is in few essential respects changed today from what it was a hundred or even a thousand years ago. The bulk of the peoples living in tradition-bound societies repeat, in the daily patterns of their economic life, much of the routine that characterized them in the distant past. Such societies may rise and fall, wax and wane, but external events—war, climate, political adventures and misadventures—are mainly responsible for their changing fortunes. Internal, self-generated economic change is but a small factor in the history of most tradition-bound states. *Tradition solves the economic problem, but it does so at the cost of economic progress.*

command A second manner of solving the problem of economic continuity also displays an ancient lineage. This is the method of imposed authority, of economic command. It is a solution based not so much on the perpetuation of a viable system by the changeless reproduction of its ways, as on the organization of a system according to the orders of an economic commander-in-chief.

Not infrequently we find this authoritarian method of economic control superimposed upon a traditional social base. Thus, the pharaohs of Egypt exerted their economic dictates above the timeless cycle of traditional agricultural practice on which the Egyptian economy was based. By their orders, the supreme rulers of Egypt brought into being the enormous economic effort that built the pyramids, the temples, the roads. Herodotus, the Greek historian, tells us how the pharaoh Cheops organized the task.

[He] ordered all Egyptians to work for himself. Some, accordingly, were appointed to draw stones from the quarries in the Arabian mountains down to the Nile, others he ordered to receive the stones when transported in vessels across the river. . . . And they worked to the number of a hundred thousand men at a time, each party during three months. The time during which the people were thus harassed by toil lasted ten years on the road which they constructed, and along which they drew the stones; a work, in my opinion, not much less than the Pyramid.[4]

The mode of authoritarian economic organization was by no means confined to ancient Egypt. We encounter it in the despotisms of medieval and classical China that produced, among other things, the colossal Great Wall, or in the slave labor by which many of the great public works of

[4] *Histories,* trans. Cary (London: 1901), Book II, p. 124.

ancient Rome were built, or, for that matter, in any slave economy, including that of the pre–Civil War United States. Of course, we find it today in the dictates of the communist economic authorities. In less drastic form we find it also in our own society; for example, in the form of taxes—that is, in the preemption of part of our income by the public authorities for public purposes.

Economic command, like tradition, offers solutions to the twin problems of production and distribution. In times of crisis, such as war or famine, it may be the only way in which a society can organize its manpower or distribute its goods effectively. Even in America, we commonly declare martial law when an area has been devastated by a great natural disaster. On such occasions we may press people into service, requisition homes, impose curbs on the use of private property such as cars, or even limit the amount of goods a family may consume.

Quite aside from its obvious utility in meeting emergencies, command has a further usefulness in solving the economic problem. Unlike tradition, the exercise of command has no inherent effect of slowing down econonmic change. Indeed, the exercise of authority is the most powerful instrument society has for *enforcing economic change*. Authority in modern China or Russia, for example, has effected radical alterations in the systems of production and distribution. But again, even in our own society, it is sometimes necessary for economic authority to intervene in the normal flow of economic life, to speed up or bring about change. The government may, for instance, utilize its tax receipts to lay down a network of roads that will bring a backwater community into the flux of active economic life. It may undertake an irrigation system that will dramatically change the economic life of a vast region. It may deliberately alter the distribution of income among social classes.

the impact of command

To be sure, economic command that is exercised within the framework of a democratic political process is very different from that exercised by a dictatorship: there is an immense social distance between a tax system controlled by Congress and outright expropriation or labor impressment by a supreme and unchallengeable ruler. Yet while the means may be much milder, the *mechanism* is the same. In both cases, command diverts economic effort toward goals chosen by a higher authority. In both cases, it interferes with the existing order of production and distribution, to create a new order ordained from "above."

This does not in itself serve to commend or condemn the exercise of command. The new order imposed by the authorities may offend or please our sense of social justice, just as it may improve or lessen the economic efficiency of society. Clearly, command can be an instrument of a democratie as well as of a totalitarian will. There is no implicit moral judgment to be passed on this second of the great mechanisms of economic control. Rather, it is important to note that no society—certainly no modern society —is without its elements of command, just as none is devoid of the influence of tradition. *If tradition is the great brake on social and economic change, economic command can be the great spur to change.* As mechanisms for assuring the successful solution to the economic problem, both serve their purposes, both have their uses and their drawbacks. Between them, tradition and command have accounted for most of the long history of man's economic efforts to cope with his environment and with himself. The fact that human society has survived is testimony to their effectiveness.

the market   But there is also a third solution to the economic problem, a third way of maintaining socially viable patterns of production and distribution. This is the *market organization of society*—an organization that, in truly remarkable fashion, allows society to insure its own provisioning with a minimum of recourse to either tradition or command.

Because we live in a market-run society, we are apt to take for granted the puzzling—indeed, almost paradoxical—nature of the market solution to the economic problem. But assume for a moment that we could act as economic advisers to a society that had not yet decided on its mode of economic organization. Suppose, for instance, that we were called on to act as consultants to one of the new nations emerging on the continent of Africa, or Asia.

We could imagine the leaders of such a nation saying, "We have always experienced a highly tradition-bound way of life. Our men hunt and cultivate the fields and perform their tasks as they are brought up to do by the force of example and the instruction of their elders. We know, too, something of what can be done by economic command. We are prepared, if necessary, to sign an edict making it compulsory for many of our men to work on community projects for our national development. Tell us, is there any other way we can organize our society so that it will function successfully—or better yet, *more* successfully?"

Suppose we answered, "Yes, there is another way. Organize your society along the lines of a market economy."

"Very well," say the leaders. "What do we then tell people to do? How do we assign them to their various tasks?"

"That's the very point," we would answer. "In a market economy, no one is assigned to any task. In fact, the main idea of a market society is that each person is allowed to decide for himself what to do."

There is consternation among the leaders. "You mean there is no assignment of some men to mining and others to cattle raising? No manner of designating some for transportation and others for weaving? You leave this to people to decide for themselves? But what happens if they do not decide correctly? What happens if no one volunteers to go into the mines, or if no one offers himself as a railway engineer?"

"You may rest assured," we tell the leaders, "none of that will happen. In a market society, all the jobs will be filled because it will be to people's advantage to fill them."

Our respondents accept this with uncertain expressions. "Now look," one of them finally says, "let us suppose that we take your advice and allow our people to do as they please. Let's talk about something specific, like cloth production. Just how do we fix the right level of cloth output in this 'market society' of yours?"

"But you don't," we reply.

"We don't! Then how do we know there will be enough cloth produced?"

"There will be," we tell him. "The market will see to that."

"Then how do we know there won't be *too much* cloth produced?" he asks triumphantly.

"Ah, but the market will see to that too!"

"But what is this market that will do these wonderful things? Who runs it?"

"Oh, nobody runs the market," we answer. "It runs itself. In fact there really isn't any such *thing* as 'the market.' It's just a word we use to describe the way people behave."

"But I thought people behaved the way they wanted to!"

"And so they do," we say. "But never fear. They will want to behave the way you want them to behave."

"I am afraid," says the chief of the delegation, "that we are wasting our time. We thought you had in mind a serious proposal. What you suggest is inconceivable. Good day, sir."

Could we seriously suggest to such an emergent nation that it entrust itself to a market solution of the economic problem? That will be a problem to which we shall return at the very end of our book. But the perplexity that the market idea would rouse in the mind of someone unacquainted with it may serve to increase our own wonderment at this most sophisticated and interesting of all economic mechanisms. How does the market system assure us that our mines will find miners, our factories workers? How does it take care of cloth production? How does it happen that in a market-run nation each person can indeed do as he wishes and, withal, fulfill needs that society as a whole presents?

economics and the market system   Economics, as we commonly conceive it and as we shall study it in much of this book, is primarily concerned with these very problems. Societies that rely primarily on tradition to solve their economic problems are of less interest to the professional economist than to the cultural anthropologist or the sociologist. Societies that solve their economic problems primarily by the exercise of command present interesting economic questions, but here the study of economics is necessarily subservient to the study of politics and the exercise of power.

It is a society that solves its economic problems by the market process that presents an aspect especially interesting to the economist. Clearly, many (although not all) of the problems we encounter in America today have to do with the workings or misworkings of the market system. And precisely *because* our contemporary problems often arise from the operations of the market, we study economics itself. Unlike the case with tradition and command, where we quickly grasp the nature of the economic mechanism of society, when we turn to a market society we are lost without a knowledge of economics. For in a market society, it is not at all clear that even the simplest problems of production and distribution will be solved by the free interplay of individuals without guidance from tradition or command; nor is it clear how and to what extent the market mechanism is to be blamed for society's ills—after all, we can find poverty and misallocation and pollution in nonmarket economies too!

In subsequent parts of this book we shall analyze these puzzling questions in more detail. But the task of our initial exploration must now be clear. As our imaginary interview with the leaders of an emergent nation has suggested, the market solution appears very strange to someone brought up in the ways of tradition or command. Hence the question arises: How did the market solution itself come into being? Was it imposed, full-blown, on our society at some earlier date? Or did it arise spontaneously and without forethought? This is the focusing question of economic history to which we now turn, as we retrace the evolution of our own market system out of the tradition- and authority-dominated societies of the past.

1	*Key Concepts and Key Words*

Provisioning wants
1. Economics is at bottom the study of how mankind assures its material sufficiency, of how societies arrange for their *material provisioning*.

Scarcity
2. Economic problems arise because the wants of most societies exceed the gifts of nature, giving rise to the general condition of *scarcity*.

3. Scarcity, in turn (whether it arises from nature's stinginess or man's appetites), imposes two severe tasks on society:

Production
   a) It must mobilize its energies for *production*—producing not only enough goods, but the right goods, and

Distribution
   b) It must resolve the problem of *distribution*, arranging a satisfactory solution to the problem of Who Gets What?

Division of labor

4. These problems exist in all societies, but they are especially difficult to solve in advanced societies in which there exists a far-reaching *division of labor*. People in wealthy societies are far more socially interdependent than people in simple societies.

5. Over the course of history, there have evolved three types of solutions to the two great economic problems. These are *Tradition, Command,* and the *Market System.*

Tradition

6. Tradition solves the problems of production and distribution by enforcing a continuity of tasks and rewards through social institutions such as the caste system. *Typically, the economic solution imposed by tradition is a static one,* in which little change occurs over long periods of time.

Command

7. Command solves the economic problem by imposing allocations of effort or reward by *governing authority*. Command can be a means for achieving rapid and far-reaching economic *change*. It can take an extreme totalitarian or a mild democratic form.

Market

8. The market system is a complex mode of organizing society in which order and efficiency emerge "spontaneously" from a seemingly uncontrolled society. We shall investigate the market system in great detail in the chapters to come.

---

1   Questions

1. If we could produce all the food we needed in our own backyards, and if technology were so advanced that we could all make anything we wanted in our basements, would an "economic problem" exist?

2. Suppose that everyone were completely versatile—able to do everyone else's work just as well as his own. Would a division of labor still be useful in society? Why?

3. Modern economic society is sometimes described as depending on "organization men" who allow their lives to be directed by the large corporations for which they work. Assuming that this description has some glimmer of truth, would you think that modern society should be described as one of Tradition, Command, or the Market?

4. In what way do your own plans for the future coincide with or depart from the occupations of your parents? Do you think that the so-called generational split is observable in all modern societies?

5. Economics is often called the science of scarcity. How can this label be applied to a society of considerable affluence such as our own?

6. What elements of Tradition and Command do you think are indispensable in a

modern industrial society? Do you think that modern society could exist without any dependence on Tradition or without any exercise of Command?

7. Much of production and distribution involves the creation or the handling of *things*. Why are production and distribution *social* problems rather than engineering or physical problems?

8. Do you consider mankind's wants to be insatiable? Does this imply that scarcity must always exist?

9. Take the main problems that disturb us in America today: neglect, poverty, inflation, pollution, racial discrimination. To what extent do you find such problems in societies run by Tradition? By Command? What is your feeling about the responsibility the market system bears for these problems in America?

2 *The Pre-market Economy*

"Nobody ever saw a dog make a fair and deliberate exchange of one bone for another with another dog," wrote Adam Smith in *The Wealth of Nations*. "Nobody ever saw one animal by its gestures and natural cries signify to another, this is mine, that yours; I am willing to give this for that." [1]

Smith was writing about "a certain propensity in human nature . . . ; the propensity to truck, barter, and exchange one thing for another." That such a propensity exists as a universal characteristic of humankind is perhaps less likely than Smith believed, but he was certainly not mistaken in putting the act of exchange at the very center of his scheme of economic life. For there can be no doubt that exchange, buying and selling, lies at the very heart of a market society such as he was describing. And so, as we now begin to study the rise of the market society, what could be more natural than to commence by tracing the pedigree of markets themselves?

It comes as something of a surprise, perhaps, to discover how very ancient is that pedigree. Communities have traded with one another at least as far back as the last Ice Age. We have evidence that the mammoth hunters of the Russian steppes obtained Mediterranean shells in trade, as did also the Cro-Magnon hunters of the central valleys of France. In fact, on the moors of Pomerania in northeastern Germany, archeologists have come across an oaken box, replete with the remains of its original leather shoulder strap, in which were a dagger, a sickle head, and a needle—all of Bronze Age manufacture. According to the conjectures of experts, this was very likely the sample kit of a prototype of the traveling salesman, an itinerant representative who collected orders for the specialized production of his community. [2]

And as we proceed from the dawn of civilization to its first organized societies, the evidences of trade and of markets increase rapidly. As Miriam Beard has written:

[1] *The Wealth of Nations* (New York: Modern Library, 1937), p. 13.
[2] *Cambridge Economic History of Europe* (Cambridge, England: Cambridge University Press, 1952), II, 4.

Millenia before Homer sang, or the wolf suckled Romulus and Remus, the bustling damkars (traders) of Uruk and Nippur . . . were buckling down to business. Atidum the merchant, in need of enlarged office facilities, was agreeing to rent a suitable location from Ribatum, Priestess of Shamash, for one and one-sixth shekels of silver per year—so much down and the rest in easy installments. Abu-wakar, the rich shipper, was delighted that his daughter had become Priestess of Shamash and could open a real estate office near the temple. Ilabras was writing to Ibi: "May Shamash and Marduk keep thee! As thou knowest, I had issued a note for a female slave. Now the time to pay is come." [3]

Thus, at first glance it seems we can discover evidences of market society deep in the past. But these disconcerting notes of modernity must be interpreted with caution. If markets, buying and selling, even highly organized trading bodies, were well-nigh ubiquitous features of ancient society, they must not be confused with the equally ubiquitous presence of a *market society*. Trade existed as an important adjunct to society from earliest times, but the fundamental impetus to production, or the basic allocation of resources among different uses, or the distribution of goods among social classes was largely divorced from the marketing process. That is, *the markets of antiquity were not the means by which those societies solved their basic economic problems*. They were subsidiary to the great processes of production and distribution rather than integral to them; they were "above" the critical economic machinery rather than within it. As we shall see, between the deceptively contemporary air of many markets of the distant past and the reality of our contemporary market economy lies an immense distance over which society would take centuries to travel.

THE ECONOMIC ORGANIZATION OF ANTIQUITY

We must ourselves traverse that distance if we are to understand how contemporary market society came into being and, indeed, if we are to understand what it is. Only by immersing ourselves in the societies of the past, only by seeing how they did, in fact, solve their economic problems, can we begin to understand clearly what is involved in the evolution of the market society that is our own environment.

Needless to say, it would make an enormous difference which of the many pre-market societies of the past we visited as general observers. To trace economic history from the monolithic temple-states of Sumer and Akkad to the "modernity" of classical Greece or Rome is to undertake a cultural journey of immense distance. Yet, traveling only as economic historians, we will find that it makes much less difference in which of the societies of antiquity we light. For as we examine these societies, we can see that, underlying their profound dissimilarities of art or political rule or religious belief, there are equally profound similarities of economic struc-

[3] *A History of the Business Man* (New York: Macmillan, 1938), p. 12.

ture, similarities we call to mind less frequently because they are in the "background" of history and rarely adorn its more exciting pages. But these identifying characteristics of economic organization are the ones that now interest us as we turn our gaze to the past. What is it that we see?

agricultural
foundation
of ancient
societies

The first and perhaps the most striking impression is the overwhelmingly agricultural aspect of all these economies.

In a sense, of course, all human communities, no matter how industrialized, live off the soil: All that differentiates, an "agricultural" society from an "industrial" one is the number of the nonagricultural population that its food growers can support. Thus, an American farmer, working a large acreage with abundant equipment, maintains more than forty nonfarmers; while an Asian peasant, tilling his tiny plot with little more than a stick-plow, is often hard pressed to sustain his own family.

Over all of antiquity, the capacity of the agricultural population to sustain a nonfarming population was very limited. Exact statistics are unavailable, but we can project backwards to the situation that prevailed in all these ancient nations by looking at the underdeveloped regions of the world today, where the levels of technique and the productivity of agriculture bear a close—too close—resemblance to antiquity. Thus in India, in Egypt, in the Philippines, Indonesia, Brazil, Colombia, Mexico, we find that it takes two farm families to support one nonfarm family; while in tropical Africa, a survey made some years ago told us that "the productivity of African agriculture is so low that it takes anywhere from two to ten people—men, women, and children—to raise enough food to supply their own needs and those of *one* additional—non-food-growing—adult."[4] Those sad findings are still largely true.

Antiquity was not *that* badly off; indeed, at times it produced impressive agricultural outputs. But neither was it remotely comparable to American farm productivity, with its enormous capacity to support a nonagricultural population. All ancient societies were basically rural economies. This did not preclude, as we shall see, a very brilliant and wealthy urban society nor a far-flung network of international trade. Yet the typical economic personage of antiquity was neither trader nor urban dweller. He was a tiller of the soil, and it was in his rural communities that the economies of antiquity were ultimately anchored.

But this must not lead us to assume that economic life was therefore comparable to that of a modern agricultural community like Denmark or New Zealand. Contemporary farmers, like businessmen, are very much bound up in the web of transactions characteristic of a market society. They sell their output on one market; they buy their supplies on another. The

[4] George H. T. Kimble, *Tropical Africa* (New York: Twentieth Century Fund, 1960), I, 572. (Italics added.)

accumulation of money, and not of wheat or corn, is the object of their efforts. Books of profit and loss regularly tell them if they are doing well or not. The latest news of agricultural technology is studied and is put into effect if it is profitable.

None of this properly describes the "farmer" of ancient Egypt, of antique Greece or Rome, or of the great Eastern civilizations. With few exceptions, the tiller of the soil was a peasant, and a peasant is a social creature very different from a farmer. He is not technologically alert but, on the contrary, clings with stubborn persistence—and often with great skill— to his well-known ways. He must, since a small error might mean starvation. He does not buy the majority of his supplies but, to a large extent, fashions them himself; similarly, he does not produce for a "market," but principally for himself. Finally, he is often not even free to consume his own crop, but typically must hand over a portion—a tenth, a third, half, or even more— to the owner of his land.

For in the general case, the peasant of antiquity did not own his land. We hear of the independent citizen-farmers of classical Greece and republican Rome, but these were exceptions to the general rule in which peasants were but tenants of a great lord. And even in Greece and Rome, the independent peasantry tended to become swallowed up as the tenantry of huge commercial estates. Pliny mentions one such enormous estate or *latifundium* (literally, "broad farm") with a quarter of a million livestock and a population of 4,117 slaves.

Hence the peasant, who was the bone and muscle of the economies of antiquity, was in himself a prime example of the nonmarket aspect of these economies. Although some cultivators freely sold a portion of their own crop in the city marketplaces, the great majority of agricultural producers scarcely entered the market at all. For many of these producers—especially when they were slaves—this was, accordingly, an almost cashless world, where a few coppers a year, carefully hoarded and spent only for emergencies, constituted the only link with a world of market transactions.*

Thus, whereas the peasant's legal and social status varied widely in different areas and eras of antiquity, in a broad view the tenor of his economic life was singularly constant. Of the web of transactions, the drive for profits of the modern farmer, he knew little or nothing. Generally poor, tax-ridden, and oppressed, prey to nature's caprices and to the exploitation of war and peace, bound to the soil by law and custom, the peasant of antiquity—like the peasant today who continues to provide the agricultural underpinnings to some countries of the East and South—was dominated by the economic rule of tradition. His main stimulus for change was command

---

* This is not, let us note, only an ancient condition. Traveling in Morocco, John Gunther reported of the local peasant-serfs, "formerly they got no wages—what would they need money for—but this is changing now." *Changing now—in 1953!* From *Inside Africa* (New York: Harper, 1955), p. 104.

—or, rather, obedience. Labor, patience, and the incredible endurance of the human being were his contributions to civilization.

economic life of the cities

The basic agricultural cast of ancient society and its typical exclusion of the peasant cultivator from an active market existence make all the more striking another common aspect of economic organization in antiquity. This is the diversity, vitality, and ebullience of the economic life of the cities.

Whether we turn to ancient Egypt, classical Greece, or Rome, we cannot help but be struck by this contrast between the relatively static countryside and the active city. In Greece, for example, a whole panoply of goods passed across the docks of the Piraeus: grain from Italy, metal from Crete and even Britain, books from Egypt, perfume from still more distant origins. Isocrates, in the *Panegyricus,* boasts: "The articles which it is difficult to get, one here, one there, from the rest of the world; all these it is easy to buy in Athens." So, too, Rome developed a thriving foreign and domestic commerce. By the time of Augustus, 6,000 loads of ox-towed barges were required to feed the city annually,[5] while in the city forum a crowd of speculators converged as on "an immense stock exchange."[6]

Thus, something that at least superficially approximated our own society was visible in many of the larger urban centers of antiquity. And yet we must not be beguiled into the conclusion that this was a market society similar to our own. In at least two respects, the differences were profound.

The first of these was the essentially restricted character and scope of the market function of the city. Unlike the modern city, which is not only a receiver of goods shipped in from the hinterlands but also an important exporter of goods and services back to the countryside, the cities of antiquity tended to assume an economically parasitic role vis-à-vis the rest of the economy. Much of the trade that entered the great urban centers of Egypt, Greece, and Rome (over and above the necessary provisioning of the city masses) was in the nature of luxury goods for its upper classes, rather than raw materials to be worked and then sent out to a goods-consuming economy. The cities were the vessels of civilization; but as centers of economic activity, they were separated by a wide gulf from the country, making the cities enclaves of economic life rather than nourishing components of integrated rural-urban economies.

slavery

Even more important was a second difference between the ancient city economies and a contemporary market society. This was their reliance on *slave labor.*

[5] *Cambridge Economic History of Europe,* II, 47.
[6] W. C. Cunningham, *An Essay on Western Civilization* (New York: 1913), p. 164.

For slavery on a massive scale was a fundamental pillar of nearly every ancient economic society. In Greece, for instance, the deceptively modern air of the Piraeus masks the fact that much of the purchasing power of the Greek merchant was provided by the labor of 20,000 slaves who labored under sickening conditions in the silver mines of Laurentium. At the height of "democratic" Athens, it is estimated that at least one-third of its population were slaves. In Rome of 30 B.C., some 1,500,000 slaves—on the latifundia, in the galleys, the mines, the "factories," the shops—provided a major impetus in keeping the economic machinery in motion.[7] Seneca even tells us that a proposal that they wear special dress was voted down lest, recognizing their own number, they might know their strength.

Slaves were not, of course, the only source of labor. Groups of free artisans and workmen, often banded together in *collegia* or fraternal bodies, also serviced the Roman city, as did similar free workmen in Greece and elsewhere. In many cities, especially latter-day Rome, a mass of unemployed (but not enslaved) laborers provided a source of casual work. Yet, without the motive power of the slave, it is doubtful if the brilliant city economies of the past could have been sustained. And this brings us to the central point. It is that the flourishing market economy of the city rested atop an economic structure run by tradition and command. Nothing like the free exercise and interplay of self-interest guided the basic economic effort of antiquity. If an astonishingly modern urban market structure greets our eye, we must not forget that its merchants are standing on the shoulders of innumerable peasants and slaves.

the social surplus The presence of great agglomerations of urban wealth amid a far poorer rural setting alerts us to another characteristic of ancient economic society. This is the special relationship between its wealth and its underlying economic organization.

In any society, wealth implies a *surplus* has been wrung from nature, that a social organization has not only solved its economic production problem but has achieved a margin of effort above that required for its own existence. Perhaps what first astonishes us when we regard the civilizations of the Ancient World is the size of surplus that could be got from a basically poor peasant population. The temples of the ancient Assyrian kings, the extraordinary treasures of the Aztecs, the pyramids and pleasure craft of the pharaohs of Egypt, the Acropolis of Athens, and the magnificent roads and architecture of Rome all testify to the ability of an essentially agricultural civilization to achieve a massive surplus, to pry considerable amounts of labor loose from the land, support it at whatever low level, and put it to work building for posterity.

[7] K. J. Beloch, *Die Bevölkerung der Griechisch-Römischen Welt* (Leipzig: 1886), p. 478.

But the stupendous achievements of the past testify as well to something else. The surplus productive potential that society manages to achieve (whether by technology or by adroit social organization) can be applied in many directions. It can be directed to agricultural improvements, such as irrigation ditches or dams, where it is apt to increase the bounty of the harvest still further. It can be applied to the tools and equipment of the city workman, where it is apt to raise his ability to produce. Or the surplus may be used to support a nonworking religious order, or a class of courtiers and idle nobility. If it were not for its amazing capacity to produce a surplus, the United States could never support its armed forces—anymore than the USSR could, if *its* economy did not also give rise to more output than it required for sheer self-perpetuation.

Thus, the social form taken by the accumulation of wealth reveals a great deal about any society. "To whom does the surplus accrue?" is a question that invariably sheds important light on the structure of power within that society.

wealth and power

To whom did the wealth of antiquity accrue? At first glimpse, it seems impossible to answer in a phrase. Emporers, nobles, religious orders, merchant traders—all enjoyed the wealth of antiquity at one time or another. But at second look, an interesting and significant generalization becomes possible: Most wealth did not go to those who played a strictly *economic* role. Although there are records of clever slaves in Egypt and Rome who became wealthy, and although rich merchants and bankers are visible throughout the annals of antiquity, theirs was not the primary route to wealth. Rather, *in ancient civilization, wealth was generally the reward for political, military, or religious power or status, and not for economic activity.*

There was a reason for this. Societies tend to reward most highly the activities they value most highly; and in the long and turbulent centuries of antiquity, political leadership, religious tutelage, and military prowess were unquestionably more necessary for social survival than trading expertise. In fact, in many of these societies, economic activity itself was disdained as essentially ignoble. As Aristotle wrote in his *Politics*, "in the best-governed polis . . . the citizens may not lead either the life of craftsmen or of traders, for such a life is devoid of nobility and hostile to perfection of character." It was a theme on which Cicero would later expand in his essay *De Officiis* (Book I):

The toil of a hired worker, who is paid only for his toil and not for artistic skill, is unworthy of a free man and is sordid in character. For in his case, money is the price of slavery. Sordid too is the calling of those who buy wholesale in order to sell retail, since they would gain no profits without a great deal of lying. . . . Trade on a small retail scale is sordid, but if it is on a large wholesale scale including the import of many wares from everywhere and their distribution to many people without any misrepresentation, it is not to be too greatly censured. . . .

Especially, added the great lawyer, "if those who carry on such trade finally retire to country estates, after being surfeited or at least satisfied with their gains."

Over and above the lesser social function of the merchant compared with the general, the consul, or the priest, this disdain of wealth obtained from "ignoble" economic activity reflected an economic fact of great importance: Society had not yet integrated the production of wealth with the production of goods. Wealth was still a surplus to be seized by conquest or squeezed from the underlying agricultural population; it was not yet a natural adjunct of a system of continuously increasing production in which some part of an expanding total social output might accrue to many classes of society.

And so it would be for many centuries. Until the smallest as well as the largest activities of society would receive their price tag, until purchases and sales, bids and offers would penetrate down to the lowest orders of society, the accumulation of wealth would always remain more a matter of political, military, or religious power than of economics. To sum it up: *In pre-market societies, wealth tended to follow power; not until the market society would power tend to follow wealth.*

"economics" and social justice in antiquity

Before we move on to view the economic system of antiquity in transition and evolution, we must ask one more question: What did contemporary economists think of it?

The answer we find is an interesting one: There were no contemporary "economists." Historians, philosophers, political theorists, writers on manners and morals abounded during the long span of history we here call "antiquity," but economists, as such, did not exist. The reason is not far to seek. The economists of society—that is, the mode by which society organized itself to meet the basic tasks of economic survival—was hardly such as to provoke the curiosity of a thoughtful man. There was little or no "veil" of money to pierce, little or no complexity of contractual relationship in the marketplace to unravel, little or no economic rhythm of society to interpret. As the harvest flourished, as the justice or injustice of the tax-gathering system varied, as the fortunes of war and politics changed, so went the lot of the peasant proprietor, the slave, the petty craftsman, and trader. As relative military strength rose or fell, as individual merchants fared luckily or otherwise, as the arts prospered or declined, so went the pulse of trade. As his prowess in war or politics permitted, as his chance at ransoms, local monopolies, or marriage dictated, so fared the individual acquisitor of wealth. In all of this, there was little to tax the analytic powers of economic-minded observers.

If there was a problem of economics—aside from the eternal problems of poor harvests, fortunes of war, and so on—it was inextricably mingled with the problem of social justice. As far back as the early Assyrian tablets, we have records of reformers who sought to alleviate taxes on the peasantry, and throughout the Bible—indeed, down through the Middle Ages—a strain of primitive communism, of egalitarian sharing, runs through the background of religious thought. In the Book of Leviticus, for example, there is mentioned the interesting custom of the *jubilee*, a limit of fifty years on leases, after which each landowner was to "return to each man unto his possession." * But despite the fact that religion was concerned with riches and poverty, and thus with the distributive problem of economics, the span of antiquity saw little or no systematic inquiry into the *social system* that produced riches or poverty. If riches were an affront, this was due to the personal failings of greedy men; and if social justice were to be obtained, it must be achieved by personal redistribution, by alms and charity. The idea of an "economic" study of society, as contrasted with a political or moral one, was conspicuous largely by its absence.

There was, however, one exception we should note. Aristotle, the great pupil of Plato, turned his powerful scrutiny to economic affairs, and with him the systematic study of economics, as such, truly begins. Not that Aristotle, any more than the majority of the Church fathers, was a radical social reformer. Much is summed up in his famous sentence, "From the hour of their birth, some are marked out for subjection, others for rule." [8] But the student of the history of economic thought turns first to Aristotle for questions whose treatment he can subsequently trace down through the present time: questions such as, "What is value?" "What is the basis of exchange?" "What is interest?"

We will not linger here over Aristotle's formulations of these ideas. But one point we might note, for it accords with what we have already seen of the attitude of antiquity to economic activity itself. When Aristotle examined the economic process, he differentiated it into two branches—not production and distribution, as we have done, but *use* and *gain*. More specifically, he differentiated between *oeconomia*—whence "economics,"—and *chrematistiké*, from which we have no precise derivative term. By *oeconomia*, the Greek philosopher meant the art of household management, the administration of one's patrimony, the careful husbanding of resources. *Chrematistiké*, on the other hand, implied the use of nature's resources or of human skill for acquisitive purposes; *chrematistiké* was trade for trade's sake, economic activity that had as its motive and end not use, but profit. Aristotle approved of *oeconomia* but not of *chrematistiké*, and within the

---

* That is, lands that had been forfeited in debt, etc., were to be restored to their original owners. The wrath of the later prophets such as Amos indicates that the injunction must have been observed largely in the breach.

[8] *Politics,* Book I.

scope of the essentially limited market structure of antiquity, where the city trader all too frequently exploited the country peasant, it is not hard to see why. The much more difficult problem of whether a market society, in which *everyone* strives for gain, might warrant approval or disapproval never appears in Aristotle's writings, as it never appeared in ancient history. The market society, with its genuinely perplexing questions of economic order and economic morality, had yet to come into being. Until it did, the philosophy needed to rationalize that order was understandably lacking.

ECONOMIC SOCIETY IN THE MIDDLE AGES

Our conspectus of economic organization has thus far scanned only the great civilizations of antiquity. Now we must turn in somewhat closer focus to a society far nearer in time and, what is more important, immediately precedent to ours in terms of social evolution. This is the vast expanse of history we call the Middle Ages, an expanse that stretches over and describes the Western world, from Sweden to the Mediterranean, "beginning" with the fall of Rome and "ending" with the Renaissance.

Modern scholarship emphasizes more and more the diversity that characterizes that enormous span of time and space, a diversity not alone of social appearance from century to century but of contrast from locality to locality within any given period. It is one thing to speak of "life" in the Middle Ages if one has in mind a tenth-century peasant community in Normandy where, it is estimated, the average inhabitant probably never saw more than two or three hundred persons in his lifetime or commanded a vocabulary of more than six hundred words; [9] it is another if we mean the worldly city of Florence, about which Boccaccio wrote so engagingly.

Even more relevant for our purposes is the need to think of the Middle Ages in terms of economic variety and change. The early years of feudal economic life are very different from the middle or later years, particularly insofar as general well-being is concerned. The commencement of feudalism coincided with a period of terrible retrenchment, deprivation, depopulation. During the fifth century, the population of Rome actually fell from 1,500,000 to 300,000. But by the twelfth century, towns had again expanded (after 600 years!) to the limits of their old Roman walls and even spilled out beyond; and by the beginning of the fourteenth century, a very considerable prosperity reigned in many parts of Europe.[*] Then came a series of catastrophes: a ghastly two-year famine in 1315; thereafter, in 1348, the Black Death, which carried off between one-third and two-thirds of the urban population;

[9] George G. Coulton. *Medieval Village, Manor and Monastery* (New York: Harper, Torchbooks, 1960), p. 15.

[*] There is some evidence that in England around the year 1500, real wages for common laborers achieved a level that they would not again surpass for at least three centuries. (*Economica*, November 1956, pp. 296–314.)

a century-long devastating struggle between England and France and among the petty principalities of Germany and Italy. All these misfortunes pulled down the level of economic existence to dreadful depths. Neither stasis nor smooth linear progress, but enormous and irregular secular tides mark the long history of feudalism, and they caution us against a simplistic conception of its development.

Our purpose, however, is not to trace these tides, but rather to form a generalized picture of the *economic structure* that, beneath the swings of fortune, marks the feudal era as a unique way station of Western economic history. And here we can begin by noting the all-important development that underlay the genesis of that economic structure. *This was the breakdown of large-scale political organization.*

the fall of Rome

For as Rome "fell" and as successive raids and invasions from north, east, and south tore apart the European countryside, the great administrative framework of law and order was replaced by a patchwork quilt of small-scale political entities. Even in the ninth century, when Charlemagne's Holy Roman Empire assumed such impressive dimensions on the map, beneath the veneer of a unified "state" there was, in fact, political chaos: Neither a single language, nor a coordinated central government, nor a unified system of law, coinage, or currency, nor, most important, any consciousness of "national" allegiance bound the statelets of Charlemagne's day into more than temporary cohesion.

We note this striking difference between antiquity and the Middle Ages to stress the tremendous economic consequences that came with political dissolution. As safety and security gave way to local autarky and anarchy, long voyages of commodities became extremely hazardous, and the once-vigorous life of the great cities impossible. As a common coin and a common law disappeared, merchants in Gaul could no longer do business with merchants in Italy, and the accustomed network of economic connections was severed or fell into disuse. As disease and invasion depopulated the countryside, men turned of necessity to the most defensive forms of economic organization, to forms aimed at sheer survival through self-sufficiency. A new need arose, a need to compress the viable organization of society into the smallest possible compass. For centuries, this insularity of economic life, this extreme self-reliance would be the economic hallmark of the Middle Ages.

manorial organization of society

The need for self-sufficiency brought with it a new basic unit of economic organization: the *manorial estate.*

What was such an estate like? Typically, it was a large tract of land, often including many thousands of acres, which was "owned" by a feudal lord, spiritual or temporal.* The word "owned" is properly in quotation marks, for the manor was not first and foremost a piece of economic property as such. Rather, it was a social and political entity in which the lord of the manor was not only landlord, but protector, judge, police chief, administrator. Although himself bound into a great hierarchy in which each lord was some other lord's servant (and even the pope was *servus servorum Dei*), the feudal noble was, within the confines of his own manor, quite literally "lord of the land." He was also undisputed owner and master of many of the people who lived on the land, for the serfs (or villeins) of a manor, although not slaves, were in many respects as much the property of the lord as were his (or their) houses, flocks, or crops.

At the focal point of the estate was the lord's homestead, a great manor house, usually armed against attack from marauders, walled off from the surrounding countryside, and sometimes attaining the stature of a genuine castle. In the enclosed courtyard of the manor were workshops in which cloth might be spun or woven, grapes pressed, food stored, simple ironwork or blacksmithing work performed, coarse grain ground. Extending out around the manor was a patchwork of fields, typically subdivided into acre or half-acre "strips," each with its own cycle of crops and rest. Half or more of all these belonged directly to the lord; the remainder "belonged," in various senses of that legal term, to the hierarchy of free, half-free, and unfree families who made up an estate.

The exact meaning of the word "belonged" hinged on the obligations and rights accruing to a serf, a freeman, or whatever other category one might be born into. Note, however, that even a freeman who "owned" his land could not sell it to another feudal lord. At best, his ownership meant that he could not himself be displaced from his land short of extraordinary circumstances. A lesser personage than a freeman did not even have this security. A typical serf was literally tied to "his" plot of land. He could not, without specific permission and, usually, without specific payment, leave his homestead for another, either within the domain of the manor or within that of another. With his status came, as well, a series of obligations that lay at the very core of the manorial economic organization. These consisted of the necessity to perform labor for the lord—to till his fields, to work in his shops, to provide him with a portion of one's own crop. From manor to manor, and from age to age, the labor dues varied: In some localities they amounted to as much as four or even five days of labor a week, which meant that only by the labor of a serf's wife or children could his own fields be maintained. And finally, the serfs owed small money-payments: head taxes, like the *chevage;* death duties, like the *heriot; merchet,* a marriage fee; or dues to use the lord's mill or his ovens.

---

* That is, the lord might be the abbot or the bishop of the locality, or he might be a secular personage, a baron who came into his possessions by inheritance or by being made a knight and given lands for exceptional service in battle or for other reasons.

There was, however, an extremely important *quid pro quo* for all this. If the serf gave the lord his labor and much of the fruits of his toil, in exchange the lord provided some things that the serf alone could not have obtained.

providing
security

The most important of these was a degree of physical security. It is difficult for us to reconstruct the violent tenor of much of feudal life, but one investigator has provided a statistic that may serve to make the point. Among the sons of English dukes, 46 percent of those born between 1330 and 1479 died violent deaths. Their life expectancy when violent death was excluded was thirty-one years; when violent death was included, it was but twenty-four years.[10] The peasant, although not a warrior and therefore not occupationally exposed to the dangers of continual combat, assassination, and so on, was preeminently fair prey for the marauding lord, defenseless against capture, unable to protect his poor possessions against destruction. Hence we can begin to understand why even free men became serfs by "commending" themselves to a lord who, in exchange for their economic, social, and political subservience, offered them in return the invaluable cloak of his military protection.

In addition, the lord offered a certain element of *economic* security. In times of famine, it was the lord who fed his serfs from the reserves in his own manorial storehouses. And, although he had to pay for it, the serf was *entitled* to use the lord's own beasts and equipment in cultivating his own strips as well as those of the lord himself. In an age when the average serf possessed almost no tools himself, this was an essential boon.[11]

These facts should not incline us to an idyllic picture of feudal life. The relation between lord and serf was often and even usually exploitative in the extreme. Yet we must see that it was also mutually supportive. Each provided for the other services essential for existence in a world where overall political organization and stability had virtually disappeared.

[10] T. H. Hollingsworth, "A Demographic Study of the British Ducal Families," *Population Studies*, XI (1957–58). I am indebted to Goran Ohlin for this reference.

[11] For a picture of life among the various classes in medieval Europe, one might turn to Eileen Power's *Medieval People* (Garden City, N.Y.: Doubleday, Anchor Books, 1954), a scholarly but charming account of the reality of human existence that lies behind history. For a sense of the violent tenor of the times, see J. Huizinga, *The Waning of the Middle Ages* (Garden City, N.Y.: Doubleday, Anchor Books, 1954), Chap. I. Let me call attention also to two other books that convey a vivid sense of feudal economic life. One is by H. S. Bennett, *Life on the English Manor* (Cambridge: Cambridge University Press, 1965); the other, by Marc Bloch, *French Rural History* (Berkeley: University of California Press, 1966). *French Rural History*, especially, is one of the real masterworks of economic history. Less concerned with economic life (one has to read between the lines to ferret it out), but marvelous as a microhistory of medieval life, is the account of a tiny, heresy-ridden town in 14th century southern France, *Montaillou, The Land of Promised Error*, by Emmanuel Le Roy Ladurie (New York: George Braziller, 1978).

economics of manorial life Despite the extreme self-sufficiency of manorial life, there is much here that resembles the economic organization of antiquity.

To begin with, like those earlier societies, this was clearly a form of economic society organized by tradition. Indeed, the hand of custom—the famous "ancient customs" of the medieval manor court, which served frequently as the counsel for the otherwise undefended serf—was never stronger. Lacking strong, unified central government, even the exercise of command was relatively weak. As a result, the pace of economic change, of economic development, although by no means lacking, was extremely slow during the early years of the medieval period.

Second, even more than with antiquity, this was a form of society that was characterized by a striking absence of money transactions. Unlike the latifundium of Rome, which sold its output to the city, the manor supplied only itself, and perhaps a local town. No manorial estate was ever quite so self-sufficient that it could dispense with monetary links with the outside world; even serfs bought a few commodities and sold a few eggs; and the lord, on occasion, had to buy considerable supplies he could not produce for himself. But on the whole, very little money changed hands. As Henri Pirenne, an authority on medieval economic history, has put it:

> . . . the tenants paid their obligations to their lord in kind. Every serf . . . owed a fixed number of days of labour and a fixed quantity of natural products or of goods manufactured by himself, corn, eggs, geese, chickens, lambs, pigs, and hempen, linen or woollen cloth. It is true that a few pence had also to be paid, but they formed such a small proportion of the whole that they cannot prevent the conclusion that the economy of the domain was a natural economy . . . since it did not engage in commerce it had no need to make use of money. . . .[12]

town and fair It would, however, be a misrepresentation of medieval life to conclude that cash and cash transactions and the bargaining of a market society were wholly foreign to it. Rather, as was the case with antiquity, we must think of medieval economic society as consisting of a huge, static, virtually moneyless foundation of agricultural production atop which flourished a considerable variety of more dynamic activities.

For one thing, in addition to manors, there also existed the shrunken descendants of Roman towns (and as we shall later see, the nuclei of new towns) and these small cities obviously required a network of markets to serve them. Every town had its stalls to which peasants brought some portion of their crop for sale. More important, towns were clearly a different social unit from manors, and the laws and customs of the manors did not apply to their problems. Even when towns fell under manorial protection, townspeople little by little won for themselves freedom from feudal obliga-

[12] *Economic and Social History of Medieval Europe* (New York: Harcourt, Harvest Books, 1956), p. 105.

tions of labor and, more important, from feudal obligations of law.* In contrast to the "ancient customs" of the manor, a new, evolving "law of merchants" regulated much of the commercial activity within the town walls.

Another locus of active economic life was the fair. The fair was a kind of traveling market, established in fixed localities for fixed dates, in which merchants from all over Europe conducted a genuine international exchange. Held usually but once a year, the great fairs were tremendous occasions, a mixture of social holiday, religious festival, and a time of intense economic activity. At some fairs, like those at Champagne in France or Stourbridge in England, a wide variety of merchandise was brought for sale: silks from the Levant, books and parchments, horses, drugs, spices. Anyone who has ever been to the Flea Market, the famous open-air bazaar outside Paris, or to a country fair in New England or the Middle West has savored something of the atmosphere of such a market. One can imagine the excitement that fairs must have engendered in the still air of medieval life.

guilds   And finally, within the towns themselves, we find the tiny but highly important centers of medieval "industrial" production. For even at its grandest, the manor could not support every craft needed for its maintenance, much less its extension. The services or products of glaziers and masons, expert armorers and metalworkers, fine weavers and dyers had to be bought when they were needed, and typically they were to be found in the medieval institutions as characteristic of town life as the manors themselves were of life in the country.

These institutions were the *guilds*—trade, professional, and craft organizations of Roman origin. Such organizations were the "business units" of the Middle Ages; in fact, one could not usually set oneself up in "business" unless one belonged to a guild. Thus, the guilds were a kind of exclusive union, but not a union of workers so much as of managers. The dominant figures in the guild were the guildmasters—independent manufacturers, working in their own houses and banding together to elect their own guild government, which then laid down the rules concerning the internal conduct of affairs. Under the master guildsmen were their few journeymen (from the French *journée,* or "day"), who were paid by the day, and their half-dozen or so apprentices, ten to twelve years old, who were bound to them for periods of three to twelve years as their legal wards. In time, an apprentice could become a journeyman and then, at least in medieval ro-

---

* Hence the saying, "City air makes men free"; for the serf who escaped to a city and remained there a year and a day was usually considered to have passed from the jurisdiction of his lord to that of the city burghers.

mance, graduate to the status of a full-fledged guildmaster on completion of his "masterpiece."

Any survey of medieval town life delights in the color of guild organization: the broiders and glovers, the hatters and scriveners, the ship-
wrights and upholsterers, each with its guild hall, its distinctive livery, and
its elaborate set of rules. But if life in the guilds and at the fairs provides a
sharp contrast with the stodgy life on the manor, we must not be misled by
surface resemblances into thinking that it represented a foretaste of modern
life in medieval dress. It is a long distance from the guild to the modern
business firm, and it is well to fix in mind some of the differences.

functions of
the guild
In the first place, the guild was much more than just an institution for
organizing production. While most of its regulations concerned wages and
conditions of work and specifications of output, they also dwelt at length on
"noneconomic" matters: on the charitable contributions expected from each
member, on his civic role, on his appropriate dress, and even on his daily
deportment. Guilds were the regulators not only of production but of social
conduct: When one member of the mercer's guild in London "broke the
hed" of another in an argument over some merchandise, both were fined
£10 and bonded for £200 not to repeat the disgrace. In another guild,
members who engaged in a brawl were fined a barrel of beer, to be drunk
by the rest of the guild.

But between guild and modern business firm there is a much more
profound gulf than this pervasive paternalism. *Unlike a modern firm, the*
purpose of a guild was not first and foremost to make money. Rather, it was
to preserve a certain orderly way of life—a way that envisaged a decent
income for its master craftsmen but that was certainly not intended to allow
any of them to become a "big" businessman or a monopolist. On the contrary, guilds were specifically designed to ward off any such outcome of an
uninhibited struggle among their members. The terms of service, the wages,
the route of advancement of apprentices and journeymen were all fixed by
custom. So, too, were the terms of sale: A guild member who cornered the
supply of an item was guilty of *forestalling*, for which rigorous penalties
were invoked, and one who bought wholesale to sell at retail was similarly
punished for the faults of *engrossing* or *regrating*. Thus, competition was
strictly limited and profits were held to prescribed levels. Advertising was
forbidden, and even technical progress in advance of one's fellow guildmen
was considered disloyal.

In the great cloth guilds of Florence in the fourteenth century, for
instance, no merchant was permitted to tempt a buyer into his shop or to
call out to a customer standing in another's doorway, nor even to process
his cloth in a manner different from that of his brethren. Standards of cloth

production and processing were subject to the minutest scrutiny. If a scarlet dye, for instance, were found to be adulterated, the perpetrator was condemned to a crushing fine and, failing payment, to loss of his right hand.[13]

Surely the guilds represent a more "modern" aspect of feudal life than the manor, but the whole temper of guild life was still far removed from the goals and ideals of modern business enterprise. There was no free play of price, no free competition, no restless probing for advantage. Existing on the margin of a relatively moneyless society, the guilds perforce sought to take the risks out of their slender enterprises. Their aim was not increase, but preservation, stability, orderliness. As such, they were as drenched in the medieval atmosphere as the manors.

medieval economics   Beyond even these differences, we must note a still deeper chasm between medieval economic society and that of a market economy. This is the gulf between a society in which economic activity is still inextricably mixed with social and religious activity, and one in which economic life has, so to speak, emerged into a special category of its own. In our next chapter we shall be talking about the ways in which a market society creates a special sphere of economic existence. But as we complete our introduction to medieval economic society, the main point to which we should pay heed is that no such special sphere then existed. *In medieval society, economics was a subordinate and not a dominant aspect of life.*

And what was dominant? The answer is, of course, that in economic matters as in so many other facets of medieval life, the guiding ideal was religious. It was the Church, the great pillar of stability in an age of disorder, that constituted the ultimate authority on economics, as on most other matters.

But the economics of medieval Catholicism was concerned not with the credits and debits of successful business operation so much as with the credits and debits of the souls of business operators. As R. H. Tawney, one of the great students of the problem, has written:

. . . the specific contributions of medieval writers to the technique of economic theory were less significant than their premises. Their fundamental assumptions, both of which were to leave a deep imprint on social thought of the sixteenth and seventeenth centuries, were two: that economic interests are subordinate to the real business of life, which is salvation; and that economic conduct is one aspect of personal conduct, upon which, as on other parts of it, the rules of morality are binding. Material riches are necessary . . . since without them men cannot support themselves and help one another. . . . But economic motives are suspect. Because they are powerful appetites men fear them, but they are not mean

[13] G. Renard, *Histoire du Travail à Florence* (Paris: 1913), pp. 190ff.

enough to applaud them. Like other strong passions, what they need, it is thought, is not a clear field, but repression. . . .[14]

Thus, what we find throughout medieval religious thought is a pervasive uneasiness with the practices of economic society. Essentially, the Church's attitude toward trade was wary and nicely summed up in the saying, *"Homo mercator vix aut numquam Deo placere potest"*—the merchant can scarcely or never be pleasing to God.

***the just
price***
We find such a suspicion of business motives in the Church's concern with the idea of a "just price." What was a just price? It was selling a thing for what it was worth, and no more. "It is wholly sinful," wrote Thomas Aquinas, "to practise fraud for the express purpose of selling a thing for more than its just price, inasmuch as a man deceives his neighbor to his loss." [15]

But what *was* a thing "worth"? Presumably, what it cost to acquire it or make it. Suppose, however, that a seller had himself paid too much for an article—then what was a "just price" at which he might resell it? Or suppose a man paid too little—was he then in danger of spiritual loss, offsetting his material gain?

These were the questions over which the medieval "economist-theologians" mulled, and they testify to the mixture of economics and ethics characteristic of the age. But they were not merely theoretical questions. We have records of the dismay that economic theology brought to actual participants in the economic process. One St. Gerald of Aurillac in the tenth century, having bought an ecclesiastical garment in Rome for an unusually low price, learned from some itinerant merchants that he had picked up a "bargain"; instead of rejoicing, he hastened to send to the seller an additional sum, lest he fall into the sin of avarice.[16]

St. Gerald's attitude was no doubt exceptional. Yet if the injunction to charge fair prices did not succeed in staying men's appetites for gain, it did stay their unbridled enthusiasm. Men in ordinary business frequently stopped to assess the condition of their moral balance sheets. Whole towns would, on occasion, repent of usury and pay a heavy amend, or merchants like Gandoufle le Grand would, on their deathbeds, order restitution made to those from whom interest had been extracted. Men of affairs in the twelfth and thirteenth centuries occasionally inserted codicils in their wills urging their sons not to follow their footsteps into the snares of trade, or

[14] *Religion and the Rise of Capitalism* (New York: Harcourt, 1947), p. 31.

[15] A. E. Monroe, ed., "Summa Theologica," in *Early Economic Thought* (Cambridge, Mass.: Harvard University Press, 1924), p. 54.

[16] Pirenne, *Economic and Social History of Medieval Europe,* p. 27.

they would seek to make restitution for their commercial sins by charitable contributions. One medieval merchant of London founded a divinity scholarship with £14, "forasmoche as I fynde myn conscience aggrugged that I have deceived in this life divers persons to that amount." [17]

the
disrepute
of gain

Thus, the theological cast of suspicion injected a wholly new note into the moneymaking process. For the first time, it associated the making of money with *guilt*. Unlike the acquisitor of antiquity who unashamedly reveled in his treasures, the medieval profiteer counted his gains in the knowledge that he might be imperiling his soul.

Nowhere was this disapproval of moneymaking more evident than in the Church's horror of usury—lending money at interest. Moneylending had, since Aristotle's day, been regarded as an essentially parasitic activity, an attempt to make a "barren" commodity, money, yield a return. But what had always been a vaguely disreputable and unpopular activity became, under Church scrutiny, a deeply evil one. Usury was decreed to be a *mortal* sin. At the Councils of Lyons and Vienne in the thirteenth and fourteenth centuries, the usurer was declared a pariah of society, to whom no one, under pain of excommunication, might rent a house; whose confession might not be heard; whose body might not have Christian burial; whose very will was invalid. Anyone even defending usury was to be suspected of heresy.

These powerful churchly sentiments were not produced merely by theological scruples. On the contrary, many of the Church's injunctions against both usury and profiteering arose from the most secular of realities. Famine, the endemic scourge of the Middle Ages, brought with it the most heartless economic gouging; loans commanded 40 to 60 percent—for bread. Much of the dislike of profit seeking and interest taking rose from its identification with just such ruthless practices, with which medieval times abounded.

Finally, another, perhaps even more fundamental, reason underlay the disrepute of gain and profit. This was the essentially static organization of economic life itself. Let us not forget that that life was basically agricultural and that agriculture, with its infinite complexity of peasant strips, was far from efficient. To quote once more from Henri Pirenne:

. . . the whole idea of profit, and indeed the possibility of profit, was incompatible with the position occupied by the great medieval landowner. Unable to produce for sale owing to the want of a market, he had no need to tax his ingenuity in order to wring from his men and his land a surplus which would merely be an encumbrance, and as he was forced to consume his own produce, he was content

---

[17] S. L. Thrupp, *The Merchant Class in Medieval London* (Chicago: University of Chicago Press, 1948), p. 177. Also Renard, *Histoire du Travail à Florence*, pp. 220ff.

to limit it to his needs. His means of existence was assured by the traditional functioning of an organization which he did not try to improve.[18]

What was true of the country was also true of the city. The idea of an *expanding* economy, a *growing* scale of production, an *increasing* productivity was as foreign to the guildmaster or fair merchant as to the serf and lord. Medieval economic organization was conceived of as a means of reproducing, but not enhancing, the material well-being of the past. Its motto was perpetuation, not progress. There is little wonder that in such a static organization, profits and profit seeking were viewed as essentially disturbing rather than welcome economic phenomena.

PREREQUISITES OF CHANGE

We have traced the broad outlines of the economic organization of the West roughly up to the tenth or twelfth century. Once again, it is wise to emphasize the diversity of currents concealed within a landscape we have too often been forced to treat as undifferentiated. At best, our journey into antiquity and the Middle Ages can give us a few glimpses of the prevailing flavor of the times, a sense of the ruling economic climate, of the main institutions and ideas by which men organized their economic efforts.

But one thing is certain. We are very far from the temper and tempo of modern economic life. The few stirrings we have witnessed in the slow world of the manor and the town are but the harbingers of a tremendous change, which, over the course of the next centuries, would dramatically alter the basic form of economic organization itself, replacing the old ties of tradition and command with new ties of market transactions.

We shall have to wait until our next chapter to witness the actual process of change itself. But perhaps it will help us put into focus both what we have already seen and what we are about to witness if we anticipate our line of advance. We now have an idea of a pre-market society, a society in which markets exist but that does not yet depend on a market mechanism to solve the economic problem. What changes will be required to transform such a society into a true market economy?

1. *A new attitude toward economic activity will be needed.*

For such a society to function, men must be free to seek gain. The suspiciousness and unease that surrounded the ideas of profit, of change, of social mobility must give way to new ideas that would encourage those very attitudes and activities. In turn this meant, in the famous words of Sir Henry Maine, that the *society of status* must give way to the *society of contract,* that the society in which men were born to their stations in life

---

[18] *Economic and Social History of Medieval Europe,* p. 63.

must give way to a society in which they were free to define those stations for themselves.

Such an idea would have seemed to the medieval mind without any possible rationale. The idea that a general free-for-all should determine men's compensations, with neither a floor to prevent them from being ground down nor a ceiling to prevent them from rising beyond all reason, would have appeared senseless—even blasphemous. If we may listen again to R. H. Tawney:

> To found a science of society upon the assumption that the appetite for economic gain is . . . to be accepted, like other natural forces . . . would have appeared to the medieval thinker as hardly less irrational or less immoral than to make the premise of social philosophy the unrestrained operation of such necessary human attributes as pugnacity or the sexual instinct.[19]

Yet some such freeing of the quest for economic gain, some such aggressive competition in the new contractual relationship of man to man would be essential for the birth of a market society.

2. *The monetization of economic life will have to proceed to its ultimate conclusion.*

One prerequisite of a market economy should by now be clear: Such an economy must involve the process of exchange, of buying and selling, at every level of society. But for this to take place, men must have the where-withal to enter a market; that is, they must have cash. And, in turn, if society is to be permeated with cash, men must earn money for their labors. In other words, *for a market society to exist, nearly every task must have a monetary reward.*

Even in our highly monetized society, we do not pay for every service: most conspicuously not for the housekeeping services of a wife. But all through the pre-market era, the number of unpaid services—the amount of work performed by law without monetary compensation—was vastly larger than in our society. Slave labor was, of course, unpaid. So was most serf labor. Even the labor of apprentices was remunerated more in kind, in food and lodging, than in cash. Thus, probably 70 to 80 percent of the actual working population of an ancient or medieval economy labored without anything resembling full payment in money.

Clearly, in such a society the possibilities for a highly involved exchange economy were limited. But a still more important consequence must be noted. The absence of a widespread monetization of tasks meant the absence of a widespread *market for producers.* Nothing like the flow of "purchasing power" that dominates and directs our own productive efforts

---

[19] *Religion and the Rise of Capitalism*, pp. 31–32.

could be forthcoming in a society in which money incomes were the exception rather than the rule.

> **3.** *The pressures of a free play of market "demand" will have to take over the regulation of the economic tasks of society.*

All through antiquity and the Middle Ages, as we have seen, tradition or command solved the economic problem. These were the forces that regulated the distribution of social rewards. But in a market society, another means of control must rise to take their place. *An all-encompassing flow of money demand, itself stemming from the total monetization of all economic tasks, must become the great propulsive mechanism of society.* Men must go to their tasks not because they are ordered there, but because they will make money there; and producers must decide on the volume and the variety of their output not because the rules of the manor or the guild so determine, but because there is a market demand for particular things. From the top to the bottom of society, in other words, a new marketing orientation must take over the production and distribution tasks. The whole replenishment, the steady provisioning, the very progress of society must now be subject to the guiding hand of a universal demand for labor and goods.

What forces would ultimately drive the world of medieval economic organization into a world of money, of universal markets, of profit seeking? The stage is now set for us to attempt to answer this profoundly important and difficult question. Let us turn to a consideration of the causes capable of effecting so vast a change.

2	*Key Concepts and Key Words*

Markets 1. We must differentiate between markets, which have a very ancient pedigree, and market societies, which do not. *In a market society, the economic problem itself*—both production and distribution—*is solved by means of a vast exchange between buyers and sellers.* Many ancient societies had markets, but these markets did not organize the fundamental activities of these societies.

Peasant farming 2. The economic societies of antiquity had several features in common, which contrast sharply with those of modern market economies:
- They rested on an agricultural base of *peasant farming.*
- Their cities were—from an economic point of view—parasitic *centers of consumption, not active centers of production.*

Slavery • *Slavery* was a common and very important form of labor.
Surplus • They produced very considerable *surpluses.*

Wealth and power

3. As a result, in the economic societies of antiquity we find the economic side of life subservient to the political side. Priest, warrior, and statesman were superior to merchant or trader; *wealth followed power,* not—as in market societies to come—the other way around.

Feudalism

4. Medieval economic life emerged from the catastrophic disorganization that followed the decline of Roman law and order. It was characterized by a unique form of organization called the *manorial* system in which:

Lords
- *Local lords were the centers of political, military, economic, and social power.*

Serfs
- *Most peasants were bound as serfs* to a particular lord, for whom they were required to work and to whom they owed both labor and taxes or dues.
- *Physical security* against brigands or other lords was provided by the lord, as well as some economic security in times of distress.

Manorial system

5. *The manorial system,* particularly in its earlier days (sixth to tenth centuries), *was a static economic system,* in which monetary payments played only a minor role. Self-sufficiency was the main purpose and the most outstanding characteristic of the manor.

Fairs

6. Side by side with the manor existed the economic life of the *towns.* Here monetary exchange always played a more important role, as did the organization of a more active economic life in the institution of *fairs.*

Guilds

7. The *guild* was the main form of organizing production in the towns and cities. *Guilds were very different from modern-day businesses,* insofar as they discouraged competition or profit seeking and sought to impose general rules on the methods of production, rates of pay, practices of marketing, and so on.

Usury

8. All through medieval times, the Church—the main social organization of the age—was suspicious of buying and selling activity. In part this reflected a dislike of the exploitative practices of the times, in part it was a consequence of an ancient contempt for moneymaking (remember Aristotle's dislike of *chrematistiké*) and especially for moneylending (usury). The religious leaders of the day worried about "just" prices, and did not admit that unregulated buying and selling gave rise to just prices.

Market society

9. Three profound and pervasive changes would be needed to convert medieval society into a market society:
- *A new attitude toward moneymaking* as a legitimate activity would have to replace the medieval suspicion of profit seeking.

Monetization
- *The web of monetization would have to expand* beyond its narrow confines—that is, buying and selling would have to control the output of all products and the performance of nearly all tasks.
- The flux of *"demand" and "supply" would have to be allowed to take over the direction of economic activity* from the dictates of lords and the usages of custom.

1. What differences, if any, characterize the economic attitudes and behavior of the American farmer and the American businessman? Can this comparison also describe the behavior and attitude of the Egyptian peasant and the Egyptian merchant? What accounts for the difference between the two societies?

2. Julius Caesar and J. P. Morgan were both wealthy and powerful men. What is the difference in the origins of their wealth and their power? Does power still follow wealth in modern economic societies? Does wealth still follow power in nonmarket societies? If not, why not?

3. To what uses was the surplus of society put in ancient Rome? in feudal society? in modern America? in the USSR? What significance attaches to these different uses? What do they tell us about the structure of these societies?

4. What do you think of the validity of Aristotle's distinction between economic activity for *use* and for *gain?*

5. In what ways is a serf a different *economic* creature from a modern farm worker? How is a slave different from an industrial worker?

6. What changes would have to take place within a guild before it resembled a modern business?

7. The Bible has numerous hostile references to moneymaking—"it is easier for a camel to go through the eye of a needle than for a rich man to enter into the kingdom of God." How do you account for this ancient churchly antipathy toward wealth? Is religion today still suspicious of moneymaking? Why?

8. Is the idea of a "just" price (or a "just" wage) still encountered in our own society? What is usually meant by these terms? Do you think these ideas are compatible with a market system?

9. The manorial system persisted for nearly 1,000 years. Why do you think change was so slow in coming?

10. Ancient Greece and Rome were a great deal more "modern" in their temper than feudal Europe. Yet neither was remotely a modern economic system. Why not?

3

The Emergence of
the Market Society

Tradition, changelessness, order—these were the key concepts of economic society in the Middle Ages, and our preceding chapter introduced us to this unfamiliar and static way of economic life. But our purpose in this chapter is different. It is no longer to describe those factors that preserved the economic stability of medieval society, but to identify those forces that eventually burst it asunder.

Once again, we need to begin with a word of caution. Our chapter spans an immense variety of historical experience. We must beware of thinking that the forces of change that dominate this chapter were identical from region to region or from century to century, or that the transition they effected was uniform throughout the broad expanse of Europe. On the contrary, the great evolution that we will witness in these pages was not sharp and clear, but muddy and irregular. At the same time that the first evidences of a truly modern market society were beginning to manifest themselves in the medieval cities of Italy or Holland, the most archaic forms of feudal relationship still persisted in the agricultural sectors of these nations, and indeed in the city life of other nations. We must bear in mind that the historic processes of this chapter extended from the tenth to the seventeenth (and even eighteenth and nineteenth) centuries and manifested themselves in no two countries in precisely the same way.

With these cautions in mind, now let us turn to the great evolution itself. What agents were powerful enough to effect the major historic changes needed to bring about a market society?

the itinerant merchant We meet the first of these forces of change in an unexpected guise. It is a small irregular procession of armed men, jogging along one of the rudimentary roads of medieval Europe: standard-bearer with colors in the lead, then a military chief, then a group of riders carrying bows and swords, and finally a caravan of horses and mules laden with casks and bales, bags and packs.

Someone unacquainted with medieval life might easily take such a troop for part of the baggage train of a small army. But he would be mistaken. These were not soldiers but merchants, the traveling merchants whom the English of the twelfth century called "pie-powders," from *pieds poudreux*, dusty feet. No wonder they were dusty; many of them came immense distances along routes so bad that we know of one instance where only the intervention of a local ecclesiastical lord prevented the "road" from being ploughed up as arable land. In their bags and packs were goods that had somehow made a perilous journey across Europe, or even all the way from Arabia or India, to be sold from town to town, or from halt to halt, as these merchant adventurers wound their way across the medieval countryside.

And adventurers they were indeed. For in the fixed hierarchies of the great manorial estates of Europe, there was no natural place for these unlanded peddlers of goods, with their unfeudal attributes of calculation and (often very crude) bookkeeping and their natural insistence on trade in money. The traveling merchants ranked very low in society. Some of them, without doubt, were the sons of serfs, or even runaway serfs themselves. Yet since no one could prove their bondage, they had, if only by default, the gift of "freedom." It is no wonder that in the eyes of the nobility, the merchants were upstarts and a disturbing element in the normal pattern of things.

Yet no one would have dispensed with their services. To their brightly canopied stalls at the fairs flocked the lords and ladies of the manors as well as the Bodos and Ermentrudes of the fields. After all, where else could one buy pepper, or purple dye, or acquire a guaranteed splinter from the Cross? Where else could one buy the marvelous cloths woven in Tuscany or learn such esoteric words, derived from the Arabic, as "jar" or "syrup"? If the merchant was a disturbing leaven in the mix of medieval life, he was also a pinch of active ingredient without which the mixture would have been very dull indeed.

We first note the traveling merchant in Europe in the eighth and ninth centuries, and we can follow his progress until the fourteenth and fifteenth centuries. By this time, largely through the merchants' own efforts, commerce was sufficiently organized so that it no longer required these itinerant journeyers.* For what these travelers brought, together with their wares, was the first breath of commerce and commercial intercourse to a Europe that had sunk to an almost tradeless and self-sufficient manorial stagnation. Even to towns as minuscule and isolated as Forcalquier in France—a dot on

---

* Records of an order for goods placed on the occasion of a funeral of a Swedish nobleman in 1328 include saffron from Spain or Italy, caraway seed from the Mediterranean, ginger from India, cinnamon from Ceylon, pepper from Malabar, anise from southern Europe, and Rhine and Bordeaux wines. The order was placed for immediate delivery from one local merchant, despite the fact that Sweden was then a laggard and even primitive land. Cf. Fritz Rorig, *Mittelalterliche Weltwirtschaft* (Jena: 1933), p. 17. (I am again indebted to Goran Ohlin for this reference.)

the map without so much as a road to connect its few hundred souls to the outer world—these hardy traders beat their path: We know from a primitive book of accounts that in May 1331, thirty-six itinerant merchants visited Forcalquier to transact business at the home and "shop" of one Ugo Teralh, a notary.[1] And so, in a thousand isolated communities, did they slowly weave a web of economic interdependence.

urbanization   An important by-product of the rise of the itinerant merchant was the slow urbanization of medieval life, the creation of new towns and villages. When the traveling merchants stopped, they naturally chose the protected site of a local castle or burg, or of a church. And so we find growing up around the walls of advantageously situated castles—in the *foris burgis*, whence *faubourg*, the French word for "suburb"—more or less permanent trading places, which in turn became the inner core of small towns. Nestled close to the castle or cathedral wall for protection, the new burgs were still not "of" the manor. The inhabitants of the burg—the burgesses, burghers, bourgeois —had at best an anomalous and insecure relation to the manorial world within. As we have seen, there was no way of applying the time-hallowed rule of "ancient customs" in adjudicating their disputes, since there *were* no ancient customs in the commercial quarters. Neither were there clear-cut rules for their taxation or for the particular degees of fealty they owed their local masters. Worse yet, some of the growing towns began to surround themselves with walls. By the twelfth century, the commercial burg of Bruges, for example, had already swallowed up the old fortress like a pearl around a grain of sand.

Curiously, it was this very struggle for existence in the interstices of feudal society that provided much of the impetus for the development of a new social and economic order within the city. In all previous civilizations, cities had been the outposts of central government. Now for the first time, they existed as independent entities outside the main framework of social power. As a result, they were able to define for themselves—as they *had* to define for themselves—a code of law and social behavior and a set of governing institutions that were eventually to displace those of the feudal countryside.

The process was long drawn out, for the rate of growth of towns was often very slow. In the nearly two centuries between 1086 and 1279, for example, the town of Cambridge, England, added an average of but one house *per year*.[2] One important reason for this almost imperceptible rate of expansion was the difficulty of moving men or materials over the terrible roads. Not the least consequence of the decline of Roman power had been

[1] *Cambridge Economic History of Europe*, II, 325–26.
[2] George Gordon Coulton, *Medieval Panorama* (New York: World Publishing, Meridian Books, 1955), p. 285.

the decay of its once magnificent system of highways, the very stones of which were pilfered for building materials during the years of worst social disorganization. Until the roads recovered, economic movement was perforce limited and limping. And it is worth remarking that in many ports of Europe, a system of transportation as efficient as that of ancient Rome was not enjoyed until the eighteenth or even nineteenth century.

Yet if growth was slow, it was steady; and in some locales it was much faster than in Cambridge. During the 1,000 years of the Middle Ages, nearly 1,000 towns were fathered in Europe, a tremendous stimulus to the commercialization and monetization of life, for each town had its local marts, its local toll gates, often its local mint, its granaries and shops, its drinking places and inns, its air of "city life," which contrasted so sharply with that of the country. The slow, spontaneous growth of urban ways was a major factor in introducing a marketing flavor to European economic life.

the Crusades

The rise of the itinerant merchant and the town were two great factors in the slow evolution of a market society out of medieval economic life; a third factor was the Crusades.

It is an ironic turn to history that the Crusades, the supreme religious adventure of the Middle Ages, should have contributed so much toward the establishment of a society to which the Church was so vigorously opposed. If we consider the Crusades, however, not from the point of view of their religious impulse, but simply as great expeditions of exploration and colonization, their economic impact becomes much more understandable.*

The Crusades served to bring into sudden and startling contact two very different worlds. One was the still slumbering society of European feudalism with all its rural inertia, its aversion to trade, and its naïve conceptions of business; the other was the brilliant society of Byzantium and Venice, with its urban vitality, its unabashed enjoyment of moneymaking, and its sophisticated business ways. The crusaders, coming from their draughty castles and boring manorial routines, thought they would find in the East only untutored heathen savages. They were astonished to be met by a people far more civilized, infinitely more luxurious, and much more money-oriented than they.

One result was that the simple-minded crusaders found themselves the pawns of commercial interests that they little understood. During the first three Crusades, the Venetians, who provided ships, gulled them as shamelessly as country bumpkins at a fair. The fact that they were fleeced, however, did not prevent the crusaders from reaching the Holy Land, albeit with inconclusive results. But in the notorious Fourth Crusade (1202–1204),

---

* We might note here some of the complex interaction of the process we are watching. For the Crusades were not only a cause of European economic development, but also a *symptom* of the development that had previously taken place.

Dandolo, the wily 94-year-old doge of Venice, managed to subvert the entire religious expedition into a gigantic plundering operation for Venetian profit.

First Dandolo held up the voyagers for an initial transportation price of 85,000 silver marks, an enormous sum for the unmoneyed nobility to scrape up. Then, when the funds had been found, he refused to carry out his bargain until the crusaders agreed first to attack the town of Zara, a rich commercial rival of Venice. Since Zara was a *Christian*, not an "infidel" community, Pope Innocent III was horrified and suggested that the attack be directed instead against heathen Egypt. But Egypt was one of Venice's best customers, and this horrified Dandolo even more. The crusaders, stranded and trapped, had no choice: Zara soon fell—after which, at Dandolo's urging, Christian Constantinople was also sacked. The "heathen" Orient was never reached at all, but Venice profited marvelously.

It was not only Venice that gained, however. The economic impact on the crusaders themselves was much more formidable than the religious. On many this impact was disastrous, as knights who had melted down their silver plate to join the Crusades came back penniless to their ruined manor houses. To others, however, the Crusades brought a new economic impetus. When in 1101, for example, the Genoese raided Caesarea, a Palestinian seaport, 8,000 soldiers and sailors reaped a reward of some forty-eight *solidi* each, plus two pounds of pepper—and thus were 8,000 petty capitalists born.[3] And in 1204 when Constantinople fell, not only did each knight receive twenty marks in silver as his share of the booty, but even the squires and archers were rewarded with a few marks each.

Thus, the Crusades provided an immense fertilizing experience for Europe. The old, landed basis of wealth came into contact with a new moneyed basis that proved much more powerful. Indeed, the old conception of life itself was forcibly revised before a glimpse of an existence not only wealthier, but gayer and more vital. As a means of shaking a sluggish society out of its rut, the Crusades played an immense role in speeding along the economic transformation of Europe.

growth of national power   Yet another factor in the slow commercialization of economic life was the gradual amalgamation of Europe's fragmented economic and political entities into larger wholes. As the disintegration of economic life following the breakup of the old Roman Empire had shown, a strong economic society requires a strong and broad political base. Hence, as political Europe began its slow process of reknitting, once again its economic tempo began to rise.

One of the most striking characteristics of the Middle Ages, and one of its most crippling obstacles to economic development, was the medieval

[3] *Cambridge Economic History of Europe,* II, 306.

crazy quilt of compartmented, isolated areas of government. Over a journey of a hundred miles, a traveling merchant might fall under a dozen different sovereignties, each with different rules, regulations, laws, weights, measures, money. Worse yet, at each border there was apt to be a toll station. At the turn of the thirteenth and fourteenth centuries, there were said to be more than thirty toll stations along the Weser River and at least thirty-five along the Elbe; along the Rhine, a century later, there were more than sixty such toll stations, mostly belonging to local ecclesiastical princes. Thomas Wykes, an English chronicler, described the system as "the raving madness of the Teutons." But it was not only a German disease. There were so many toll stations along the Seine in France in the late fifteenth century that it cost half its final selling price to ship grain 200 miles down the river.[4] Indeed, among the European nations, England alone enjoyed an internally unified market during the middle and late Middle Ages. This was one powerful contributory factor to England's emergence as the first great European economic power.

The amalgamation of Europe's fragmented markets was essentially a political as well as an economic process; it followed the gradual centralization of power that changed the map of Europe from the infinite complexity of the tenth century to the more or less "modern" map of the sixteenth. Here, once again, the burgeoning towns played a central and crucial role. It was the city burghers who became the allies of the nascent monarchies, thereby disassociating themselves still further from their local feudal lords while, in turn, supplying the shaky monarchs with an absolutely essential prerequisite for kingship: cash.

Thus, monarch and bourgeois combined to bring about the slow growth of centralized governments, and from centralized government, in turn, came not alone a unification of law and money but a direct stimulus to the development of commerce and industry as well. In France, for example, manufacturing was promoted by royal patronage of the famous Gobelin tapestry and Sèvres porcelain works, and business was created for innumerable craftsmen and artesans by the demands of the royal palaces and banquet halls. In other fields, growing national power also imparted a new encouragement: Navies had to be built, armies had to be equipped, and these new "national" armed forces, many of whom were mercenaries, had to be paid. All this set into faster motion the pumps of monetary circulation.

exploration   Another economic impetus given by the gradual consolidation of political power was the official encouragement of exploration. All through the long years of the Middle Ages, a few intrepid adventurers, like Marco Polo, had

---

[4] *Cambridge Economic History of Europe*, II, pp. 134–35.

beat their way to remote regions in search of a short route to the fabled riches of India; and as a matter of fact, by the early fourteenth century, the route to the Far East was well enough known so that silk from China cost but half the price of that from the Caspian area, only half the distance away.

Yet the network of all these hazardous and brave penetrations beyond Europe formed only the thinnest of spider webs. There still remained the systematic exploration of the unknown, and this awaited the kingly support of state adventurers. Columbus and Vasco da Gama, Cabral and Magellan did not venture on their epoch-making journeys as individual merchants (although they all hoped to make their fortunes thereby) but as adventurers in fleets bought with, and equipped by, royal money, bearing the royal mark of approval, and sent forth in hope of additions to the royal till.

The economic consequences of those amazing adventures were incalculably great. For one thing, they opened up an invigorating flow of precious metals into Europe. Gold and silver, coming from the great Spanish mines in Mexico and Peru, were slowly redistributed to other nations as Spain paid in gold specie for goods it bought abroad. As a result, prices rose throughout Europe—between 1520 and 1650 alone, it is estimated that they increased 200 to 400 percent, bringing about both stimulus and stress to industry, but setting in motion a great wave of speculation and commerce.

In addition, of course, the longer-run results of exploration brought an economic stimulus of still greater importance. The establishment of colonies in the sixteenth and seventeenth centuries and the subsequent enjoyment of trade with the New World provided a tremendous boost in propelling Europe into a bustling commercial society. The discovery of the New World was, from the beginning, a catalytic and revolutionizing influence on the Old.

change in religious climate

The forces of change that we have thus far summarized were actually visible. At any time during the long transition from a nonmarket into a market society, we could have witnessed with our own eyes the traveling merchants, the expanding towns, the Crusades, the evidences of a growing national power. Yet these were not the only forces that undermined the feudal system and brought into being its commercial successor. There were, as well, powerful but invisible currents of change, currents that affected the intellectual atmosphere, the beliefs, and the attitudes of Europe. One of these, of special importance, was a change in the religious climate of the times.

In our last chapter we saw how deeply the Catholic church was imbued with theological aversions to the principle of gain—and especially to interest taking or usury. An amusing story of the times sums up the position of the Church very well. Humbertus de Romanis, a monk, tells of someone who found a devil in every nook and cranny of a Florentine cloister, although in the marketplace he found but one. The reason, Humbertus explains, was that it took only one to corrupt a marketplace, where every man harbored a devil in his own heart.[5] In such a disapproving climate, it was hard for the commercial side of life to thrive.

To be sure, for all its fulminations against gain and usury, the Church itself grew in time to a position of commanding economic importance. Through its tithes and benefices, it was the largest collector and distributor of money in all of Europe; and in an age in which banks and safe deposit boxes did not exist, it was the repository of much feudal wealth. Some of its suborders, such as the Knights Templar, became immensely wealthy and served as banking institutions, lending to needy monarchs on stiff terms. Nonetheless, all this faintly disreputable activity was undertaken despite, and not because of, the Church's deepest convictions. For behind the ecclesiastical disapproval of wealth seeking was a deep-seated theological conviction, a firm belief in the transient nature of this life on earth and the importance of preparing for the Eternal Morrow. The Church lifted its eyes, and sought to lift the eyes of others, above the daily struggle for existence. It strove to minimize the importance of life on earth and to denigrate the earthly activities to which an all too weak flesh succumbed.

What changed this dampening influence on the zest of wealth making? According to the theories of the German sociologist Max Weber and the English economic historian R. H. Tawney, the underlying cause lay in the rise of a new theological point of view contained in the teachings of the Protestant reformer John Calvin (1509–1564).

Calvinism   Calvinism was a harsh religious philosophy. Its core was a belief in *predestination,* in the idea that from the beginning God had chosen the saved and the damned, and that nothing man could do on earth could alter that inviolable writ. Furthermore, according to Calvin, the number of the damned exceeded by a vast amount the number of the saved, so that for the average person the chances were great that this earthly prelude was but the momentary grace given before eternal Hell and Damnation commenced.

Perhaps only a man of Calvin's iron will could have borne life under such a sentence. For we soon find that in the hands of his followers in the Lowlands and England, the inexorable and inscrutable quality of the original doctrine began to be softened. Although the idea of predestination was still preached, it was now allowed that in the tenor of one's worldly life there was a *hint* of what was to follow. Thus, the English and Dutch divines taught that whereas even the saintliest-seeming man might end in Hell, the frivolous or wanton one was certainly headed there. Only in a blameless life lay the slightest chance of demonstrating that Salvation was still a possibility.

[5] Beard, *A History of the Business Man,* p. 160.

And so the Calvinists urged a life of rectitude, severity, and, most important of all, diligence. In contrast to the Catholic theologians who tended to look upon worldly activity as vanity, the Calvinists sanctified and approved of endeavor as a kind of index of spiritual worth. Indeed in Calvinist hands there grew up the idea of a man *dedicated* to his work: "called" to it, as it were. Hence the fervid pursuit of one's calling, far from evidencing a distraction from religious ends, came to be taken as evidence of a dedication to a religious life. The energetic merchant was, in Calvinist eyes, a *godly* man, not an ungodly one; and from this identification of work and worth, it was not long before the notion grew up that the more successful a man was, the more worthy he was. Calvinism thus provided a religious atmosphere that, in contrast to Catholicism, encouraged wealth seeking and the temper of a businesslike world.

Perhaps even more important than its encouragement in seeking wealth was the influence of Calvinism on the *use* of wealth. By and large, the prevailing attitude of the prosperous Catholic merchants had been that the aim of worldly success was the enjoyment of a life of ease and luxury, while Catholic nobility displayed on occasion a positively grotesque disdain for wealth. In an orgy of gambling that gripped Paris at the end of the seventeenth century, a prince who sent his mistress a diamond worth 5,000 *livres* had it pulverized and strewn over her reply when she rejected it as being too small. The same prince eventually gambled away an income of 600,000 *livres* a year. A *maréchal* whose grandson turned up his nose at a gift of a purse of gold threw it into the street: "Let the street cleaner have it then." [6]

The Calvinist manufacturer or trader had a very different attitude toward wealth. If his religion approved of diligence, it most emphatically did not approve of indulgence. Wealth was to be accumulated and put to good use, not frittered away.

the
Protestant
ethic

Calvinism promoted an aspect of economic life of which we have hitherto heard very little: *thrift.* It made saving, the conscious abstinence from the enjoyment of income, a virtue. It made investment, the use of saving for productive purposes, an instrument of piety as well as profit. It even condoned, with various *quids* and *quos*, the payment of interest. In fact Calvinism fostered a new conception of economic life. In place of the old ideal of social and economic stability, of knowing and keeping one's "place," it brought respectability to an ideal of struggle, of material improvement, of economic growth.

Economic historians still debate the precise degree of influence that

[6] Werner Sombart, *Luxury and Capitalism* (New York: Columbia University Press, 1938), pp. 120ff. Also Thirion, *La Vie Privée des Financiers au XVIIIe Siècle* (Paris: 1895), p. 292.

may properly be attributed to "the Protestant Ethic" in bringing about the rise of a new gain-centered worldly philosophy. After all, there was nothing much that a Dutch Calvinist would have been able to teach an Italian Catholic banker about the virtues of a businesslike approach to life. Yet, looking back on the subsequent course of economic progress, it is striking that without exception it was the Protestant countries with their "Puritan streak" of work and thrift that forged ahead in the economic race. As one of the powerful winds of change of the sixteenth and seventeenth centuries, the new religious outlook must be counted as a highly favorable stimulus for the evolution of the market society.

breakdown of the manorial system

The enumeration of all these currents does not exhaust the catalog of forces bearing against the old fixed economic order in Europe. The list could be expanded and greatly refined.* Yet with all due caution, we can now begin to comprehend the immense coalition of events—some as specific as the Crusades, some as diffuse as a change in religious ideals—that jointly cooperated to destroy the medieval framework of economic life and to prepare the way for a new dynamic framework of market transactions.

One important aspect of this profound alteration was the gradual *monetization of feudal obligations.* In locality after locality we can trace the conversion of the old feudal payments in *kind*—the days of labor or chickens or eggs a lord received from his tenants—into payments of *money* dues and money rents with which they now discharged their obligations to him.

A number of causes lay behind this commutation of feudal payments. One was the growing urban demand for food, as town and city populations began to swell. In concentric circles around the town, money filtered out into the countryside, at one and the same time raising the capacity of the rural sector to buy urban goods and whetting its desire to do so. At the same time, in a search for larger cash incomes to buy a widening variety of goods, the nobility looked with increasing favor on receiving its rents and dues in money rather than in kind. In so doing, however, it unwittingly set into motion a cause for the further serious deterioration of the manorial system. Usually, the old feudal services were converted into *fixed* sums of money payments. This temporarily eased the cash position of the lord, but soon placed him in the squeeze that always hurts the creditor in times of

---

* An extremely important influence (to which we will specifically turn in our next chapter) was the rise of a new interest in technology, founded on scientific inquiry into natural events. Another important causative factor was the development of modern business concepts and techniques. The German economic historian Werner Sombart has even said that if he were forced to give a single date for the "beginning" of modern capitalism he would choose 1202, the year in which appeared the *Liber Abaci*, a primer of commercial arithmetic. Similarly, the historian Oswald Spengler has called the invention of double-entry bookkeeping in 1494 an achievement worthy of being ranked with that of Columbus or Copernicus.

inflation. And even when dues were not fixed, rents and money dues lagged sufficiently behind the growing monetary needs of the nobility so that still further feudal obligations were monetized to keep the lord in cash. But as prices rose and the monetized life style expanded still further, these too failed to keep him solvent.

The result was that the rural nobility, which now depended increasingly on rents and dues for its income, steadily lost its economic power.* Indeed, beginning in the sixteenth century, we find a new class coming into being—the *impoverished* nobility. In the year 1530 in the Gevaudan district of France, we find that 121 lords had an aggregate income of 21,400 *livres*, but one of these seigneurs accounted for 5,000 *livres* of the sum, another for 2,000—and the rest averaged but a mean 121 *livres* apiece.[7] In fact, the shortage of cash afflicted not only the lesser nobility but even the monarchy itself. Maximilian I, Emperor of the Holy Roman Empire, on occasion lacked the cash to pay for even the overnight lodgings of his entourage on tour; and when two of his grandchildren married children of the King of Hungary, all the trappings of the weddings—2,000 caparisoned horses, jewels, and gold and silver plate—were borrowed from merchant bankers to whom Maximilian had written wheedling letters begging them not to forsake him in his moment of need.

rise of the cash economy

Clearly, the manorial system was incompatible with a cash economy; for while the nobility was pinched between rising prices and costs, and static incomes, the merchant classes, to whom cash naturally gravitated, steadily increased their power. In the Gevaudan district, for example, where the richest lord had his income of 5,000 *livres*, the richest town merchants had incomes up to 65,000 *livres*. In Germany, while Maximilian scratched for cash, the great banking families of Augsburg commanded incomes far larger than Maximilian's entire kingly revenue. In Italy, the Gianfigliazzi of Florence, who began as "nobodies" lending money to the Bishop of Fiesole, ended up stripping him of his possessions and leaving him a pauper; while in Tuscany, the lords who looked down their noses at usurers in the tenth century lost their estates to them in the twelfth and thirteenth. All over Europe men of mean social standing turned the monetary economy to good account. One Jean Amici of Toulouse made a fortune in English booty during the Hundred Years War; Guillaume de St.-Yon grew rich by selling meat at rapacious prices to Paris; and Jacques Coeur, the most extraordinary figure of all, rose from merchant to King's coiner, then to King's purchasing

---

* This process of economic decline was considerably hastened by the ineptitude of the nobility as managers of their estates. The descendants of the crusaders were not much more businesslike than their ancestors.

[7] *Cambridge Economic History of Europe,* I, 557–58.

agent, then to financier not for, but *of*, the King, during the course of which he accumulated a huge fortune, estimated at 27-million *écus*.[*]

APPEARANCE OF THE ECONOMIC ASPECT OF LIFE

Behind all these profoundly disturbing events, we can discern an immense process of change that literally revolutionized the economic organization of Europe. Whereas in the tenth century, cash and money transactions were only peripheral to the solution of the economic problem, by the sixteenth and seventeenth centuries cash and transactions were already beginning to provide the very molecular force of economic cohesion.

But over and above this general monetization of life, another and perhaps even more profound change was taking place. This was the emergence of a separate *economic* sphere of activity visible within, and separable from, the surrounding matrix of social life. It was the creation of a whole aspect of society that had never previously existed, but was thenceforth to constitute a commanding facet of human existence.[8]

In antiquity and feudal times, as we have seen, one could not easily separate the economic motivations or even the economic actions of the great mass of men from the normal round of existence itself. The peasant following his immemorial ways was hardly conscious of acting according to "economic" motives; indeed, he did not—he heeded the orders of his lord or the dictates of custom. Nor was the lord himself economically oriented. His interests were military or political or religious, and not basically oriented toward the idea of gain or increase. Even in the towns, as we have seen, the conduct of ordinary business was inextricably mixed with non-economic concerns. The undeniable fact that men were acquisitive, not to say avaricious, did not yet impart its flavor to life in general; the making of money, as we have been at some pains to indicate, was a tangential rather than a central concern of ancient or medieval existence.

labor, land,
and capital
come into
being

With the ever-widening scope of monetization, however, a genuinely new element of life came slowly to the fore. Labor, for example, emerged as an activity quite different from the past. No longer was "labor" part of an explicit social relationship in which one man (serf or apprentice) worked for another (lord or guildmaster) in return for at least an assurance of subsistence. Labor was now a mere quantum of effort, a "commodity" to be disposed of in the marketplace for the best price it could bring, quite devoid of any reciprocal responsibilities on the part of the buyer, beyond the

---

[*] Note, however, that Coeur eventually fell from power, was imprisoned, and died in exile. The counting house was not yet fully master of the castle.

[8] The following section owes much to the insights of Karl Polanyi's famous *The Great Transformation* (Boston: Beacon Press, 1957, paperback ed.), Part II.

payment of wages. If those wages were not enough to provide subsistence—well, that was not the buyer's responsibility. He had bought his "labor," and that was that.

This emergence of "pure" labor—labor as a quantity of effort detached from a man's life and bought on the market in fixed amounts—had a parallel in two other main elements of economic life. One of these was land. Formerly conceived of as the territory of a great lord, as inviolable as the territory of a modern nation-state, land was now also seen in its economic aspect as something to be bought or leased for the economic return it yielded. An estate that was once the core of political and administrative power became a "property" with a market price, available for any number of uses, even as a site for a factory. The dues, the payments in kind, the intangibles of prestige and power that once had flowed from the ownership of land gave way to the single return of *rent;* that is, to a money return derived from putting land to *profitable* use.

The same transformation became true of property. As it was conceived in antiquity and throughout most of the Middle Ages, property was a sum of tangible wealth, a hoard, a treasury of plate, bullion, or jewels. Very logically, it was realized in the form of luxurious homes, in castles and armaments, in costly robes and trappings. But with the monetization and commercialization of society, property, too, became expressible in a monetary equivalent: a man was now "worth" so many *livres,* or *écus,* or pounds, or whatever. Property became *capital,* manifesting itself no longer in specific goods, but as an abstract sum of infinitely flexible use whose "value" was its capacity to earn *interest* or *profits.*

None of these changes, it should be emphasized, was planned, clearly foreseen, or for that matter, welcomed. It was not with equanimity that the feudal hierarchies saw their prerogatives nibbled away by the mercantile classes. Neither did the tradition-preserving guildmaster desire his own enforced metamorphosis into a "capitalist," a man of affairs guided by market signals and beset by competition. But perhaps for no social class was the transition more painful than for the peasant, caught up in a process of history that dispossessed him from his livelihood and made him a landless laborer.

enclosures   This process, which was particularly important in England, was the *enclosure movement,* a by-product of the monetization of feudal life. Starting as early as the thirteenth century, the landed aristocracy, increasingly squeezed for cash, began to view their estates not merely as the ancestral fiefs but as potential sources of cash revenue. In order to raise larger cash crops, they therefore began to "enclose" the pasture that had previously been deemed "common land." Communal grazing fields, which had in fact always belonged to the lord despite their communal use, were now claimed for the exclusive benefit of the lord and turned into sheepwalks. Why sheepwalks? Because a rising demand for woolen cloth was making sheep raising a highly profitable occupation. The medieval historian Eileen Power writes:

> The visitor to the House of Lords, looking respectfully upon that august assembly, cannot fail to be struck by a stout and ungainly object facing the throne—an ungainly object upon which in full session of Parliament, he will observe seated the Lord Chancellor of England. The object is a woolsack, and it is stuffed as full of pure history as the office of the Lord Chancellor itself. . . . The Lord Chancellor of England is seated upon a woolsack because it was upon a woolsack that this fair land rose to prosperity.[9]

The enclosure process in England proceeded at an irregular pace over the long centuries; not until the late eighteenth and early nineteenth centuries did it reach its engulfing climax.[*] By its end, some ten million acres, nearly *half* the arable land of England, had been "enclosed"—in its early Tudor days by the more or less high-handed conversion of the "commons" to sheep raising; in the final period, by the forcible consolidation of strips and plots into tracts suitable for commercial farming, for which tenants presumably received "fair compensation."

From a strictly economic point of view, the enclosure movement was unquestionably salutary in that it brought into productive employment land that had hitherto yielded only a pittance. Indeed, particularly in the eighteenth and nineteenth centuries, enclosure was the means by which England "rationalized" its agriculture and finally escaped from the inefficiency of the traditional manorial strip system. But there was another, crueler side to enclosure. As the common fields were enclosed, it became ever more difficult for the tenant to support himself. In the fifteenth and sixteenth centuries, when the initial enclosure of the commons reached its peak, as many as three-fourths to nine-tenths of the tenants of some estates were simply turned off the farm. Whole hamlets were thus wiped out. Sir Thomas More described it savagely in Book I of his *Utopia*:

> Your sheep that were wont to be so meek and tame, and so small eaters, now, as I hear say, be become so great devourers and so wild, that they eat up and swallow down the very men themselves. They consume, destroy and devour whole fields, houses and cities. For look in what parts of the realm doth grow the finest, and therefore dearest wool, there noblemen and gentlemen, yea and certain abbots, holy men God wot, not contenting themselves with the yearly revenues and profits that were wont to grow to their forefathers and predecessors of their land . . . leave no ground for tillage, they enclose all into pastures, they throw down houses,

---

[9] *Medieval People* (Garden City, N.Y.: Doubleday, Anchor Books, 1954), p. 125.

[*] In other European nations an enclosure process also took place, but at a much slower pace. In France, Italy, and southern Germany, the small-holder peasant persisted long after he had virtually ceased to exist in England; in northeastern Germany, on the other hand, the small peasant was deprived of his holdings and turned into a landless proletarian.

they pluck down towns and leave nothing standing, but only the church to make of it a sheep house. . . .

The enclosure process provided a powerful force for the dissolution of feudal ties and the formation of the new relationships of a market society. By dispossessing the peasant, it "created" a new kind of labor force—landless, without traditional sources of income, however meager, impelled to find work for wages wherever it might be available.

emergence of an agricultural proletariat

Together with this agricultural proletariat, we begin to see the emergence of an urban proletariat, partly brought about by a gradual transformation of guilds into more "businesslike" firms, partly by the immigration into the cities of some of the new landless peasantry. And then to exacerbate the whole situation, from the middle of the eighteenth century, a rising population (itself traceable in large measure to the increase in food output resulting from the enclosures) began to pour growing numbers into the labor market. As a result of this complicated interplay of causes and effects, we find England plagued with the problem of the "wandering poor." One not untypical proposal of the eighteenth century was that they be confined in what a reformer candidly termed "Houses of Terror."

Thus did the emergence of a market-oriented system grind into being a "labor force," and though the process of adjustment for other classes of society was not so brutal, it, too, exacted its social price. Tenaciously the guildmasters fought against the invasion of their protected trades by manufacturers who trespassed on traditional preserves or who upset established modes of production with new machinery. Doggedly the landed nobility sought to protect its ancient privileges against the encroachment of the moneyed *nouveaux riches.*

Yet the process of economic enlargement, breaking down the established routines of the past, rearranging the power and prestige of all social classes, could not be stopped. Ruthlessly it pursued its historic course and impartially it distributed its historic rewards and sacrifices. Although stretched out over a long period, it was not an evolution but a slow revolution that overtook European economic society. Only when that society had run its long gauntlet, suffering one of the most wrenching dislocations of history, would the world of transactions appear "natural" and "normal" and the categories of "land," "labor," and "capital" become so matter-of-fact that it would be difficult to believe they had not always existed.

factors of production

Yet, as we have seen, it was not at all "natural" and "normal" to have free, wage-earning, contractual labor or rentable, profit-producing land or fluid, investment-seeking capital. They were *creations* of the great transformation of a pre-market into a market society. Economics calls these creations the *factors of production,* and much of economics is concerned with analyzing the manner in which these three basic constituents of the productive process are combined in the market mechanism.

What we must realize at this stage of our inquiry, however, is that "land," "labor," and "capital" do not exist as eternal categories of *social* organization. Admittedly, they are categories of *nature,* but these eternal aspects of the productive process—the soil, human effort, and the artifacts that can be applied to production—do not take on, in every society, the specific separation that distinguishes them in a market society. In pre-market economies, land, labor, and capital are inextricably mixed and mingled in the figure of slave and serf, lord and guildmaster—none of whom enters the production process as the incarnation of a specific economic function offered for a price. The slave is not a "worker," the guildmaster is not a "capitalist," nor is the lord a "landlord." Only when a social system has evolved in which labor is sold, land is rented, and capital is freely invested do we find the categories of economics emerging from the flux of life.

property in men

Nowhere do we see this astonishing social process more clearly illustrated than in the evolution of the concept of property in man himself. In ancient society, as we have seen, men owned men. That is, a slave was literally the chattel of his owner, to be used, abused, or even put to death under certain circumstances. In the Middle Ages, this idea of human property evolved into the conception of serfdom. A serf was also the property of his master and subject to the ties and bonds we have discussed, but the ownership was not so all-embracing and entailed reciprocal obligations on the part of the lord.

Finally, we reach modern commercial society, in which each person has property *in himself.* A worker who has become a "factor of production" owns his own labor, which he is free to sell as advantageously as possible, something that no slave or serf could do. At the same time, the free worker, who is no man's property, is also no man's obligation. The employer buys his employees' labor, not their lives. All responsibility for the laborer ends when he leaves his employer's office or factory, which is the owner's "property."

economics and the market society

Modern economics thus describes the manner in which a certain kind of society, with a specific history of acculturation and institutional evolution, solves its economic problems. It may well be that in another era there will no longer be "land," "labor," and "capital." If, for example, a pure communist society ever evolves, the method by which the social product will be assured or distributed need not bear any more relation to our present system of wage payments or rental incomes or profit shares than our own system bears to its feudal predecessor. In that case, "economics" as we know it will have to be revised to correspond to the new social relationships by which the production and distribution problems will be solved.

But the emergence of a market society, with its new factors of production, was not the only creation of the forces of change we have examined in this chapter. Along with the new relationships of man to man in the marketplace, there arose a new form of *social control* to take over the guidance of the economy from the former aegis of tradition and command.

rise of the "profit motive" What was this new form of control? Essentially, it was a pattern of social behavior, of normal, everyday action that the new market environment imposed on society. And what was this pattern of behavior? In the language of the economist, it was the drive to *maximize one's income* (or to minimize one's expenditures) by concluding the best possible bargains on the marketplace. In ordinary language, it was the drive to buy cheap and sell dear, or, in business terminology, the *profit motive*.

The market society had not, of course, invented this motive. Perhaps it did not even intensify it. But it did make it a *ubiquitous* and *necessitous* aspect of social behavior. Although men may have *felt* acquisitive during the Middle Ages or antiquity, they did not enter en masse into market transactions for the basic economic activities of their livelihoods. And even when, for instance, a peasant sold his few eggs at the town market, rarely was the transaction a matter of overriding importance for his continued existence. Market transactions in a fundamentally nonmarket society were thus a subsidiary activity, a means of supplementing a livelihood that, however sparse, was largely independent of buying or selling.

With the monetization of labor, land, and capital, however, transactions became *universal* and *critical* activities. Now everything was for sale, and the terms of transactions were anything but subsidiary to existence itself. To a man who sold his labor on a market, in a society that assumed no responsibility for his upkeep, the price at which he concluded his bargain was all-important. So it was with the landlord and the budding capitalist. For each of these a good bargain could spell riches—and a bad one, ruin. Thus, the pattern of economic maximization was generalized throughout society and given an inherent urgency that made it a powerful force for shaping human behavior.

THE INVENTION OF ECONOMICS

The new market society did more than merely bring about an environment in which men were not only free, but *forced*, to follow their self-interest. It also brought a puzzle of great importance and considerable difficulty. The puzzle was to understand the workings of a world in which profit-seeking individuals were no longer constrained to follow the ways of their fore-fathers or to shape their economic activities according to the dictates of a ruling lord or king.

the
"philos-
ophy"
of trade

The new order needed a "philosophy"—a reasoned explanation of how such a society would hang together, would "work." And such a philosophy was by no means self-evident. In many ways the new world of profit-seeking individuals appeared as perplexing and fraught with dangers to its con-temporaries as it did to the imaginary village elders to whom we described it in our last chapter.

Hence it is not surprising that the philosophers of trade disagreed. In England, a group of pamphleteers and merchants, the so-called Mercan-tilists, put forward an explanation of economic society that stressed the importance of gold and extolled the role of the merchant whose activities were most likely to bring "treasure" into the state by selling goods to for-eigners. In France, a school of thinkers we call the Physiocrats held quite different ideas. They extolled the virtues of the farmer, not the merchant. All wealth ultimately came from nature's bounty, the Physiocrats argued, dismissing merchants and even manufacturers as belonging to a "sterile" class that added nothing to the wealth produced by the farmer. Labor was assumed to be poor, although not necessarily "wretched."

With such diverse views, it is obvious that nothing like unanimity prevailed concerning proper economic policy. Should competition be regu-lated or left alone? Should the export of gold be prohibited, or should "treasure" be permitted to enter or leave the kingdom as the currents of trade dictated? Should the agricultural producer be taxed because he was the ultimate source of all wealth, or should taxes fall on the prosperous merchant class? The answers to these perplexing questions awaited the advent of Adam Smith (1723–1790), patron saint of our discipline and a figure of towering intellectual stature. His masterwork, *The Wealth of Nations*, published in 1776, the year of the American Revolution, gave to the world the first full account of something it dearly wanted to know—how its own economic mechanism worked.

the growing
wealth of
nations

The world that Smith described was very different from our own. It was a world of very small enterprises: Smith's famous description of a pin factory describes a manufacturing establishment that employs ten people. It was still hampered by medieval guild restrictions: In Smith's time, no master hatter in England could employ more than two apprentices; in the famous Sheffield silver trade, no master cutler could employ more than one. Still more important, it was a world in which government-protected monop-olies were accorded to certain fields of commerce, such as the trade with the East Indies. Yet, for all the differences from modern economic society, the basic vision that Smith gave to his time can still elucidate the tasks of economics in our own time.

Two main problems occupied Smith's attention. The first is implicit in the title of the book. This is Smith's theory of the most important tendency of a society of "perfect liberty"—its *tendency to grow.*°

Economic growth—that is, the steady increase in the output of goods and services enjoyed by a society—was hardly a concern for philosophers of tradition-bound societies, or even of societies ruled by imperial-minded emperors. But what Smith discerned amid the seeming turmoil of a market society was a hidden mechanism that would operate to enlarge the "wealth of nations"—at any rate, those nations that enjoyed a system of perfect liberty and did not tamper with it.

What was it that drove society to increase its riches? Basically, it was the tendency of such a society to encourage a steady rise in the *productivity* of its labor, so that over time, the same number of working people could turn out a steadily larger output.

And what lay behind the rise in productivity? The answer, according to Smith, was the gain in productiveness that was to be had by achieving an ever-finer *division of labor.* Here Smith's famous pin factory serves as an example:

One man draws out the wire, another straits it, a third cuts it, a fourth points it, a fifth grinds it at the top for receiving the head; to make the head requires two or three distinct operations; to put it on is a peculiar business; to whiten it is another; it is even a trade by itself to put them into paper. . . . I have seen a small manufactory of this kind where ten men only were employed and where some of them consequently performed two or three distinct operations. But though they were poor, and therefore but indifferently accomodated with the necessary machinery, they could, when they exerted themselves, make among them about twelve pounds of pins in a day. There are in a pound upwards of four thousand pins of middling size. Those ten persons, therefore, could make among them upwards of forty-eight thousand pins in a day. . . . But if they had all wrought separately and independently . . . they could certainly not each of them make twenty, perhaps not one pin in a day.

Adam Smith's growth model

This begins to unravel the reasons why a society of free enterprise tends to grow. But it does not fully explain the phenomenon. For what is it that drives such a society to a division of labor? And how do we know that the tendency to growth will not peter out, for one reason or another?

° By "perfect liberty" Smith emphasized that all agents in such a society were free to enter, or not to enter, into economic arrangements, in sharp contrast to the *obligations* imposed on serfs and slaves. That "liberty" may not have appeared very precious to the "freely contracting" owner of labor power in a London slum. Nonetheless, there was a difference—a legal difference—that Smith correctly identified as crucial for the system of capitalism.

This leads us to the larger picture that Smith had in mind. We would call it a growth model, although Smith used no such modern term himself. What we mean by this is that Smith shows us both a *propulsive force* that will put society on an upward growth path and a *self-correcting* mechanism that will keep it there.

First the driving force. One of the fundamental building blocks of Smith's conception of human nature was what he called the "desire for betterment"—what we have already described as the profit motive. And what does the desire for betterment have to do with growth? The answer is very important. *It impels every manufacturer to expand his business in order to increase his profits.*

And how does this business expansion result in a higher division of labor? The answer is very neat. The main road to profit consists in equipping workmen with the necessary machinery that Smith mentions in his description of the pin factory, for it is this machinery that will increase their productivity. Thus, the path to growth lies in what Smith called *accumulation*, or in more modern terminology, in the process of *capital investment*. As capitalists seek money, they invest in machines and equipment. As a result of the machines and equipment, their men can produce more. Because they produce more, society's output grows.

the dynamics of the system   This answers the first part of our query. But there is still the question of how we know that society will continue to grow, that its trajectory will not flatten out. Here we come to the cleverest part of Smith's model. For at first look, it might seem as if the drive to increase capital investments would be self-defeating. The reason is that the steady increase in the demand for workmen to run the new machines would drive up their wages; and as wages rose, they would cut into the manufacturer's profits. In turn, as profits were eaten away, the very source of new investment would dry up and the growth curve would soon level off.

Not so, according to Smith. To be sure, the rising demand for workmen *would* tend to drive up wages. But this was only half the picture. The same upward tendency of wages would also tend to increase the supply of workingmen. The reason is not implausible. In Smith's day, infant mortality was shockingly high: "It is not uncommon," Smith remarked, ". . . in the Highlands of Scotland for a mother who has borne twenty children not to have two alive." But as wages rose, infant and child mortality would tend to diminish, and therefore more of the population would arrive at working age (ten or younger in Smith's day).

The outcome must already be clear. Along with an increase in the demand for workingmen (and working children) comes an increase in their supply. This increase in the number of available workers meant that the competition for jobs would increase. Therefore the price of labor would *not* rise, at least not enough to choke off further growth. Like a vast self-regulating machine, the mechanism of capital accumulation would provide the very thing it needed to continue unhampered: a force to prevent wages from eating up profits. And so the growth process could go on undisturbed.

We will not concern ourselves here with the full details of Smith's growth model. And of course, his "model" is not directly applicable to the modern world, where (at least in industrialized nations) most children do not die before they reach working age and where his "safety valve" therefore has no relevance. But nonetheless, in Smith's model we get a sense of the imaginative reach and capacity for enlightenment that economic analysis can bring.*

the market mechanism The wealth (we would say the output) of nations was not, however, the only major problem on which Smith's treatise threw a clarifying light. There was also the question of how a market system held together, of how it provided an orderly solution to the problems of production and distribution.

This brings us to Smith's description and explanation of *the market mechanism*. Here Smith begins by elucidating a perplexing problem. The actors in Smith's drama, as we know, are driven by the desire for self-betterment and guided mainly by their self-interest. "It is not from the benevolence of the butcher, the brewer or the baker that we expect our dinner," writes Smith, "but from their regard to their self-interest. We address ourselves not to their humanity, but to their self-love, and never talk to them of our necessities, but of their advantages."

The problem here is obvious. How does a market society prevent self-interested, profit-hungry men from holding up their fellow citizens for ransom? How does a socially workable arrangement emerge from such a socially dangerous set of motivations?

The answer introduces us to a central mechanism of a market society, the mechanism of *competition*. For each man, out to do the best for himself with no thought of others, is faced with a host of similarly motivated individuals who are in exactly the same position. Each is only too eager to take advantage of his competitor's greed if it urges him to raise his price above the level "set" by the market. If a pin manufacturer tried to charge more than his competitors, they would take away his trade; if a workman asked

---

* It seems necessary to add a word to the student who gets sufficiently interested in Smith's model to look into the *Wealth* itself. He will look in vain, in this vast, discursive book for a clear-cut exposition of the interactions we have just described. The model is implicit in Smith's exposition, but it lies around the text like a disassembled machine, requiring us to put it together in our minds. Nonetheless it is there, if one fits together the pieces. For a full exposition, see A. Lowe, "Adam Smith's System of Equilibrium Growth," and W. A. Eltis, "Adam Smith's Theory of Economic Growth," both in *Essays on Adam Smith*, eds. Skinner and Wilson (Oxford: Clarendon Press), 1975, as well as my own essay in that volume.

for more than the going wage, he would not be able to find work; if a land-lord sought to exact a rent steeper than another with land of the same quality, he would get no tenants.

the market and allocation

But the market mechanism does more than impose a competitive safeguard on the price of products. It also arranges for the production of the right *quantities* of the goods that society desires. Suppose that consumers want more pins than are being turned out, and fewer shoes. The public will buy out the existing supply of pins, while business in the shoe stores will be dull. Pin prices will tend to rise as the public scrambles for shrinking supplies, and prices of shoes will tend to fall as merchants try to get rid of their burdensome stocks.

And now, once again, a restorative force comes into play. As pin prices rise, so will the profits of the pin business, and as shoe prices sag, so will profits in shoemaking. Again, self-interest and the desire for betterment go to work. Pin manufacturers will expand their output to take advantage of higher prices; shoe factories will curtail production to cut their losses. Employers in the pin business will seek to hire more factors of production —more workers, more space, more capital equipment; and employers in the shoe business will reduce their use of the factors of production, letting workers go, giving up leases on land, cutting down on their capital in-vestment.

Hence pin output will rise and shoe output will fall. *But this is exactly what the public wanted in the first place!* Through what Smith called, in a famous phrase, "an invisible hand," the selfish motives of men are trans-muted by the market mechanism to yield the most unexpected of results: social well-being.

the self-regulating system

Thus Smith showed that a market system, far from being chaotic and dis-orderly, is in fact the means by which a solution of the strictest discipline and order is provided for the economic problem.

First, he has explained how the motive of self-interest provides the necessary impetus to set the mechanism to work. Next, he has shown how competition prevents any individual from exacting a price higher than that set by the marketplace. Third, he has made clear how the changing desires of society lead producers to increase production of wanted goods and to diminish the production of goods that are no longer as highly desired.

Not least, he has shown that the market system is a *self-regulating* process. For the beautiful consequence of a competitive market is that it is its own guardian. If prices or profits or wages stray away from the levels determined by the market system, forces exist to drive them back into line. Thus a curious paradox emerges; the competitive market, which is the acme of individual economic freedom, is at the same time the strictest of economic taskmasters. One may appeal the ruling of a planning board or win the dispensation of a minister, but there is no appeal, no dispensation, from the anonymous pressures of the competitive marketplace. Economic freedom is thus more illusory than it appears. You may do as you please, but if you please to do that which the market disapproves of, the price of freedom is ruin.

the market system and the rise of capitalism

Does the market system really work as Smith's great treatise suggests? Much of the rest of this book will be devoted to that very question—that is, to tracing the growth and the internal order of the system whose prospects Smith's model described so brilliantly. The fact that we have suffered business cycles and depressions, and that giant business firms and labor unions have taken the place of pin factories and child workers, is evidence enough that Smith's model alone will certainly not serve us as a dependable guide through economic history. But the fact that our economy has grown prodigiously and that it has hung together, despite all its problems, is also evidence that there is an important kernel of truth in Smith's conception.

Let us therefore return to our historical narrative, to see how much of what Smith foresaw came true, and how much did not, and for what reasons. For we must remember that *The Wealth of Nations* appeared before capitalism assumed anything like its present industrial guise. After all, serfdom was not formally abolished in France until 1789; and in Germany, not until a half century later. Even in Adam Smith's England the market society had not yet reached a stage in which capitalism had achieved full legal and political status. For example, the guild regulations that irked Smith did not vanish until the medieval Statute of Artificers was repealed in 1813. Likewise in France, an immense web of regulations bound the would-be capitalist. Rules and edicts, many of them seeking to standardize production, laid down the exact number of threads to be woven into the cloths of the French textile manufacturers, and to disregard these laws was to risk pillorying—first for the cloth, then for the manufacturer.

Thus, well into the eighteenth century, we find the great revolution of the market still incomplete; or rather, we find the nearly complete process of monetization and commercialization contained uncomfortably within a frame of legal and social organization not yet fully adapted to it. We will have to observe how capitalism burst through the restrictions of the pre-capitalist, mercantilist era before we can see Adam Smith's marvelous market mechanism in full operation.

Feudalism

1. *Powerful forces of change* were operative within European feudalism, and served gradually to introduce the structure of a market society. Primary among these forces were:
   - The role of *the itinerant merchant* in introducing trade, money, and the acquisitive spirit into feudal life.
   - The *process of urbanization* as a source of economic activity, and as the locus of a new, trade-centered seat of power.
   - *The Crusades* as a force for the disruption of feudal life and the introduction of new ideas.
   - The rise of unifying, commerce-supporting *national states.*
   - The stimulus of the *Age of Exploration* and of the *gold* it brought into Europe.
   - The emergence of *new religious ideas* more sympathetic to business activity than Catholicism had been.
   - The *monetization of dues* within the manorial system.

2. As a consequence of these forces, we begin to see the *separation of economic from social life.* The processes of production and distribution were no longer indistinguishably melded into the prevailing religious, social, and political customs and practices, but now began to form a sharply distinct area of life in themselves.

Enclosures

3. With the rise of the economic aspect of life, we see *deep-seated transformations* taking place. The peasant-serf is no longer bound to the land, but becomes a free, mobile laborer; the guildmaster is no longer hobbled by guild rules but becomes an independent entrepreneur; the lord of the land becomes (in the modern sense of the word) a landlord. The transformation was a long and often violent one, especially in the complex case of the *enclosures.*

Factors of production

4. The advent of free laborers, capitalists, and landlords, each selling his services on the market for land and capital and labor, made it possible to speak of the "*factors of production.*" By this was implied two things: the *physical categories* of land, labor, and capital as distinguishable agents in the production process; and the *social relationships* among laborers, landowners, and capitalists as distinct groups or classes entering the marketplace.

Profit motive

Monetization

5. As part of this process of change, we find the emergence of the *profit motive* at all levels of society, not as an acquisitive drive (which may have existed for centuries), but as the pervasive necessity for all individuals in a *monetized society* to strive for higher incomes for economic survival.

Adam Smith

6. Along with the new economic society came a new interest in the mechanism of a market society. The greatest of the early economists was *Adam Smith,* author of *The Wealth of Nations.* Essentially a philosopher, Smith turned his powerful and far-ranging inquiry to the understanding of a society of "perfect liberty" (a society of freely contracting agents).

Productivity

Divison of labor

7. In the *Wealth*, he described two attributes of such a society. The first was its *tendency to grow*. Smith showed how growth resulted from the increase in labor *productivity* that came from the ever-finer *division of labor*. This enhancement in productivity was brought about by capitalists' *investment* in *capital equipment* as a means to higher profit.

Growth model

8. Smith actually described a *"growth model"* for a market system. The model showed that growth would continue even though the demand for labor bid up wages, imperiling profits. In Smith's model, the rise in wages also increased the supply of labor, thereby preventing a sharp increase in wages from undermining the process of capital investment.

Market mechanism

9. Smith also described the *market mechanism*. In this mechanism, *competition* played a key role in preventing individuals from exacting whatever price they pleased from buyers.

Competition

10. The *market mechanism* also revealed how changing demands for goods would change the production of goods, to match that demand. Thus the capstone of Smith's treatise was the demonstration of the *self-regulating* nature of a competitive market, in which an "invisible hand" brought socially useful ends from selfish and private means.

3	*Questions*

1. What was so disruptive to feudal life about the activities of the merchant? Are business activities today also the causes of social stress?

2. The underdeveloped nations today often resemble the economies of antiquity or of the Middle Ages, at least insofar as their poverty and stagnation are concerned. Discuss what relevance, if any, the forces of change mentioned in this chapter have on the modernization of these areas. Are there new forces of change?

3. The leading nations in the world, so far as per capita income is concerned, are the U.S., New Zealand and Australia, and the Scandinavian states. Among the less-affluent Western nations are Ireland, Spain, Portugal, and Italy. Do you think this proves the validity of the Weber-Tawney thesis as to the importance of the Protestant ethic in economic growth? Does the addition of Latin America change the argument? Japan?

4. The process of monetization and commercialization was often a violent one in Europe. Do you think the Civil War, which ended slavery and displaced the southern semifeudal plantation system, could be considered part of the same transformation in America?

5. Is economic life distinctly separate from social and political life in America?

6. Do you think most people in the United States obey the profit motive? Are most people mobile in the United States? Do you know anyone who has changed his residence because of economic considerations? His profession?

7. Profit making is certainly as old as man. Do you think we can speak of the origins of capitalism as being equally old?

8. Describe what Smith meant by the "invisible hand." What is the mechanism by which selfish interests are made compatible with—indeed, made the agent for—successful social provisioning?

9. Can you see a relation between Smith's growth model and his market model? Would the growth model work if the forces of the market did not operate?

10. What legal and political changes were necessary to change feudalism into a market system?

4   *The Industrial Revolution*

Heretofore, in our survey of economic history, we have concentrated almost entirely on two main currents of economic activity: agriculture and commerce. Yet there was, from earliest days, a third essential source of economic wealth—industry—which we have purposely let slip by unnoticed. For in contrast to agriculture and commerce, industrial manufacture did not leave a major imprint on economic society itself. As a peasant, a serf, a merchant, or a guildsman, the actor in the economic drama directly typified the basic activities of the times, but this would not have been true of someone in industry. Such a person as a "factory worker"—indeed, the very idea of an *industrial* "proletarian"—was singularly absent from the long years before the late seventeenth century. Only with the advent of Adam Smith's pin factory does he begin to enter the scene.

Let us note as well that the "industrial capitalist" was also lacking. Most of the moneymakers of the past gained their fortunes by trading, or transporting, or lending—not by making. It is amusing—more than amusing; instructive—to mark the best ways of getting rich enumerated by Leon Battista Alberti, a fifteenth-century architect, musician, and courtier. They are (1) wholesale trade; (2) seeking for treasure trove; (3) ingratiating oneself with a rich man to become his heir; (4) usury; and (5) the rental of pastures, horses, and the like. A seventeenth-century commentator adds to this: royal service, soldiering, and alchemy. Manufacturing is conspicuously absent from both lists.[1] It, too, enters the economic world only about the time of Smith.

Granted that in ancient Greece, Demosthenes had an armor and a cabinet "factory"; and from long before his time, in ancient Egypt, we even have the attendance record of workers in "factories" for the production of cloth. Yet it is clear that this form of production was far less important than either agriculture or commerce in shaping the economic texture of the times. For one thing, the typical scale of manufacture was small.

[1] Werner Sombart, *The Quintessence of Capitalism* (New York: Dutton, 1915), pp. 34–35.

Note that the very word *manufacture* (from the Latin *manus,* "hand," and *facere,* "to make") implies a system of hand, rather than machine, technology. Demosthenes' enterprises, for example, employed no more than fifty men. It is true that from time to time we do come across quite large manufacturing operations; already in the second century A.D., a Roman brickworks employed forty-six foremen; and by the time we reach the seventeenth century, enterprises with several hundred workers are not unheard of. Yet such operations were the exception rather than the rule. In 1660, for instance, a steelworker in France needed no more than three tons of pig iron a year for his output of swords or sickle blades or artistic cutlery. Similarly, most guild operations, as we have seen, were small. As late as 1843, a Prussian census showed only sixty-seven working people for every hundred masters.[2] In the past—as today in the East and Near East—most "industry" was carried on in the backs of small shops or the dim cellars of houses, in sheds behind bazaars, or in the scattered homes of workers to whom materials would be supplied by an organizing "capitalist."

pace of technical change   In addition to the smallness of the scale of industry, another aspect of the times delayed industrial manufacture from making known its social presence. This was the absence of any sustained interest in the development of an *industrial technology.* Throughout antiquity and the Middle Ages, little of society's creative energy was directed toward a systematic improvement of manufacturing techniques. It is indicative of the lack of interest attached to productive technology that so simple and important an invention as the horse collar had to await the Middle Ages for discovery; the Egyptians, Greeks, and Romans, who were capable of a magnificent technology of architecture, were simply not fundamentally concerned with the techniques of everyday production itself.[3] Even well into the Renaissance and Reformation, the idea of industrial technology hardly attracted serious thought. With the exception of Leonardo da Vinci, whose fecund mind played with inventions of the most varied kind, the serious thinkers of Europe, until well into the seventeenth century, were both ignorant of, and uninterested in, the technology of basic production.

There was good reason for this prevailing indifference: In the societies of the pre-market world, the necessary economic base for any large-scale industrial manufacture was totally lacking. In economies sustained by the

---

[2] *Cambridge Economic History of Europe,* II, 34; John U. Nef, *Cultural Foundations of Industrial Civilization* (New York: Harper, Torchbooks, 1960), p. 131; R. H. Tawney, *Equality,* 4th ed. (London: Macmillan, 1952), p. 59.

[3] E. M. Jope, in *History of Technology,* eds. Charles J. Singer et al. (New York: Oxford University Press, 1956), II, 553. There was, however, considerable improvement in mining techniques, especially for silver and copper.

labor of peasants, slaves, and serfs, economies in which the stream of money was small and the current of economic life, accidents of war and nature aside, relatively changeless from year to year, who could dream of a process in which avalanches of goods would be turned out? The very idea of industrial production on the large scale was inconceivable in such an unmonetized, static setting.*

For all these reasons, the pace of industrialization was slow. It is a question whether Europe in the year 1200 was significantly more technologically advanced than it had been in the year 200 B.C. The widespread use of waterpower in industry, for instance, did not appear until the fifteenth century, and it would be still another century before windmills provided a common means for tapping the energy of nature. The mechanical clock dates from the thirteenth century, but not for 200 years would significant improvements be made in instruments for navigation, surveying, or measuring. Movable type, that indispensable forerunner of mass communication, did not appear until 1450.

In short, despite important pockets of highly organized production, notably in the thirteenth-century Flanders cloth industry and in Northern Italian towns, not until the late sixteenth century can we discern the first signs of a general ground swell of industrial technology, and even in that day it would have been impossible to foresee that one day industry would be the dominant form of productive organization. As a matter of fact, as late as the eighteenth century, when manufacturing had already begun to reach respectable proportions as a form of social endeavor, it was not generally thought of as inherently possessing any but secondary importance. Agriculture, of course, was the visible foundation of the nation itself. Trading was regarded as useful insofar as it brought a nation gold. But at best, industry was seen as a handmaiden of the others, providing the trader with the goods to export, or serving the farmer as a secondary market for the products of the earth.†

What finally conspired to bring manufacturing into a position of overwhelming prominence?

It was a complex concatenation of events that finally brought about the eruption we call the Industrial Revolution. As with the Commercial Revolution and the Mercantile era, which preceded it and formed its indispensable preparation, it is impossible in a few pages to do justice to the many currents that contributed to that final outburst of industrial tech-

---

* Even today, one sees the difficulties of the unmonetized, static, underdeveloped societies in finding an industrial-minded, rather than commercial-minded, entrepreneurial group.

† Remember that in the mid-eighteenth century, when the French doctor François Quesnay propounded one of the first systematic explanations of economic production and distribution (called *Physiocracy*), only the farmer was regarded as a producer of net worth; and the manufacturer, while his utility was not ignored, was nonetheless relegated to the "sterile" (i.e., non-wealth-producing) classes.

nology. But if we cannot trace the process in detail, we can at least gain an idea of its impetus and of the main forces behind it if we turn now to England around 1750. Here, for the first time, industrial manufacture as a major form of economic activity began to work its immense social transformations. Let us observe the process as it took place.

England in   Why did the Industrial Revolution originally take place in England and not
1750   on the Continent? Why did the pin factory attract Smith's attention? To answer these questions we must look at the background factors that distinguished England from most other European nations in the eighteenth century.

The first of these factors was simply that England was relatively wealthy. In fact, a century of successful exploration, slave trading, piracy, war, and commerce had made her the richest nation in the world. Even more important, her riches had accrued not merely to a few nobles, but to a large upper-middle stratum of commercial *bourgeoisie*. England was thus one of the first nations to develop, albeit on a tiny scale, a prime requisite of an industrial economy: a "mass" consumer market. As a result, a rising pressure of demand inspired a search for new techniques. Very typically, the Society for the Encouragement of Arts and Manufactures (itself a significant child of the age) offered a prize for a machine that would spin six threads of cotton at one time, thus enabling the spinner to keep up with the technologically more advanced weaver. It was this that led, at least in part, to Arkwright's spinning jenny, of which we shall hear more shortly.

Second, England was the scene of the most successful and thoroughgoing transformation of feudal society into commercial society. The process of enclosures was a significant clue to a historic change that sharply marked off England from the Continent. It was that in England alone the aristocracy had made its peace with (and more than that, found its profits in) commerce. Although sharp conflicts of interest remained between the "old" landed power and the "new" monied power, by 1700 the ruling orders in England had decisively opted for adaptation rather than resistance to the demands of the market economy.[4]

Third, England was the locus of a unique enthusiasm for science and engineering. The famous Royal Society, of which Newton was an early president, was founded in 1660 and was the immediate source of much intellectual excitement. Indeed, a popular interest in gadgets, machines, and devices of all sorts soon became a mild national obsession: *Gentlemen's Magazine*, a kind of *New Yorker* of the period, announced in 1729 that it would henceforth keep its readers "abreast of every invention"—a task

[4] See Barrington Moore, *Social Origins of Dictatorship and Democracy* (Boston: Beacon Press, 1966), Chap. I.

that the mounting flow of inventions soon rendered quite impossible. No less important was an enthusiasm of the British landed aristocracy for scientific farming: English landlords displayed an interest in matters of crop rotation and fertilizer that their French counterparts would have found quite beneath their dignity.

Then there were a host of other background causes, some as fortuitous as the immense resources of coal and iron ore on which the British sat; others as purposeful as the development of a national patent system that deliberately sought to stimulate and protect the act of invention itself.° And then, as the Revolution came into being, it fed upon itself. The new techniques (especially in textiles) simply destroyed their handicraft competition around the world and thus enormously increased their own markets. But what finally brought all these factors into operation was the energy of a group of New Men who made of the latent opportunities of history a vehicle for their own rise to fame and fortune.

rise of the One such, for instance, was John Wilkinson. The son of an old-fashioned,
New Men small-scale iron producer, Wilkinson was a man possessed by the technological possibilities of his business. He invented a dozen things: a rolling mill and a steam lathe, a process for the manufacture of iron pipes, and a design for machining accurate cylinders. Typically, he decided that the old-fashioned leather bellows used in the making of iron itself were not efficient, and so he determined to make iron ones. "Everybody laughed at me," he later wrote. "I did it and applied the steam engine to blow them and they all cried: 'Who could have thought of it?' "

He followed his success in production with a passion for application; everything must be made of iron: pipes, bridges, even ships. After a ship made of iron plates had been successfully launched, he wrote a friend: "It answers all my expectations, and has convinced the unbelievers, who were nine hundred and ninety-nine in a thousand. It will be a nine-days wonder, and afterwards, a Columbus' egg." [5]

But Wilkinson was only one of many. The most famous was, of course, James Watt—well known to Adam Smith—who, together with Matthew

---

° Phyllis Deane, in *The First Industrial Revolution* (paperback ed., Cambridge: Cambridge University Press, 1965), ascribes the onset of industrialism in England to a somewhat different set of causes: a rise in population, better food-producing techniques, a boom in foreign trade, and a vast improvement in transportation. There is no doubt that these were also indispensable elements in the process. I mention Miss Deane's book so that a student will not think that there is only one "right" way of accounting for very complex historical transformations. For yet another exceedingly good general account of the process, one might turn to the fascinating book by David Landes, *Prometheus Unbound* (Cambridge: Cambridge University Press, 1969).

[5] Paul Mantoux, *The Industrial Revolution in the Eighteenth Century,* 2nd ed. (New York: Harcourt, 1928), pp. 313n, 315.

Boulton, formed the first company for the manufacture of steam engines. Watt was the son of an architect, shipbuilder, and maker of nautical instruments. At thirteen he was already making models of machines, and by young manhood he was an accomplished artisan. He planned to settle in Glasgow, but the guild of hammermen objected to his making mathematical instruments—the last remnants of feudalism thus coming into an ironic personal conflict with the man who, more than any other, would create *the* invention that would destroy guild organization. At any rate, Watt found a haven at the university and there, in 1764, had his attention turned to an early and very unsatisfactory steam engine invented by Newcomen. In his careful and systematic way, Watt experimented with steam pressures, cylinder designs, and valves, until by 1796 he had developed a truly radical and (by the standards of those days) extraordinarily powerful and efficient engine. Interestingly, Watt could never have done so well with his engines had not Wilkinson perfected a manner of making good piston–cylinder fits. Previously, cylinders and pistons were made of wood and rapidly wore out. Typically, too, it was Wilkinson who bought the first steam engine to be used for purposes other than pumping: It worked the famous iron bellows.

There was needed, however, more than Watt's skill. The new engines had to be produced and sold, and the factory that made them had to be financed and organized. Watt at first formed a partnership with John Roebuck, another iron magnate, but it shortly failed. Thereafter, luck came his way. Matthew Boulton, already a wealthy and highly successful manufacturer of buttons and buckles, took up Roebuck's contract with Watt, and the greatest combination of technical skill and business acumen of the day was born.

Even then the firm did not prosper immediately. Expenses of development were high, and the new firm was not out of debt for twelve years. Yet from the beginning, interest was high. By 1781 Boulton was able to claim that the people of London, Birmingham, and Manchester were all "steam mill mad"; and by 1786, when two steam engines were harnessed to fifty pairs of millstones in the largest flour mill in the world, all London came to see the marvel.

The steam engine was the greatest single invention, but by no means the sole mainstay, of the Industrial Revolution. Hardly less important were a group of textile inventions, of which the most famous was Arkwright's jenny, or water frame, as it was called to distinguish it from other hand-operated spinning jennies.*

---

* Essentially, what the water frame did was enable cotton thread of much greater strength to be produced. As a result, for the first time it was possible to use cotton thread instead of linen thread for the warp (the vertical threads that take most of the strain in weaving) as well as for the weft. Not until Arkwright's invention was "cotton cloth" made wholly of cotton. The new cloth was incomparably superior to the old and instantly enjoyed a huge demand.

Arkwright's career is, in itself, interesting. A barber, he plied his trade near the weaving districts of Manchester and so heard the crying need for a machine that would enable the cottage spinners to keep up with the technically more advanced weavers. Good fortune threw him into contact with a clockmaker named John Kay, whom he hired to perfect a machine that Kay had already begun with another employer-inventor. What happened thereafter is obscure: Kay left the business accused of theft and embezzlement, and Arkwright appeared as the "sole inventor" of a spinning jenny in 1769.

He now found two rich hosiers, Samuel Need and Jedediah Strutt, who agreed to set up business with him to produce water frames, and in 1771 the firm built its own spinning mill. It was an overnight success; by 1779 it had several thousand spindles and more than 300 workmen, and ran night and day. Within not many years, Arkwright had built an immense fortune for himself and founded an even more immense textile industry for England. "O reader," wrote Carlyle, looking back on his career, "what a historical phenomenon is that bag-cheeked, pot-bellied, much enduring, much inventing barber! . . . It was this man that had to give England the power of cotton." [6]

the industrial entre- preneur

It is interesting, as we watch the careers of these New Men, to draw a few generalizations concerning them. For this was an entirely new class of economically important persons. Peter Onions, who was one of the inventors of the puddling process, was an obscure foreman; Arkwright was a barber; Benjamin Huntsman, the steel pioneer, was originally a maker of clocks; Maudslay, who invented the automatic screw machine, was a bright young mechanic at the Woolwich Arsenal. None of the great industrial pioneers came of noble lineage; and with few exceptions, such as Matthew Boulton, none even possessed money capital. In agriculture, the new revolutionary methods of scientific farming enjoyed aristocratic patronage and leadership, especially from the famous Sir Jethro Tull and Lord Townshend; but in industry, the lead went to men of humble origin and descent.

Let us note, therefore, that this required a social system flexible enough to permit the rise of such obscure "adventurers." It is not until we see the catalytic effect of unleashing and harnessing the energies of talented men in the lower and middle ranks of the social order that we begin to appreciate the immense liberating effect of the preceding economic and political revolutions. In the medieval hierarchy, the meteoric careers of such New Men would have been unthinkable. In addition, the New Men were the product of the unique economic preparation of England itself. They were, of course, the beneficiaries of the rising demand and the technical inquisitiveness of the times. Beyond that, many of the small manufacturers were, themselves,

[6] Mantoux. *The Industrial Revolution in the Eighteenth Century,* p. 225.

former small proprietors who had been bought out during the late period of the enclosure movement and who determined to use their tiny capital in the promising area of manufacture.

the new   Many of these New Men made great sums of money. A few, like Boulton
rich   and Watt, were modest in their wants. Despite an iron-clad patent, they charged for their engines only the basic cost of the machine and installation plus one-third the saving in fuel the customer got. Some, like Josiah Wedgwood, founder of the great china works, actually refused on principle to take out patents. But most of them did not display such fine sensibilities. Arkwright retired a multimillionaire, living in ostentatious splendor; Huntsman, Wilkinson, and Samuel Walker (who began life as a nailsmith and stole the secret of cast steel) all went on to roll up huge fortunes.[*] Indeed, Wilkinson's iron business became a minor industrial state with a credit stronger than many German and Italian principalities. It even coined its own money, and its copper and silver tokens (with a profile and legend of John Wilkinson, Ironmaster) were much in use between 1787 and 1808.

Beyond mere avarice, the manufacturers have been described by the economic historian, Paul Mantoux, as

tyrannical, hard, sometimes cruel: their passions and greeds were those of upstarts. They had the reputation of being heavy drinkers and of having little regard for the honour of their female employees. They were proud of their newly acquired wealth and lived in great style with footmen, carriages and gorgeous town and country houses.[7]

It is not surprising, then, that Adam Smith, while recognizing their usefulness, looked with distrust on the "mean rapacity, the monopolizing spirit" of merchants and manufacturers, warning that "they neither are, nor ought to be, the rulers of mankind."[8]

Pleasant or unpleasant, the personal characteristics fade beside one overriding quality. These were all men interested in expansion, in growth, in investment for investment's sake. All of them were identified with technological progress, and none of them disdained contact with the physical process of production. An employee of Maudslay once remarked, "It was a pleasure to see him handle a tool of any kind, but he was *quite splendid* with an 18-inch file."[9] Watt was tireless in experimenting with his machines;

---

[*] In contrast to the manufacturers, the inventors did not usually fare successfully. Many of them, who did not have Watt's good fortune in finding a Boulton, died poor and neglected, fruitlessly suing for stolen inventions, unpaid royalties, ignored claims.

[7] Mantoux, *The Industrial Revolution in the Eighteenth Century*, p. 397.

[8] *The Wealth of Nations* (New York: Modern Library, 1937), p. 460.

[9] Lewis Mumford, *Technics and Civilization* (New York: Harcourt, 1934), p. 210.

Wedgwood stomped about his factory on his wooden leg, scrawling, "This won't do for Jos. Wedgwood," wherever he saw evidence of careless work. Richard Arkwright was a bundle of ceaseless energy in promoting his interests, jouncing about England over execrable roads in a post chaise driven by four horses, pursuing his correspondence as he traveled.

"With us," wrote a French visitor to a calico works in 1788, "a man rich enough to set up and run a factory like this would not care to remain in a position which he would deem unworthy of his wealth." [10] This was an attitude entirely foreign to the rising English industrial capitalist. His work was its own dignity and reward; the wealth it brought was quite aside. Boswell, on being shown Watt and Boulton's great engine works at Soho, declared that he never forgot Boulton's expression as the latter declared, "I sell here, sir, what all the world desires to have—Power."[11]

The New Men were first and last *entrepreneurs*—enterprisers. They brought with them a new energy, as restless as it proved to be inexhaustible. In an economic, if not a political, sense, they deserve the epithet "revolutionaries," for the change they ushered in was nothing short of total, sweeping, and irreversible.

industrial and social repercussions   The first and most striking element of that change was a sharp rise in the output of the newly industrialized industries. The import of raw cotton for spinning weighed 1-million pounds in 1701; 3-million pounds in 1750; 5 million in 1781. That was a respectable rate of increase. But then came the sudden burst in textile technology. By 1784, the figure was over 11-million pounds; by 1789 it was three times greater yet, and still it grew: to 43-million pounds in 1799; 56 million in 1800; 60 million in 1802.[12] So was it with much else where the new technology penetrated. The output of coal increased tenfold in forty years; that of pig iron leaped from 68,000 tons in 1788 to 1,347,000 tons in 1839.[13]

Thus, the first impact of the Industrial Revolution was an immense quickening of the pace of production in the new industrial sector of the economy, an effect we find repeated in every nation that goes through an "industrial revolution." In France, for example, the impact of industrial techniques did not make its influence felt until about 1815; between that date and 1845, the French output of pig iron grew fivefold; her coal production, sevenfold; her rate of importation, tenfold.[14]

---

[10] Mantoux, *The Industrial Revolution in the Eighteenth Century*, p. 404.

[11] H. R. Fox Bourne, *English Merchants* (London: 1866), p. 119.

[12] Mantoux, *The Industrial Revolution in the Eighteenth Century*, p. 258.

[13] J. L. and B. Hammond, *The Rise of Modern Industry* (New York: Harcourt, 1937), p. 160.

[14] A. Dunham, *The Industrial Revolution in France, 1815–48* (New York: Exposition Press, 1955), p. 432.

The Industrial Revolution, itself, did not immediately exert a comparable leverage on the *overall* increase of output. The industrial sector, to begin with, was small; and the phenomenal rates of increase in those industries where its leverage was first and most fruitfully applied were by no means mirrored in every industry. What is of crucial importance, however, is that the Industrial Revolution ushered in the technology by which large-scale, sustained growth was eventually to take place. This is a process into which we must look more carefully at the end of this chapter.

rise of the factory   But first we must pay heed to another immediate and visible result of the Industrial Revolution in England. We can describe it as the transformation of an essentially commercial and agricultural society into one in which industrial manufacture became the dominant mode of organizing economic life. To put it more concretely, the Industrial Revolution was characterized by *the rise of the factory to the center of social as well as economic life.* After 1850, the factory was not only the key economic institution of England, but it was the economic institution that shaped its politics, its social problems, the character of its daily life, just as decisively as the manor or the guild had done a few centuries earlier.

It is difficult for us today to realize the pace or the quality of change that this rise of factory work brought about. Until the mid-eighteenth century, Glasgow, Newcastle, and the Rhondda Valley were mostly waste or farm land, and Manchester in 1727 was described by Daniel Defoe as "a mere village." Forty years later, there were a hundred integrated mills and a whole cluster of machine plants, forges, leather and chemical works in the area. A modern industrial city had been created.

By the 1780s the shape of the new environment was visible. A French mineralogist visiting England in 1784 wrote:

[The] creaking, the piercing noise of the pulleys, the continuous sound of hammering, the ceaseless energy of the men keeping all this machinery in motion, presented a sight as interesting as it was new. . . . The night is so filled with fire and light that when from a distance we see, here a glowing mass of coal, there darting flames leaping from the blast furnaces, when we hear the heavy hammers striking the echoing anvils and the shrill whistling of the air pumps, we do not know whether we are looking at a volcano in eruption or have been miraculously transported to Vulcan's cave. . . .[15]

The factory provided not merely a new landscape but a new and uncongenial social habitat. In our day, we have become so used to urban industrial life that we forget what a wrench is the transition from farm to city. For the peasant, this transfer requires a drastic adjustment. No longer does he work at his own pace, but at the pace of a machine. No longer are

[15] Mantoux, *The Industrial Revolution in the Eighteenth Century,* p. 313.

slack seasons determined by the weather, but by the state of the market. No longer is the land, however miserable its crop, an eternal source of sustenance close at hand, but only the packed and sterile earth of the industrial site.

It is little wonder that the English laborer, still more used to rural than urban ways, feared and hated the advent of the machine. Throughout the early years of the Industrial Revolution, workmen literally attacked the invading army of machinery, burning and wrecking factories. During the late eighteenth century, for instance, when the first textile mills were built, whole hamlets rose in revolt rather than work in the mills. Headed by a mythical General Ludd, the Luddites constituted a fierce but fruitless opposition to industrialism. In 1813, in a mass trial that ended in many hangings and transportations, the movement came to an end.*

*conditions
of labor*   Distasteful as was the advent of the factory itself, even more distasteful were the conditions within it. Child labor, for instance, was commonplace and sometimes began at age four; hours of work were generally dawn to dusk; abuses of every kind were all too frequent. A Committee of Parliament, appointed in 1832 to look into conditions, gives this testimony from a factory overseer.

Q. At what time in the morning, in the brisk time, did these girls go to the mills?

A. In the brisk time, for about six weeks, they have gone at three o'clock in the morning and ended at ten or nearly half past at night.

Q. What intervals were allowed for rest and refreshment during those nineteen hours of labour?

A. Breakfast a quarter of an hour, and dinner half an hour, and drinking a quarter of an hour.

Q. Was any of that time taken up in cleaning the machinery?

A. They generally had to do what they call dry down; sometimes this took the whole time at breakfast or drinking.

Q. Had you not great difficulty in awakening your children to the excessive labour?

A. Yes, in the early time we had to take them up asleep and shake them.

Q. Had any of them any accident in consequence of this labour?

A. Yes, my eldest daughter . . . the cog caught her forefinger nail and screwed it off below the knuckle.

Q. Has she lost that finger?

A. It is cut off at the second joint.

Q. Were her wages paid during that time?

A. As soon as the accident happened the wages were totally stopped.[16]

* Even in our day, however, we use the word "Luddite" to describe an attempt to "fight back" at the threat of machinery.

[16] Tawney, Bland, and Brown, *English Economic History, Selected Documents* (London: Bell, 1914), p. 510.

It was a grim age. The long hours of work, the general dirt and clangor of the factories, the lack of even the most elementary safety precautions, all combined to give early industrial capitalism a reputation from which, in the minds of many people of the world, it has never recovered. Worse yet were the slums to which the majority of workers returned after their travail. Life expectancy at birth in Manchester was seventeen years—a figure that reflected a child mortality rate of over 50 percent. This is not so surprising when we read this government commissioner's report of 1839 on one such workers' quarter in Glasgow called "the wynds."

The wynds . . . house a fluctuating population of between 15,000 and 30,000 persons. This district is composed of many narrow streets and square courts and in the middle of each court there is a dunghill. Although the outward appearance of these places was revolting, I was nevertheless quite unprepared for the filth and misery that were to be found inside. In some bedrooms we visited at night we found a whole mass of humanity stretched on the floor. There were often 15 to 20 men and women huddled together, some being clothed and others naked. There was hardly any furniture there and the only thing which gave these holes the appearance of a dwelling was fire burning on the hearth. Thieving and prostitution are the main sources of income of these people.[17]

early capitalism and social justice

Without question, the times were marked by tremendous social suffering. But it is well, in looking back on the birth years of industrial capitalism, to bear several facts in mind:

1. *It is doubtful if the poverty represented a deterioration in life for the masses in general.*

In at least some sections of England, industrialism brought immediate benefits. Wedgwood (an exceptionally good employer, it is true) used to tell his employees to ask their parents for a description of the country as *they* first knew it and to compare their present state. So, too, the twelve-hour day in Arkwright's mills was a two-hour *improvement* over previous Manchester standards. Furthermore, the existing poverty was not by any means new. As we know from Hogarth's etchings, long before the Industrial Revolution, "Gin Lane" already sported its pitiful types. As one reformer of the mid-nineteenth century wrote, those whose sensibilities were revolted by the sight of suffering factory children thought "how much more delightful would have been the gambol of free limbs on the hillside; the sight of the green mead with its spangles of buttercups and daisies; the song of the bird and the humming of the bee . . . [but] we have seen children perishing from sheer hunger in the mud hovel or in the ditch by the wayside." [18]

[17] Quoted in F. Engels, *The Condition of the Working Class in England* (New York: Macmillan, 1958), p. 46.

[18] Friedrich Hayek, ed., *Capitalism and the Historians* (Chicago: University of Chicago Press, 1954), p. 180.

2. *Much of the harsh criticism to which early industrial capitalism was subjected was derived not so much from its economic but from its political accompaniments.*

For, coincident with the rise of capitalism, and indeed contributory to it, was a deep-seated change in the vantage point of political criticism. New ideas of democracy, of social justice, of the "rights" of the individual charged the times with a critical temper of mind before which *any* economic system would have suffered censure.

To be sure, the political movements by which capitalism was carried to its heights were not working-class movements, but middle-class, bourgeois movements; the rising manufacturers in England and France had little "social conscience" beyond a concern for their own rights and privileges. But the movement of political liberalism that they set in motion had a momentum beyond the narrow limits for which it was intended. By the first quarter of the nineteenth century, the condition of the working classes, now so exposed to public view in the new factory-slum environment, had begun to curry public sympathy.

Thus, one of the unexpected consequences of the Industrial Revolution was a sharp reorientation of political ideas. In the creation of an industrial working class and an industrial environment, the revolution bequeathed a new economic framework to politics. Karl Marx and Friedrich Engels were to write in 1848 that "all history" was the history of class struggle, but never did that struggle emerge so nakedly into the open as after the industrial environment had been brought into being.

Equally important was that the rise of political liberalism not only roused feelings of hostility toward the prevailing order, but initiated the slow process of amelioration. *From the outset, a reform movement coincided with capitalism.* In 1802, pauper apprentices were legally limited to a twelve-hour day and barred from night work. In 1819, the employment of children under nine was prohibited in cotton mills; in 1833, a 48- to 69-hour week was decreed for workers under eighteen (who comprised about 75 percent of all cotton-mill workers), and a system of government inspection of factories was inaugurated; in 1842, children under ten were barred from the coal mines; in 1847, a 10-hour daily limit (later raised to 10½) was set for children and women.

The nature of the reforms is itself eloquent testimony to the conditions of the times, and the fact that the reforms were bitterly opposed and often observed in the breach is testimony to the prevailing spirit. Yet capitalism, unlike feudalism, was from the beginning subject to the corrective force of democracy. Karl Marx, drawing on the material of the 1830s, drew a mordant picture of the capitalist process in all its economic squalor, but he overlooked (or shrugged off) this countervailing force whose power was steadily to grow.

3. *The most important effect of the Industrial Revolution we have left for last: its long-term leverage on economic well-being.*

The ultimate impact of the Industrial Revolution was to usher in a rise of living standards on a mass scale unlike anything that the world had ever known before.

This did not happen overnight. In 1840, according to the calculations of Arnold Toynbee, Sr., the wage of an ordinary laborer came to eight shillings a week, which was six shillings less than he needed to buy the bare necessities of life.[19] He made up the deficit by sending his children or his wife, or both, to work in the mills. If, as we have noted, some sections of the working class gained from the early impact of industrialization, others suffered a *decline* from the standard of living enjoyed in 1795 or thereabouts. A Committee of Parliament in the 1830s, for example, discovered that a hand weaver at that earlier date could have bought more than three times as many provisions with his wages as at the later date. Although not every trade suffered equally, the first flush of the Industrial Revolution brought its hardships to bear full force, while its benefits were not as immediately noticeable.

By 1870, however, the long-run effects of the Industrial Revolution were beginning to make themselves felt. The price of necessities had by then risen to fifteen shillings, but weekly earnings had crept up to meet and even exceed that sum. Hours were shorter, too. At the Jarrow Shipyards and the New Castle Chemical Works, the workweek had fallen from 61 to 54 hours; and even in the notoriously long-working textile mills, the stint was down to "only" 57 hours. It was still a far cry from an abundant society, much less an "affluent" one, but the corner had been turned.

THE INDUSTRIAL REVOLUTION IN THE
PERSPECTIVE OF THEORY

We have reviewed very briefly the salient historic features of the rise of industrial capitalism. Now we must reflect on the great economic and social changes we have witnessed and ask a pertinent economic question: *How did the process of industrialization raise material well-being?* To answer the question, we must turn to economic theory to elucidate systematically the insights we have already gained from Smith's *Wealth of Nations*.

Let us begin by asking what is necessary for a rise in the economic well-being of a society. The answer is not difficult. If we are to enjoy a greater material well-being, generally speaking, we must produce more. This is particularly true when we begin at the stage of scarcely-better-than-subsistence that characterized so much of Europe before the Industrial Revolution. For such a society to raise the standard of living of its masses,

[19] *The Industrial Revolution* (Boston: Beacon Press, 1956), p. 113.

the first necessity is unquestionably higher production. Despite all the inequities of distribution that attended the society of serf and lord, capitalist and child-employee, underlying the meanness of the times was one overriding reality: the sheer inadequacy of output. There was simply not enough to go around, and if somewhat less lopsided distributive arrangements might have lessened the moral indignity of the times, they would not have contributed much to a massive improvement in basic economic well-being. Even assuming that the wage of the city laborer and the income of the peasant could have been doubled had the rich been deprived of their share—and this is a wildly extravagant assumption—still, the prime characteristic of rural and urban life would have been its poverty.

We must add only one important qualification to this emphasis on increased output as the prerequisite of economic improvement. Overall living standards will not improve if a country's population is growing even faster than its increased output. The production of goods and services must rise *faster* than population if individual well-being is to improve.

How does a society raise its *per capita* output?

We cannot fully analyze this problem here. But our glimpse into the pin factory and our study of the Industrial Revolution in England enable us to understand a great deal about the problem. For clearly, *the key to higher output lies in enhancing the human energies of the community with the leverage of industrial capital.* Our analytic understanding of the growth must begin by looking further into this extraordinary power that capital possesses.

capital and productivity

We have already frequently used the word "capital," but we have not yet defined it. We can see that in a fundamental sense, capital consists of anything that can enhance man's power to perform economically useful work. An unshaped stone is capital to the cave man who can use it as a hunting implement. A hoe is capital to a peasant; a road system is capital to the inhabitants of a modern industrial society. Knowledge is capital, too—indeed, perhaps the most precious part of society's stock of capital.

When economists talk of capital, however, they usually confine their meaning to *capital goods*—the stock of tools, equipment, machines, and buildings that society produces in order to expedite the production process.* All these capital goods have one effect in common on the productive process: They all operate to make human labor more productive. They make

---

* Is money capital? It certainly is to the individual who possesses it. But it is not capital for society as a whole. For money only represents *claims* to society's real wealth, which is its goods and services. If an individual's money disappears, he loses his claim on those goods and services, and we can indeed say that he has lost his "capital." But if *all* money disappeared, we could not say that society had lost its claim on its own wealth. It would only have to devise another system of tickets.

it possible for a worker to produce more goods in an hour (or a week, or a year) than he could produce without the aid of that capital. Capital is therefore a method of raising per capita *productivity*, which is an individual's output in a given span of time; it is the lesson of the pin factory extended to all branches of output. For example, in a forty-hour week, a typical modern worker using power-driven mechanical equipment can physically outproduce three men working seventy hours a week with the simpler tools of a half-century ago. To put it differently, in one day a modern worker will turn out as much output as his counterpart of 1900 did in a full week—not because the modern worker works harder, but because he has at his command thousands of dollars worth of capital equipment rather than the few hundred dollars worth available to a worker in 1900.

Why does capital make labor so much more productive?

The most important reason is that capital goods enable man to use principles and devices such as the lever and the wheel, heat and cold, combustion and expansion in ways that the unaided body cannot. *Capital gives men mechanical and physicochemical powers of literally transhuman dimensions.* They magnify enormously his muscular strength; they refine his powers of control; they embody his intelligence; they endow him with endurance and resilience far beyond those of the flesh and bone. In using capital, man utilizes the natural world as a supplement to his own feeble capacities.

capital and special-ization

Another reason for the augmentation of production lies in the fact that capital facilitates the *specialization of man's labor*. Once again Smith's example serves us well. A team of men working together, each man tending to one job alone in which he is expert, can usually far outproduce the same number of men, each of whom does a variety of jobs. The prime example is, of course, the auto production line, in which a thousand men cooperate to produce an immensely larger output of cars than could be achieved if each man built a car by himself. Auto assembly lines, of course, use prodigious quantities of capital in the overhead conveyor belts, the inventories of parts on hand, the huge factory with its power system, and so on. And while not all specialization of labor depends on capital, capital is usually necessary for the large-scale industrial operations in which specialization becomes most effective.

In our next chapter we will return to these important matters in the context of the development of modern industry. But while we are still discussing the basic question of the rise of industry itself, there is a fundamental problem to be disposed of. This is the question of how capital is made in the first place, of how a society generates the capital equipment it needs in order to grow.

capital and saving   The question brings us for the first time to a relationship that we will encounter many more times in our study of economics, both in a perspective of history and from a later vantage point of theory. The relationship is between the creation of those physical artifacts we call capital, and the inescapable prior act that we call *saving*.

When we think of saving, we ordinarily picture it in financial terms; that is, as a decision not to spend part of our money income. Behind this financial act, however, lies a "real" act that we must now clearly understand. *When we save money, we also abstain from using a certain quantity of goods and services we might have bought.* To be sure, our money savings represent a claim on goods and services, a claim that we may later exercise. Until we do, however, we have freed resources that would otherwise have been used to satisfy our immediate wants. When Smith's pin manufacturer "accumulated," he deliberately forwent a higher standard of living that he could have enjoyed by spending his profits on riotous living. From these freed resources—the unused labor and capital that might have produced silks and coaches—society builds its capital, or, in more technical language, carries out the act of *investment*.

In the simplest example, we can see this real meaning of saving in the case of a primitive hunter who abstains from a full meal today so that he will not have to hunt tomorrow. By saving half of today's kill, he frees the resource of (his own) labor: Tomorrow, instead of hunting, he will make a better spear. In a much more indirect and complex fashion, when we save money we are also giving up a potential meal (or some other consumption good), so that society can then make capital out of the goods and services we would otherwise have consumed.

saving and investment   Thus, the acts of saving and investment are inextricably linked: Saving is the releasing of resources from consumption; investment is the employment of these resources in making capital. Indeed, from society's point of view, saving and investment are only two sides of the same coin. Why do we then separate them in economic discourse? The reason is that different people may perform the saving and investing functions, especially in modern societies. We are no longer hunters and spear makers. Those who release the resources of society are often not the same individuals as those who gather up those resources for investment purposes. Nonetheless, we can see that every act of investment, no matter who performs it, requires the presence of released resources.*

This does not mean that investment necessarily entails a *diminution* of consumption. A rich society does not feel its normal, recurrent saving as a

* Note, however, that an act of saving—i.e., an abstention from consumption—does not *automatically* bring about an act of purposive investment. This leads to serious problems, to which we shall turn in Chapter 7.

"pinch" on its spending, and Smith's manufacturers were not known for their modest ways. A society with unemployed factors can put its idle resources to work building capital without diminishing its expenditure on consumption. (It is still saving, of course, insofar as it is not using those newly employed resources to make consumption goods.) But—and this is a crucial point—when a *fully employed* society builds more capital, it *must* curtail its consumption. In this case, there is nowhere the needed capital-building resources can come from but their erstwhile consumption employments.

Let us go on still further. We can now see that the *rate* at which an economy can invest—that is, the size of the yearly addition it can make to its stock of capital goods—depends on its capacity to save. If its living standards are already close to the margin of existence, it will not be able to transfer much labor from consumption effort to capital-building effort. However badly it may wish for more tools, however productive those tools would prove to be, it cannot invest beyond the point at which its remaining consumption activity would no longer be adequate to maintain subsistence. At the other extreme, if a society is well-to-do, it may be able to abstain from a great deal of current consumption effort to provide for the future. Accordingly, its growth will be fast. *It is a hard economic reality that the amount of construction for the future can never exceed the amount of resources and effort that are unused, or that can be released from consumption in the present.*

growth in early capitalism

This seems to imply that the process of economic growth must perforce be very slow in a poor economy. And so it is. In England, as we have already seen, nearly three-quarters of a century elapsed before the new process of industrialization brought about an increase in productivity sufficiently large to be felt as a general improvement in the lot of the working-man. In the underdeveloped nations, as we shall see in Chapter 12, the prospect is equally or even more sluggish. At its best, growth is a gradual and cumulative rather than an "instant" phenomenon; and where the initial level of savings is low because of poverty, the rate of advance is correspondingly slower.

Perhaps we can better appreciate this overall determinant of the pace of growth if we now examine the actual social circumstances under which saving arose in early nineteenth-century England.

For who did the saving? Who abstained from consumption? Well-to-do agriculturalists and manufacturers (for all their ostentatious ways) were certainly important savers who plowed substantial sums into more new capital investments. Yet the savers were not just the manufacturers or the gentry but also another class—the industrial workers. Here, in the low level of industrial wages, a great sacrifice was made—not voluntarily, by any manner of means, but made just the same. From the resources the workers could have consumed was built the industrial foundation for the future.

We can also see something that is perhaps even more significant. This is the fact that England *had* to hold down the level of its working-class consumption in order to free productive effort for the accumulation of capital goods. In point of historic actuality, the "holding-down" was accomplished largely by the forces of the marketplace—with a liberal assist, to be sure, from the capitalists and from a government quick to oppose the demands of labor in the interests of its upper classes. But social inequities aside, the hard fact remains that had industrial wages risen very much, a vast demand for consumer goods would have turned the direction of the English economy away from capital building, toward the satisfaction of current wants. This would certainly have redounded to the immediate welfare of the English worker (although the increase in per capita consumption would have been small). At the same time, however, it would have *postponed* the day when society's overall productive powers were capable of generating an aggregate output of very large size.

This bitter choice must be confronted by every industrializing society, capitalist or socialist, democratic or totalitarian. To assuage the needs of today or to build for tomorrow is *the* decision a developing society must make. As we shall see in Chapter 12, it is a decision that lies behind much of the political and economic agony of a large part of the world today.

incentives
for growth

There remains but one last question. We have gained some insight into the mechanics of growth, but we have not yet answered the question: How are these mechanics brought about? How does society arrange the reallocation of its factors of production to bring about the creation of the capital it needs?

This query brings us again to a consideration of our original division of economic societies into three types: Traditional, Command, and Market. It also leads to some very important conclusions.

The first of these is obvious: it is that tradition-bound societies are not apt to grow. In such societies there is *no* direct social means of inducing the needed reallocation of factors. Worse yet, there are often strong social and religious barriers that create obstacles to the needed shifts in employment.

The situation is very different, however, when we turn to command societies. We have seen a striking use of command as the industrializing agency in modern times. In at least one country, the Soviet Union, Command has been the principal mechanism for a dramatic transition from peasanthood into industrialization, and in many other collectivist economies, Command is now trying to bring into effect such a transition.

In Chapter 10, we shall return to the Russian experience. Meanwhile, let us not forget that command was also one of the principal ways by which

Europe began its industrialization. In the state-directed establishment of shipyards and armories, the construction of royal palaces and estates, tapestry works and chinaware factories, a very important organizing impetus was given to the creation of an industrial sector in the mercantilist era. True, of course, that in those days, command was never so ruthlessly applied nor so widely directed as with the communist states. But however much milder the dosage, the medicine was in essence the same: the *initial* transfer of labor from the traditional pursuits of the land to the new tasks of the factory depended on a commanding authority that ordered the new pattern into being.*

the market as a capital-building mechanism

But command was by no means the main agency for the final industrialization of the West. Rather, the organizing force that put men to work in making capital equipment was the market.

How did the market bring about this remarkable transformation? It achieved its purposes by the lure of monetary rewards. It was the hope of *profits* that lured manufacturers into turning out more capital goods. It was the attraction of better *wages* (or sometimes of *any* wages) that directed workers into the new plants. It was the signal of rising prices that encouraged, and falling prices that discouraged, the production of this or that particular capital good. Here is Smith's market mechanism, joined to his growth model.

And what, we may next ask, opened the prospect of profits large enough to induce entrepreneurs to risk their savings in new capital goods? The answer brings us full circle to the focal point of this chapter. For the answer is to be found primarily in the body of technological advance constituting the core of the Industrial Revolution. It was the pin-making *machinery* that opened the possibility of a profitable and expanding pin industry.

Not that every new invention brought with it a fortune for its pioneering promoters, or that every new product found a market waiting for it. The path of technical advance is littered with inventions born "too soon" and with enterprises founded with great hopes and closed down six months later. But looking back over the vast process of capital accumulation that, beginning in the late eighteenth century, lifted first England and then America into the long flight of industrial development, there is little doubt

---

* As Barbara Ward has written in *India and the West:* "A developing society must at some point begin to save, even though it is still poor. This is the tough early stage of growth which Marx encountered in Victorian England and unfortunately took to be permanent. It is a difficult phase in any economy—so difficult that most societies got through it by *force majeure*. . . . No one asked the British laborers moving into the Manchester slums whether they wanted to save. . . . The Soviet workers who came to Sverdlovsk and Magnitogorsk from the primitive steppes had no say in the scale or the condition of their work. Nor have the Chinese in their communes today."

that the impelling force was the succession of inventions and innovations that successfully opened new aspects of nature to human control. Steam power, the cheap and efficient spinning and weaving of cloth, the first mass production of iron and, later, steel—these were the great breakthroughs of industrial science that opened the way for the massive accumulation of capital. And once the great inventions had marked out the channel of advance, secondary improvements and subsidiary inventions took on an important supporting role. To the enterpriser with a cost-cutting innovation went the prize of a market advantage in costs and correspondingly higher profit. More than that, once one pioneer in a field had gained a technical advantage, competition quickly forced everyone else in the field to catch up as quickly as they could. Most of the cost-cutting innovations involved adding mcahinery to the production process—and this in turn boosted the formation of capital.

Capitalism as a whole proved an unparalled machine for the accumulation of capital. In its development we find the first economic system in history in which economic growth became an *integral* part of daily life. As Marx and Engels were to write in the *Communist Manifesto:* "The bourgeoisie, during its scarce one hundred years, has created more massive and more colossal productive forces than have all preceding generations together." And the compliment, all the more meaningful coming from the two archenemies of its social order, was true.

4	*Key Concepts and Key Words*

Industrial Revolution

1. The Industrial Revolution *was a* great *turning period* in history, during which manufacturing and industrial activity became primary forms of social production.

2. The Industrial Revolution began in England in the mid- to late-eighteenth century (although its roots are far deeper). There are numerous reasons why it occurred there and then:
   - England was *a wealthy trading nation* with a well-developed middle class.
   - England's *aristocracy was much more commerce-minded* than the aristocracies of the Continent.
   - England was the home of a widespread vogue of *scientific investigation* and of "gentlemen farmers" interested in *agricultural innovation*.
   - England's relatively *open social structure* permitted the rise of New Men, such as Watt or Wilkinson, who brought to manufacturing a burst of new social energies.
   - Many other causes could be cited as well. The Industrial Revolution was a *many-sided,* complex chain of events.

Output
3. The Industrial Revolution brought with it changes of the greatest importance in society.
- It ushered in a slow but cumulative *rise in output* that was eventually to lift the industrial world out of an age-old poverty.
- It brought the *factory* (and the *industrial slum*) as a new environment for work and life.
- It gave rise to new kinds of *social abuses* and greatly sharpened the general *awareness of economic conditions*.

Capital building
4. The Industrial Revolution was essentially a *capital-building process* (machines, buildings, canals, railways), as a result of which the productivity of labor was greatly increased.

Productivity
5. *Capital generally enhances productivity* because it gives man far greater physical and technical capabilities than he enjoys with unaided labor alone. It also enables men to combine and *specialize* their labor, as in modern factory production lines.

Saving
6. *Capital building requires saving.* Capital can be built only if society has the use of resources normally used for filling its consumption needs. Saving releases these resources; investing puts them to use.

Investment

Consumption
7. Society cannot devote more resources or energies to capital building than those it releases from other uses (or those it has available as unemployed resources). Hence, by and large, *saving regulates the pace at which investment can proceed*. Poor societies, in which it is difficult to give up consumption, accordingly have great problems in amassing enough resources for investment.

8. The saving necessary for investment can come from agriculture, manufacturing enterprises, and many other sources. In poor nations, it must also often be wrung from workers or peasants, by denying them the use of all the nation's economic potential to fill their consumption needs.

9. Hence, *saving in poor nations is usually an involuntary process*. Capital building in many developing nations today, particularly those under collectivist regimes, is accomplished by the agency of Command. In the Industrial Revolution, it was accomplished in part by Command, but mainly by the market system. The remarkable inventions of the Industrial Revolution served as sources of profits that resulted in great accumulations of capital.

4	*Questions*

1. It is interesting to note that technical improvements in agriculture or manufacturing have generally been slow to arise in countries that have relied on slave labor. Can you think of a reason why this might be so?

2. What forces do you think would be necessary to bring a new "industrial revolu-

tion" to the underdeveloped world today? Is an industrial revolution there apt to resemble that in England in the eighteenth century?

3. Industrialization in England was marked by a sharp growth of bitter political feeling on the part of the new factory proletariat. Do you think this must be an accompaniment of industrialization everywhere, or was it a particular product of early capitalism?

4. How does capital help human productivity? Discuss this in relation to the following kinds of labor: farm labor, office help, teaching, government administration.

5. When General Motors devotes a billion dollars to new investment (building new factories, warehouses, offices, etc.), who does the saving that is required? Stockholders? Workers? The public? Buyers of cars?

6. It is estimated that the value of the capital structures and equipment in the US is some $4 trillion. Assume that half of it were wiped out in some catastrophe. What would happen to US productivity? To average US well-being? How could the damage be repaired?

7. Does all investment require saving? Why?

8. Is capital building in the US today directed by the market alone? Does the government accumulate capital? Does public capital improve productivity as well as private capital?

9. Is building a school an "investment?" Is building a hospital? a sports stadium? a housing project? a research lab? What do you think distinguishes investment, in general, from consumption?

5 The Impact of Industrial Technology

With this chapter, we enter a new major period of economic history. Formerly we dealt largely with the past, giving only an occasional glance to later echoes of the problems we have encountered. Commencing with this chapter, our focus turns toward and into the actual present. We have reached the stage of economic history whose nearest boundary is our own time. Simultaneously, our point of geographic focus shifts. As economic history enters the mid-nineteenth century, the dynamic center of events comes increasingly to be located in the United States. Not only do we now begin to enter the modern world, but the economic trends in which we will be interested take us directly into our own society.

What will be the theme of this chapter? Essentially it will continue a motif we began with the Industrial Revolution—the impact of technology on economic society. Looking back, we can see that the burst of inventions that marked the Revolution was not in any sense the completion of a historic event. Rather, it was merely the inception of a process of technological change that would continually accelerate down to the present time.

We can distinguish three or even four stages of this continuous process. The "first" industrial revolution was largely concentrated in new textile machinery, improved methods of coal production and iron manufacture, revolutionary agricultural techniques, and steam power. It was succeeded in the middle years of the nineteenth century by a "second" industrial revolution: a clustering of industrial inventions centering on steel, railroad and steamship transportation, agricultural machinery, and chemicals. By the early years of the twentieth century, there was a third wave of inventions: electrical power, automobiles, the gasoline engine. In our own time there is a fourth: the revolution of electronics, air travel, automation, and, of course, nuclear energy.

It is difficult, perhaps impossible, to exaggerate the impact of this continuing industrial revolution. Now advancing rapidly, now slowly; now on a broad front, now on a narrow salient; now in the most practical of inventions, again in the purest of theoretical discoveries, the cumulative application of science and technology to the productive process was *the* great change of the nineteenth and twentieth centuries. The initial Industrial Revolution was thus in retrospect a kind of discontinuous leap in human history; a leap as important as that which had lifted the first pastoral settlements above the earlier hunting communities. We have already noted that in the factory the new technology brought a new working place for man, but its impact was vastly greater than that alone. The enormously heightened powers of transportation and communication, the far more effective means of wresting a crop from the soil, the hugely enhanced ability to apply power for lifting, hauling, shaping, binding, cutting—all this conspired to bring about a literal remaking of the human environment, and by no means an entirely benign one.

impact of one invention

In this book we cannot do more than inquire into some of the economic consequences of the incursion of industrial technology into modern society, but it may help us gain some insight into the dimensions of that penetrative process if we follow for a short distance the repercussions of a single invention.

Let us therefore look in on the Paris Exposition of 1867, where curious visitors are gathered around an interesting exhibit: a small engine in which illuminating gas and air are introduced into a combustion chamber and ignited by a spark. The resulting explosion pushes a piston; the piston turns a wheel. There is but one working stroke in every four, and the machine requires a large flywheel to regularize its movement, but, as the historian Allan Nevins writes, the effect of the machine "was comparable to the sudden snapping on of an electric globe in a room men had been trying to light with smoky candles."[1] It was the world's first internal combustion engine.

It was not long before the engine, invented by Dr. N. A. Otto of Germany, was a regular feature of the American landscape. Adapted to run on gasoline, a hitherto uninteresting by-product of kerosene manufacture, it was an ideal stationary power plant. Writes Nevins, "Soon every progressive farm, shop, and feed-mill had its one-cylinder engine chugging away, pumping water, sawing wood, grinding meal, and doing other small jobs."[2] By 1900 there were more than 18,500 internal combustion engines in the United States; and whereas the most powerful model in the Chicago World's Fair in 1893 was 35 horsepower, at the Paris Exposition seven years later, it was 1,000 horsepower.

The internal combustion engine was an extraordinary means of increasing, diffusing, and giving mobility to a basic requirement of material progress: power. And soon the new engine opened the way for a yet more

[1] *Ford, the Times, the Man, the Company* (New York: Scribner's, 1954), I, 96.
[2] *Study in Power, John D. Rockefeller* (New York: Scribner's, 1953), II, 109.

startling advance. In 1886, Charles E. Duryea of Chicopee, Massachusetts, had already decided that the gasoline engine was a far more promising power source than steam for a self-propelling road vehicle. By 1892, he and his brother had produced the first gas-powered "automobile," a weak and fragile toy. The next model in 1893 was a better one, and by 1896 the Duryea brothers actually sold thirteen cars. In that same year, a thirty-two-year-old mechanic named Henry Ford sold his first "quadricycle." The history of the automobile industry had begun.

the automobilization of America

Its growth was phenomenal. By 1905 there were 121 establishments making automobiles, and 10,000 wage earners were employed in the industry. By 1923 the number of plants had risen to 2,471, making the industry the largest in the country. In 1960 its annual payroll was as large as the national income of the United States in 1890. Not only that, but the automobile industry had become the single greatest customer for sheet steel, zinc, lead, rubber, leather. It was the buyer of one out of every three radios produced in the nation. It absorbed twenty-five-billion pounds of chemicals a year. It was the second largest user of engineering talent in the country, bowing only to national defense. It was the source of one-sixth of all the patents issued in the nation and the object of one-tenth of all consumer spending in the country. In the mid-1970s, it was estimated that no less than one job out of every seven and one business out of every six owed their existences directly or indirectly to the car.

Even this impressive array of figures by no means exhausts the impact of the internal combustion engine and its vehicular mounting. Over eight out of every ten families today own a motor vehicle, one in three own two or more cars. As a result, some fifty thousand towns manage to flourish without rail or water connections, an erstwhile impossibility; and seven out of ten workers no longer live within walking distance of their places of employment but drive to work. In fact, 1,300,000 of them drive fifty miles or more to work. To an extraordinary extent our entire economy has become "mobilized"—which is to say, dependent for its very functioning on the existence of wheeled, self-propelled transportation. If by some strange occurrence our automotive fleet were put out of commission—say by a spontaneous change in the nature of the gasoline molecule, rendering it incombustible—the effect would be as grave and as socially disastrous as a catastrophic famine in the Middle Ages.° No wonder that the Arab oil embargo of 1974 shook the industrialized world!

° I believe it was the economist Kenneth Boulding who suggested that if the United States were to be visited by intelligent beings from another part of the universe, their initial impression would probably be that the dominant form of life here consists of hard-shelled creatures with soft pulpy insides, who are propelled by wheels, although the creatures are capable of sluggish motion on their own when not encased in their natural exoskeletons.

We dwell on the impact of the car to stress the *economic* consequences of technology. These may not be its most ultimately important consequences. We live in a world that is threatened in many ways by the extraordinary disruptive power of man's inventive capacity. Technology has progressed to the point at which whole species (including man himself) are endangered by the poisons we manufacture and carelessly spew into the air and water, by the vast quantities of heat we throw into the atmosphere, and of course by the capacity for explosive disintegration that has come with the mastery of the atomic nucleus.

Later we will look into some of these problems when we turn to the immediate issues confronting the United States. But at this point, while we are studying the general effects of man's gradually increasing technological powers, we leave aside these very large problems to focus on the ways in which technology has silently affected our economic system. Let us look into some of these effects.

urban-
ization
The first has been a *vast increase in the degree of urbanization of society.* To an extraordinary extent (as we shall see in our next chapters), technology has enhanced the ability of the farmer to support the nonfarmer. As a result, society has more and more taken on the aspects and problems of the city rather than the country. In 1790, only 24 towns and cities in all of the United States had a population of more than 2,500, and together they accounted for only 6 percent of the total population. By 1860, the 392 biggest cities held 20 percent of the population; by the late 1970s, roughly two-thirds of the nation's people lived in 212 great "standard metropolitan areas," and the belt from Boston to Washington was in fact, if not in government, one vast sprawling "city." Industrial technology has literally refashioned the human environment, bringing with it all the gains—and all the terrible problems—of city life on a mass scale.

inter-
dependence
Second, *the steady growth of industrial technology has radically lessened the degree of economic independence of the average citizen.* In our opening chapter we noted the extreme vulnerability of the "unsupported" inhabitant of a modern society, dependent on the work of a thousand others to sustain his own existence. This, too, we can now trace to the effect of the continuing industrial revolution. Technology has not only moved men off the soil and into the city, but has vastly increased the specialized nature of work. Unlike the "man of all trades" of the early nineteenth century—the farmer who could perform so many of his necessary tasks himself—the typical factory worker or office worker is trained and employed to do only one small part

of a social operation that now achieves staggering complexity. Technology has vastly increased the degree of economic interdependence of the modern community and has made the solution of the economic problem hinge on the smooth coordination of an ever-widening network of delicately connected activities.

work and its discontents

Third, *the expansion of industrial technology has radically altered the character of work.* For the greater part of man's history, work was a strenuous physical activity, largely carried on alone or in small groups in the open air, requiring considerable dexterity to match human strength to the infinite variations of the natural environment, and culminating in an end product as unambiguously identifiable as the grain in the field or the cloth on a loom.

The Industrial Revolution profoundly altered these attributes of work. Work now consisted more and more of repetitive movements that, however exhausting after a full day, rarely involved more than a fraction of a man's full muscular ability. In place of the judgments and aptitudes required to meet the variations of nature, it demanded only the ability to repeat a single task adapted to a changeless work surface. No longer alone in nature, the worker performed his job in vast sheds with regiments like himself. And most wrenching of all, in place of "his" product, what he saw emerging from the factory was an object in which he could no longer locate, much less appreciate, his own contribution.

A worker in an automobile plant reports:

I work on a small conveyor which goes around in a circle. We call it a "merry-go-round." I make up zigzag springs for front seats. Every couple of feet on the conveyor there is a form for the pieces that make up the seat springs. As the form goes by me, I clip several pieces together, using a clip gun. I then put the pieces on the form, and it goes around to where other men clip more pieces together. . . . The only operation I do is work the clip gun. It takes just a couple of seconds to shoot six or eight clips into the spring and I do it as I walk a few steps. Then I start right over again. . . .[3]

alienation

What has been the effect on workers of this basic alteration in the pace and pattern of labor? Looking around us at factories (and offices), we find that industrial technology often subjects men to stultifying and enervating discipline—that it makes work a singularly joyless and meaningless process to which they must subordinate their individual personalities. This is an aspect of technology that has disturbed observers since Adam Smith commented, two hundred years ago, that a man who endlessly performed the

[3] Charles R. Walker and Robert H. Guest, *The Man on the Assembly Line* (Cambridge: Harvard University Press, 1952), p. 46.

same task "generally becomes as stupid and ignorant as it is possible for a human creature to become." [4] Later, Karl Marx wrote with passion and perception about the terrible effects of industrial capitalism in divorcing the worker from the fruits of his own toil; and since Marx, writers in socialist as well as in capitalist nations have articulated the feelings of impotence and estrangement experienced in a vast, mechanized environment.

Is industrial technology in fact the cause of a pervasive "alienation" of man? We do not really know. Man today is certainly as much the servant as the master of his industrial apparatus. Yet we must guard against too easy an indictment of technology as the great dehumanizer. Let us not forget the terrible toll on the human personality of preindustrial labor, with its exhausted peasants and its brutalized common laborers. Further, let us bear in mind that if the repressive and disciplinary aspects of technology predominate in our time, it may be because we are still only in the inception of the industrial history of humankind. In a longer perspective, this same technology holds forth at least the promise of an eventual emancipation of man, as machinery gradually takes over his onerous, monotonous tasks.

distribution of the labor force We will return again to some of these problems of technology, as well as to its larger environmental impact. But meanwhile we must pay heed to another important aspect of the technological invasion. This is the striking alteration it has brought about in the tasks of social provisioning. It is obvious that the inventory of work skills that we possessed in 1800 would never suffice to operate the social machine of the 1980s. But even in the much shorter span since 1900, the required distribution of skills has significantly changed, as Table 5–1 shows.

Note how different is our profile of occupations today from the not too distant past. We have already commented on the sharp drop in the number of people needed to feed the nation, but we can also see a shift within the blue-collar group from unskilled to skilled and semiskilled jobs, as more people labor with capital equipment than with their hands. In addition, as the sharp increase in the number of managers and clerical workers indicates, a swifter and more complex production process requires ever more people to coordinate and oversee the actual making of goods. In 1899 there was one nonproduction worker for every thirteen production workers in manufacturing; by the end of 1970s, about one for every two.

THE RISE OF UNIONISM

Before we leave this discussion of the general impact of technology on economic society, we must briefly look into one last attribute of industrial-

[4] *The Wealth of Nations* (New York: Modern Library, 1937), p. 734.

TABLE 5·1

OCCUPA-
TIONAL
DISTRIBU-
TION OF
THE LABOR
FORCE
1900–1975

	Percentage of labor force	
	1900	1977
Managerial and professional		
Professional and technical workers	4.1	15.1
Managers, officials, and proprietors (nonfarm)	5.9	10.7
White-collar		
Clerical workers	3.1	17.8
Sales workers	4.8	6.3
Blue-collar		
Skilled workers and foremen	10.3	12.9
Semiskilled workers	12.8	15.3
Unskilled workers	12.4	4.9
Household and other service workers	8.9	14.0
Farm		
Farmers and farm managers	20.0	} 3.0
Farm laborers	17.6	

SOURCE: 1900 figures calculated from *Historical Statistics of the United States,* Series D 72–122, p. 74; 1977 figures from US Department of Labor. Totals do not add to 100 percent, owing to rounding.

ism—the rise of labor unions within the market system during the late nineteenth and early twentieth centuries.

Actually we can trace the origins of trade unionism back to early Roman times, when some workmen organized semifraternal orders. But unionism as an important social institution obviously had to await the creation of a free labor force, and that, as we know, did not occur until relatively recent times. Even after labor had been pried loose from its feudal status and thrown upon the market for survival, unionism still awaited as a final stimulus the advent of an industrial technology that brought masses of men together in the insecure and impersonal environment of the factory.

Thus, all through the nineteenth century, as industrial technology entered nation after nation, we also find a strong impetus toward union organization. In nearly every nation, it should also be noted, these movements were met at first with determined and often ferocious resistance: Under the so-called Conspiracy Doctrine and the Combination Laws (1800) of Great Britain, for example, thousands of workmen were punished for combining to raise wages—although in no case were employers punished for combining to lower them. Indeed, for a quarter of a century, British unionists were treated as rebels or common criminals, as they also were, for that matter, in France or Germany.

In America, trade union progress was also slow. The strong American belief in "rugged individualism"—a belief shared by many workers as well as by their bosses—a reliance on docile immigrant labor in the heavy industries, and the use of every legal and many illegal weapons on the part of employers kept American unionism largely limited to the skilled crafts long after the union movement had finally gained acceptance and some measure of power in Europe.

During the 1920s, for example, union membership *dropped* some 30 percent, partly as a result of an all-out attack by the National Association of Manufacturers, partly as a consequence of labor's own indifference to unionism. By 1929, less than one nonagricultural worker in five belonged to a union, and not a single industrial union of consequence had yet organized a mass-production industry.°

industrial The coming of industrial unionism in America was compressed into a few
unionism dramatic years in the mid-1930s. Then, under the combined impetus of the New Deal and the newly formed Congress for Industrial Organization (CIO), the long-pent-up pressures of labor frustration finally broke the barriers of corporate resistance. In a series of dramatic strikes, the CIO won contracts from Ford and General Motors, United States Steel and Bethlehem Steel, all bastions of antilabor resistance. It was not the terms of the contracts that mattered so much as the fact that in signing any contract at all, the companies *for the first time* recognized the unions as bargaining agents for their workers regarding wages, hours, and working conditions.

As a result, unionism boomed. By 1940 the number of the unionized had jumped from less than 4 million to over 8 million, and big-business resistance to union was effectively finished.

It is difficult today to reconstruct that era, not so very long past, when Walter Reuther, the great organizer of the United Auto Workers, was thrown down a flight of concrete stairs and kicked by the hired strongmen of the Ford Motor Company, when coal miners carried rifles to fight the local police, or when strikers actually seized and occupied General Motors and Chrysler plants. The tumultuous history of this turning point in labor history has today given way to a much calmer era, in which tensions and conflicts continue to mark the relations of business and labor (as they always will in a market society), but the attitudes and actions of the anti-labor past already seem to be ancient history.

We cannot trace here the full story of American unionism (including the very important and checkered history of its efforts at self-government),

---

° Craft unions seek to organize the workers of a particular skill (regardless of where they work) into one union; examples are the Newspaper Guild and the carpenters' or the plumbers' unions. Industrial unions, on the other hand, join all the members of a given industry (regardless of their craft or level of skill); examples are the Steelworkers and the United Auto Workers.

but one point seems worth making before we return to our main narrative. It is that a high point in union membership seems to have been reached in the late 1950s, when about 32 percent of all nonagricultural employment belonged to affiliates of the AFL-CIO or to independent unions. Since then there has been a stagnation in union growth, all the more noticeable against a rising total labor force. Today, less than a quarter of the total labor force is unionized, and even in manufacturing industries, only about one-third of all employees belong to an AFL–CIO union.

new trends in the labor movement

Why has the union movement ceased to grow? The single most cogent reason seems to lie in the very shift in the job spectrum we have already examined. Blue-collar jobs, where trade unionism has traditionally been strongest, are now a static or perhaps slowly declining fraction of the work force. Conversely, the fastest growing area of employment is in the service and white-collar sectors, where the antipathy to unionism has traditionally been greatest.

Out of this shift in occupations may come a new era in labor relations —and in labor problems. It is unlikely, as we have seen, that industrial unionism will experience much further dynamic growth. But this does not mean that the power of organized labor is therefore on the wane. For the stability or shrinkage in industrial unionism has been compensated for in recent years by a sudden rise of union activity in the service and white-collar areas, particularly in the public sector. Strikes of sanitation workers and teachers can be very disruptive and, more important, may be difficult to settle without large wage increases. Unlike the case of a union dealing with a corporation, a union dealing with a municipality or a state does not have to temper its demands to the ability of its adversary to pay wages out of its *sales*. Instead, wage increases are ultimately limited only by the amount of additional *tax revenues* that the union can force the public authority to allocate to its members. Thus, restraints on public wages are very hard to impose.

There is a second and even more cogent reason for labor's gain in the balance of power between employer and worker. Traditionally, the employer has held the whip hand over the union, because in all labor disputes, sooner or later, the pressure of sheer need would compel the union to agree to the employer's offer. But this inherent inequality is changing as technology increases the general affluence of the economy. When workers' bank balances and union treasuries are full, and when it is easy for strikers to find temporary employment, the traditional pressures on the union to "settle" lose much of their effect.

All this implies that considerable labor problems may lie ahead for which there are no simple solutions. We will look into some of these when we study inflation and unemployment in Chapter 9. What is necessary is to recognize that many problems that we tend to blame on this union leader or on that company or public official have their roots in a much deeper change of situation—indeed, that they ultimately spring, as we have said, from the power of technology to increase productivity and to alter the occupational mix. Another way of putting it is that technology has rearranged the priorities of society, lessening the pressing nature of the production problem and exacerbating that of the distribution problem; and while such reflections do not solve our problems, they help us to understand them better.

MASS PRODUCTION

Thus far we have examined some of the diffuse effects of industrial technology on the lifeways of society. Now we must turn back to a more technical aspect of the industrial process—but one that in many ways underlies the larger and more general effects we have been studying. This is the development of a new method of industrial production first visible after the 1860s, although not fully realized until the turn of the twentieth century. This is the method of *mass production*.

Allan Nevins has decided what mass-production techniques looked like in the early Ford assembly lines.

Just how were the main assembly lines and lines of component production and supply kept in harmony? For the chassis alone, from 1,000 to 4,000 pieces of each component had to be furnished each day at just the right point and right minute; a single failure, and the whole mechanism would come to a jarring standstill. . . . Superintendents had to know every hour just how many components were being produced and how many were in stock. Whenever danger of shortage appeared, the shortage chaser—a familiar figure in all automobile factories—flung himself into the breach. Counters and checkers reported to him. Verifying in person any ominous news, he mobilized the foreman concerned to repair deficiencies. Three times a day he made typed reports in manifold to the factory clearing-house, at the same time chalking on blackboards in the clearing-house office a statement of results in each factory-production department and each assembling department.[5]

Such systematizing in itself resulted in astonishing increases in productivity. With each operation analyzed and subdivided into its simplest components, with a steady stream of work passing before stationary men, with a relentless but manageable pace of work, the total time required to assemble a car dropped astonishingly. Within a single year, the time required to assemble a motor fell from 600 minutes to 226 minutes; to build a chassis, from 12 hours and 28 minutes to 1 hour and 33 minutes. A stopwatch man was told to observe a 3-minute assembly in which men assembled rods and piston, a simple operation. The job was divided into three jobs, and half the men turned out the same output as before.[6]

[5] *Ford, the Times, the Man, the Company,* I, 507.
[6] *Ford,* pp. 504, 506.

But what interests us in the context of our study is not the technical achievements of mass production as much as its economic results; for increases in productivity bring reductions in cost. Even though the machinery needed for mass production is extremely expensive, output increases so fast that costs *per unit* of output drop dramatically.

Imagine, for instance, a small plant turning out 1,000 items a day with the labor of ten men and a small amount of equipment. Suppose each man is paid $10, each item before manufacture costs 10¢, and the daily amount of "overhead"—that is, the daily share of costs such as rent, plant maintenance, office salaries, and wear and tear on equipment—comes to $100. Then our total daily cost of production is $300 ($100 of payroll, $100 of raw material costs, and $100 of overhead). Divided among 1,000 items of output, our cost per item is 30¢.

Now imagine that our product lends itself to mass-production techniques. Our payroll may then jump to $1,000 and, with our much larger plant and equipment, our daily overhead to $5,000. Nevertheless, mass production may have boosted output as much as 100 times. Then our total daily cost of production will be $16,000 ($1,000 of payroll, $5,000 of overhead, and $10,000 of raw material costs). Divided among our 100,000 items of output, our cost per item has fallen to 16¢. Despite a quintupling of overall expense, our cost per unit has almost halved.

This is not a far-fetched example of what economists call *the economies of large-scale production*. A glance at Table 5–2 shows how mass production techniques did, in fact, boost output of Ford cars by more than one hundred times while reducing their cost by seven-eighths.

Nor do the dynamics of the industrial process come to a halt with these formidable economies of large-scale production. For this technological

TABLE 5·2

Year	Unit sales, Ford cars	Price of typical model *(touring)*
1907–1908	6,398	$2,800 (Model K)
1908–1909	10,607	850
1909–1910	18,664	950
1910–1911	34,528	780
1911–1912	78,440	690
1912–1913	168,304	600 ⎫ Model T
1913–1914	248,307	550
1914–1915	221,805 (10 mos.)	490
1915–1916	472,350	440
1916–1917	730,041	360

Compiled from Nevins, *Ford, the Times, the Man, the Company*, pp. 644, 646–47.

achievement brings into the market system itself a new element of primary importance. That element is *size*.

It is not difficult to see why. Once a firm—by virtue of adroit management, improved product, advantages of location, or whatever other reason—steps out decisively in front of its competitors in size, *economies of large-scale production operate to push it out still further in front*. Bigger size usually means lower cost, at least for a young, expanding industry. Lower cost means bigger profits. Bigger profits mean the ability to grow to still larger size. Thus, the techniques of large-scale manufacturing bring about a situation threatening to alter the whole meaning of competition. From a mechanism that prevents any single firm from dominating the market, competition now becomes a force that may drive an ever-larger share of the market into the hands of the largest and most efficient producer.*

the great entre- preneurs
We shall have much more to say about the economics of the drive to bigness when we study the evolution of the market system in Chapter 6. Yet it may be helpful if we look once again at the actual historic scene in which this internal growth took place. For the processes of economic change described in this chapter did not occur in a vacuum. They were brought about by a social "type" and a business milieu that powerfully accelerated and abetted the process of industrial enlargement, much as the New Men had speeded along the initial industrializing process in England in the late eighteenth century.

The agents of change during the late nineteenth century in America were very much the descendants of their industrial forebears a century earlier. Like Arkwright and Watt, many of the greatest American entrepreneurs were men of humble origin, endowed with an indomitable drive for business success. There was Carnegie in steel, Harriman in railroads, Rockefeller in oil, Frick in coke, Armour and Swift in meat packing, McCormick in agricultural machinery—to mention but a few. To be sure, the *typical* businessman was very different from these Horatio Alger stereotypes of the business hero. Economic historians, such as F. W. Taussig, looking back over the careers of the business leaders of the late nineteenth century, have discovered that the average entrepreneur was not a poor, industrious immigrant lad, but the son of well-circumstanced people often in business affairs themselves. Nor was the average businessman nearly so successful as a Carnegie or a Rockefeller.

---

* In an important book, *The Visible Hand, The Managerial Revolution in American Business* (Harvard University Press, 1977), Alfred D. Chandler looks into why some industries displayed a tendency toward the emergence of big business (such as steel), and others did not (such as furniture). The crucial elements, he shows, were a cost-cutting, mass-producing technology which did not develop in all industries and an equally important technology of mass distribution, also not available to every industry.

captains Yet in nearly every line of business, at least *one* "captain of industry"
of appeared who dominated the field by his personality and ability. Though
industry few achieved their supreme degree of pecuniary success, the number who
climbed into the "millionaire class" was impressive. In 1880, it was estimated
that there were 100 millionaires in the country. By 1916, the number had
grown to 40,000.

Interesting and significant differences distinguish these nineteenth-
century business leaders from those of a century earlier. The American
captains of industry were not typically men whose leadership rested on
inventive or engineering skills. With the growth of large-scale production,
the engineering functions became the province of salaried production experts, of second-echelon plant managers. What was required now was the
master touch in guiding industrial strategy, in making or breaking alliances,
choosing salients for advance, or overseeing the logistics of the whole
operation. More and more, the great entrepreneurs were concerned with
the strategy of finance, of competition, of sales, rather than with the cold
technics of production itself.

Then, too, we must make note of the entrepreneurial tactics and tone
of the period. In a phrase that has stuck, Matthew Josephson once called
the great men of business in this era "the robber barons." In many ways,
they did indeed resemble the predatory lords of the medieval era. For
example, in the 1860s, a small group of California entrepreneurs under the
guiding hand of Collis Huntington performed the astonishing feat of building a railroad across the hitherto impassable Rockies and Sierras. Aware
that Huntington and his associates would thereby have a monopolistic
control of all rail traffic to California, Congress authorized the construction of three competing lines. But the legislators had not taken the measure
of the wily pioneers. Before their own line was completed, they secretly
bought the charter of one competitive line; and when the second proved
somewhat harder to buy out, they simply built it out, recklessly flinging
their lines into its territory until it, too, was forced to surrender. Thereafter
it was no great trick to buy out the third, having first blocked it at a critical
mountain pass. Only one competitive source of transportation remained:
the Pacific Mail Steamship Company. Fortunately, this was owned by
the obliging Jay Gould, a famous robber baron in his own right; and for
the payment of a proper tribute, he agreed to eliminate San Francisco as
a cargo port. There was now *no* way of bringing goods across the nation
into southern California except those the Huntington group controlled.
Counting the smaller lines and subsidiaries that passed into their grasp,
nineteen rail systems, in all, came under their domain. It was not surprising
that to the residents of California, the resulting unified system was known
as "the Octopus" and that its average freight rate was the highest in the
nation.

And it was not just the railroad industry that used economic power to create a monopoly position. In whiskey and in sugar, in tobacco and cattle feed, in wire nails, steel hoops, electrical appliances, tinplate, in matches and meat there was an octopus similar to that which fastened itself on California. One commentator of the late 1890s pictured the American citizen as born to the profit of the Milk Trust and dying to that of the Coffin Trust.

If the robber barons milked the public as consumers (and to an even greater extent bilked them as stockholders), they also had no compunctions about cutting each other down to size. In the struggle for financial control of the Albany and Susquehanna Railroad, for instance, James Fisk and J. P. Morgan found themselves in the uncomfortable position of each owning a terminal at the end of a single line. Like their feudal prototypes, they resolved the controversy by combat, mounting locomotives at each end and running them full tilt into each other—after which the losers still did not give up, but retired, ripping up the line and tearing down trestles as they went. In similar spirit, the Huntington group that built the Central Pacific hired Gen. David Colton to run a subsidiary enterprise for them, and the general wrote to his employers:

I have learned one thing. We have got *no true* friends outside of us five. We cannot depend upon a human soul outside of ourselves, and hence we must all be good-natured, stick together, and keep to our own counsels.

Whereupon he proceeded to swindle his friends out of several millions.

With this buccaneering went as well another identifying mark of the times: what the economist Thorstein Veblen was to call Conspicuous Consumption. One repentant member of the gilded age recalled in his memoirs parties at which cigarettes were wrapped in money for the sheer pleasure of inhaling wealth; a dog that was presented with a $15,000 diamond collar; an infant, resting in a $10,000 cradle, attended by four doctors who posted regular bulletins on the baby's (excellent) health; the parade of fabulous chateaux stuffed with fabulous and not-so-fabulous works of art on New York's Fifth Avenue; and the collection of impecunious European royalty as sons-in-law of the rich.

The age was a rollicking, sometimes cruel, but always dynamic one. Yet what interests us here is not to recount its colorful social history as much as to understand its deeper economic consequences. It is impossible to consider the period with which we have been concerned without taking into account the social type of the robber baron and the milieu in which he operated. Bold, aggressive, acquisitive, competitive, the great entrepreneur was the natural agent to speed along the process for which the technology of the day prepared the way. But as yet we have only begun to sketch out the changes wrought by the joint impact of strong men and ever-more-complex machinery.

Technical progress

1. The Industrial Revolution brought not one but *successive waves of technical progress* and economic advance.

2. In studying the impact of these industrial discoveries, we must broaden our lens to look beyond the effect on productivity alone (although that was no doubt the single most important result). Industrialization brought:

Urbanization
   • A vast increase in *urbanization*.
   • A cumulative rise in the degree of *economic interdependence* of individuals within society.
Alienation
   • A new climate for and character of work, including *the disturbing problems of monotonous industrial work* (alienation).
   • A *sweeping redistribution of occupations* away from unskilled toward semi-skilled, technical, and managerial labor.
Unions
   • The rise of *unionism*.

Mass production

3. The new technology brought as well a change in the character of both production and competition. Production became more and more a process of highly integrated subassemblies, making possible the *mass production* of goods. The **Economies of scale** large amounts of capital required for mass production led to very great *economies of scale*.

Destructive competition

4. With the advent of mass production, *the nature of competition also changed into a destructive force*. Economies of scale led to situations in which a leading firm could undersell all competitors and thus dominate a market.

"Robber baron"

5. The dynamic potential of the new technology was given further impetus by the *aggressive "robber baron" era* of business leadership.

| 5 | *Questions* |

1. Describe the social, as well as economic, repercussions of the following inventions: the typewriter, the jet airplane, television, penicillin. Which do you think is greater in each case—the social or economic impact?

2. The philosopher Karl Jaspers has claimed that modern technology brings an "immense joylessness." Do you agree? Is factory work unpleasant, to your mind? office work, in a very large organization such as an insurance company? Do you think the nature of industrial work can be basically changed?

3. White-collar jobs have always proved harder to unionize than so-called blue-collar (factory-floor) jobs. Why do you think this is so? Do you think it might change?

4. Suppose that you have a business in which you hire five men, to whom you pay $2 an hour; suppose further that you have overhead costs of $100 a day and that you pay $1 in materials cost for each item that your business manufactures. Assuming that you keep all five men, what is your average cost per unit of output if your plant turns out 10 items per 8-hour day? 100 items? 1,000?

5. Which is more economical, a plant with a payroll of $400 a week, with $100 of overhead a week, and with an output of 100 units per week, or a plant with a payroll of $80,000 a week, an overhead of $100,000 a week, and an output of 50,000 units per week?

6. How do you explain economies of large-scale production? Why do certain businesses, such as cigarette manufacture, seem to enjoy them, whereas other businesses, such as barbering, do not?

6 The Change in Market Structure

So far we have investigated the impact of the new technology of mass production mainly insofar as it exerted its pervasive influence on socioeconomic life, and we have only glanced at its effects on the workings of the market system proper. Now we must look more carefully into this latter problem. For under the joint impetus of the drive of bold entrepreneurs and the self-feeding tendencies of economies of large-scale production, dramatic changes began to appear in many sectors of the economy by the end of the nineteenth century. A system originally characterized by large numbers of small enterprises was starting to give way to one in which production was increasingly concentrated in the hands of a relatively few, very big and very powerful business units.

By 1900, for example, the number of textile mills, although still large, had dropped by a third from the 1880s; over the same period, the number of manufacturers of agricultural implements had fallen by 60 percent, and the number of leather manufacturers by three-quarters. In the locomotive industry, two companies ruled the roost in 1900, contrasted with nineteen in 1860. The biscuit and cracker industry changed from a scatter of small companies to a market in which one producer had 90 percent of the industry's capacity by the turn of the century. Meanwhile, in steel there was the colossal US Steel Corporation, which alone turned out over half the steel production of the nation. In oil, the Standard Oil Company tied up between 80 to 90 percent of the nation's output. In tobacco, the American Tobacco Company controlled 75 percent of the output of cigarettes and 25 percent of cigars. Similar control rested with the American Sugar Company, the American Smelting and Refining Company, the United Shoe Machinery Company, and dozens more.

From an overall view, the change was even more impressive. In the early 1800s, according to the calculations of Myron W. Watkins, no single plant controlled as much as 10 percent of the output of a manufacturing industry. By 1904, 78 enterprises controlled over half the output of their industries, 57 controlled 60 percent or more, and 28 controlled 80 percent or more. From industry to industry, this degree of "concentration" varied—from no significant concentration at all in printing and publishing, for instance, to the highly concentrated market structure of industries like copper or rubber. But there was no mistaking the overall change. In 1896, railroads excepted, there were not a dozen $10-million companies in the nation. By 1904, there were over 300 of them, with a combined capitalization of over $7 billion. Together, these giants controlled more than two-fifths of the industrial capital of the nation and affected four-fifths of its important industries.[1]

Clearly, something akin to a major revolution in market structure had taken place. Let us examine more closely the course of events that led up to it.

change in competition The initial impact of the trend to big business was an unexpected one. Rather than diminishing the degree of competitiveness of the market structure, it extended and intensified it. In the largely agricultural, handicraft, and small-factory economy of the early nineteenth century, "the" market consisted mainly of small, localized markets, each insulated from the next by the high cost of transportation and each supplied by local producers who had neither the means nor the motivation to invade the market on anything resembling a national scale.

The rise of mass production radically changed this fragmented market structure and, with it, the type of competition within the market. As canals and railroads opened the country and as new manufacturing techniques vastly increased output, the parochial quality of the market system changed. More and more, one unified and interconnected market bound together the entire nation, and the petty semimonopolies of local suppliers were invaded by products from large factories in distant cities.

Quickly, a second development followed. As the new production techniques gained momentum, aggressive businessmen typically not only built, but overbuilt. "As confident entrepreneurs raced to take advantage of every ephemeral rise in prices, of every advance in tariff schedules, of every new market opened by the railroads and puffed up immigration," write Thomas Cochran and William Miller in a history of these industrializing times, "they recklessly expanded and mechanized their plants, each seeking the greatest share of the new melon." [2]

The result was a phenomenal burst in output but, simultaneously, a serious change in the nature of competition. Competition now became not only more extensive, but more *expensive*. As the size of the plant and the

---

[1] John Moody, *The Truth about Trusts* (Chicago: Moody, 1904). See also Ralph Nelson, *Merger Movements in American Industry, 1895–1956* (Princeton, N.J.: National Bureau of Economic Research, 1959).

[2] *The Age of Enterprise*, rev. ed. (New York: Harper, Torchbooks, 1961), p. 139.

complexity of equipment grew, so did the "fixed charges" of a business enterprise—the interest on borrowed capital, the depreciation of capital assets, the cost of administrative staff, the rent of land, and "overhead" generally. These costs tended to remain fairly constant, regardless of whether sales were good or bad. Unlike the payment of wages to a working force, which dropped when men were fired, there was no easy way to cut down the steady drain of payments for these fixed expenditures. The result was that the bigger the business, the more vulnerable was its economic health when competition cut into its sales.

The ebullience of the age, plus the steady growth of a technology that required massive investments, made competition increasingly drastic. As growing giant businesses locked horns, railroad against railroad, steel mill against steel mill, each sought to assure the coverage of its fixed expenses by gaining for itself as much of the market as it could. The outcome was the emergence of "cutthroat competition" among massive producers, replacing the more restricted, local competition of the small-business, small-market world. In 1869, for example, the New York–Chicago railway freight rate on a hundredweight of grain crashed from $1.80, on February 4, to 40¢ twenty days later, climbed back to $1.88 in July, and then plummeted to 25¢ in August when another "war" broke out. In the oil fields, the coal fields, among the steel and copper producers, similar price wars repeatedly occurred as producers sought to capture the markets they needed to achieve a profitable level of production. All this was unquestionably favorable to the consumer, as indeed competitive situations always are, but it threatened literal bankruptcy for the competing enterprises themselves—and furthermore, bankruptcy on a multimillion-dollar scale.

limitation of competition

In these circumstances, it is not difficult to understand the next phase of economic development. The giants decided not to compete.

But how were they to avoid competition? Since common law invalidated any contract binding a competitor to fixed prices or production schedules, there seemed no alternative but voluntary cooperation: trade associations, "gentleman's agreements," or "pools," informal treaties to divide the market. By the 1800s, there were a cordage pool and a whiskey pool, a coal pool, a salt pool, and endless rail pools, all calculated to relieve the individual producers from the mutually suicidal game of all-out competition. But to little avail. The division of the market worked well during good times; but when bad times approached, the pools broke down. As sales fell, the temptation to cut prices was irresistible, and thus began again the old, ruinous game of competition.

The robber-baron ethics of the day contributed to the difficulties. "A starving man will usually get bread if it is to be had," said James J. Hill, a

great railway magnate, "and a starving railway will not maintain rates." [3]
Typically, at a meeting of railroad heads called to agree upon a common
freight schedule, the president of one road slipped out, during a brief recess,
to wire the new rates to his road, so that it might be the first to undercut
them. (By chance, his wire was intercepted, so that when the group next
met, it was forced to recognize that even among thieves there is not always
honor.)

trusts,   During the 1880s, a more effective device for control became available. In
mergers,   1879, Samuel Dodd, lawyer for the new Standard Oil Company, had a
and growth brilliant idea for regulating the murderous competition that regularly
wracked the oil industry. He devised the idea of a trust. Stockholders of
companies that wished to join in the Standard Oil Trust were asked to
surrender their actual shares to the board of directors of the new trust.
Thereby they would give up working control over their companies, but in
return they would get "trust certificates" that entitled them to the same
share in the profits as their shares earned. In this way, the Standard Oil
directors wielded control over all the associated companies, while the former stockholders shared fully in the profits.

Eventually, as we shall see, the trusts were declared to be illegal. But
by that time, still more effective devices were created. In 1888, the New
Jersey legislature passed a law allowing a corporation chartered in the state
to buy stock in another corporation. This was a privilege that had not previously been available to corporations chartered anywhere in the United
States. The result was the rapid appearance of the corporate merger, the
coming together of two corporations to form a new, bigger one. In manufacturing and mining alone, there were 43 mergers in 1895 (affecting 41-
million dollars worth of corporate assets); 26 mergers in 1896, 69 mergers
in 1897. Then in 1898 there were 303—and finally in 1899, a climactic, *1,208*
mergers combined some $2.26 billion in corporate assets. [4] Another great wave
of mergers occurred in the 1920s. In all, from 1895 to 1929, some $20 billion
in industrial corporate wealth was merged into larger units.*

---

[3] Cochran and Miller, *The Age of Enterprise,* p. 141.

[4] *Historical Statistics of the United States,* Series V, pp. 30–31.

* We must take a footnote to call attention to a development that deserves a chapter in
itself. This is the importance of the *corporation,* as a marvelously adaptive legal form of
organizing production, in spurring on the growth of the economy. Unlike the personal
proprietorship or partnership, the corporation existed quite independently of its owners,
survived their deaths, and could enter into binding contracts in "its" own name. Further,
by limiting the liability of its owners to the value of the stock they had bought, it
protected a capitalist against limitless loss. Much has been written, quite rightly, about
the abuses of corporations, but it is important to recognize how valuable was this
ingenious legal innovation in encouraging the accumulation of capital and in creating the
organizational means to supervise and direct that capital into production.

Another effective means of limiting competition was the *holding company*. Having passed a law permitting its corporations to buy stock in one another, New Jersey now allowed its corporations to do business in any state. Thus the legal foundation was laid for a central corporation that could control subsidiary enterprises by the simple means of buying a controlling share of their stock. By 1911, when the Standard Oil combine was finally dissolved, Standard Oil of New Jersey had used this device to acquire direct control over seventy companies and indirect control over thirty more.

Yet we must not think that it was only the movement toward trustification and merger that brought about the emergence of the giant firm with its ability to limit—or eliminate—competition. *Equally, perhaps more, important was simply the process of internal growth.* Ford and General Motors, General Electric and AT&T, du Pont and Carnegie Steel (later to be the core of US Steel) grew essentially because their market was expanding and they were quick, able, efficient, and aggressive enough to grow faster than any of their competitors. All of them gobbled up some small businesses along the way, and most of them benefited from agreements not to compete. But their gradual emergence to a position of dominance within their industries was not, in the last analysis, attributable to these facts. It was the dynamism of their own business leadership, coupled with a production technique that made enormous size both possible and profitable.

threat of economic feudalism

Certainly, size became enormous. By the end of the nineteenth century, some business units were already considerably larger than the states in which they were located. Charles William Eliot pointed out in 1888 that a single railway with headquarters in Boston not only employed three times as many people as the entire government of the Commonwealth of Massachusetts, but enjoyed gross receipts nearly six times that of the state government that had created it. But by comparison with the findings of the Pujo Committee of the US Senate, not quite twenty-five years later, the railway was still small. The committee pointed out that the Morgan banking interests held 341 directorships in 112 corporations whose aggregate wealth exceeded by three times the value of *all* the real and personal property of New England. And not only was the process of trustification eating away at the competitive structure of the market, but the emergence of enormous financially controlled empires posed as well a political problem of ominous portent. As Woodrow Wilson declared, "If monopoly persists, monopoly will always sit at the helm of government. I do not expect to see monopoly restrain itself. If there are men in this country big enough to own the government of the United States, they are going to own it." [5]

---

[5] Richard Hofstadter, *The Age of Reform* (New York: Knopf, 1955), p. 231.

Not surprisingly, from many quarters the trend to bigness was vehemently
opposed. From the 1880s on, a series of state laws strove to undo the trusts
that squeezed their citizens. Louisiana sued the Cottonseed Oil Trust; New
York, the Sugar Trust; Ohio, the Oil Trust—but to little avail. When one
state, like New York, clamped down on its trusts, other states, seeing the
revenue available from a change in corporate headquarters, virtually invited
the trust to set up business there. When the Supreme Court ruled that
corporations, as "persons," could not be deprived of property without "due
process of law," state regulation became almost totally useless.

It was soon clear that if something further were to be done, the federal
government would have to do it. "Congress alone can deal with the trusts,"
said Senator Sherman in 1890, "and if we are unwilling or unable, there will
soon be a trust for every production and a master to fix the price for every
necessity of life." [6]

The result was the Sherman Anti-Trust Act, which, on its surface, was
an effective remedy for the problem. "Every contract, combination . . . or
conspiracy, in restraint of trade" was declared to be illegal. Violators were
subject to heavy fines and jail sentences, and triple damages could be
obtained by persons who proved economic injury because of unfair price
rigging.

Indeed, under the Sherman Act a number of trusts were prosecuted;
and in a famous action in 1911, the great Standard Oil Trust was ordered
dissolved. Yet, despite the breakup of a few trusts, the act was singularly
weak. Fines for violations were too small to be effective, and in any case,
few were levied: not until Franklin Roosevelt's time would the Antitrust
Division of the Department of Justice have as much as a million dollars with
which to investigate and control the affairs of a multibillion-dollar economy.
In fact, during the first fifty years of its existence, only 252 criminal
actions were instituted under the Sherman law. And then too, the prevailing judicial opinion of the 1890s and early 1900s was not much in
sympathy with the act. The Supreme Court early dealt it a severe blow by
finding, in the American Sugar Refining case, that manufacturing was not
"commerce," and therefore the American Sugar Refining Company, which
had bought controlling stock interests in its four largest competitors, was
not to be considered as acting "in restraint of trade." It is not surprising
that the concentration of business was hardly slowed in such a climate of
opinion. As a humorist of the times put it, "What looks like a stone wall to
a layman is a triumphal arch to a corporation lawyer."

These weaknesses led to further acts in 1914: primarily, the Clayton
Anti-Trust Act, prohibiting specific kinds of price discrimination and mergers by the acquisition of stock in competing corporations; and the Federal
Trade Commission, which sought to define and prevent "unfair" business
practices. As we shall see later, these acts were not without their effect. Yet,

[6] Cochran and Miller, *The Age of Enterprise,* p. 171.

undermining the entire antitrust movement there remained one critical and vitiating fact. The purpose of antitrust was essentially to restore competitive conditions to markets that were in danger of becoming monopolized by giant firms. Against this tendency, antitrust legislation could pose a deterrent only insofar as the monopolization process resulted from the outright *combination* of erstwhile competitors. Against a much more fundamental condition—the ability of large businesses to enjoy decisive advantages over small businesses in finance, merchandising, and research—it could offer no remedy. While antitrust effort concentrated its fire against collusion or amalgamation, it was powerless against the fact of spontaneous internal growth.

the Berle and Means study

And therefore growth continued. Through most of the first quarter of the twentieth century, the biggest corporations not only grew, but grew much *faster* than their smaller competitors. As Adolf Berle and Gardiner Means pointed out in a famous study in 1932, between 1909 and 1928, the 200 largest nonfinancial corporations increased their gross assets over 40 percent more rapidly than all nonfinancial corporations.[7] Looking into the future, Berle and Means concluded:

> Just what does this rapid growth of the big companies promise for the future? Let us project the trend of the growth of recent years. If the wealth of the large corporations and that of all corporations should each continue to increase for the next twenty years at its average annual rate for the twenty years from 1909 to 1929, 70 percent of all corporate activity would be carried on by two hundred corporations in 1950. If the more rapid rates of growth from 1924 to 1929 were maintained for the next twenty years, 85 percent of corporate wealth would be held by two hundred huge units. . . . If the indicated growth of the large corporations and of the national wealth were to be effective from now until 1950, half of the national wealth would be under the control of big companies at the end of that period.[8]

Indeed, warned the authors, if the trend of the past continued unchecked, it was predictable that in 360 years, all the corporate wealth in the nation would have become fused into one gigantic enterprise, which would then have an expected life-span equal to that of the Roman Empire.

the national market: periphery and center

Has the Berle and Means projection come true? The question brings to a climax our long survey of the changing market structure. We have been concerned with gathering up the various forces that created and shaped the market as a great system of economic control. Now we must see what the outcome of that process has been.

[7] *The Modern Corporation and Private Property* (New York: Macmillan, 1948), p. 36.
[8] *Ibid.*, pp. 40–41.

Let us begin by looking at the market system in the United States today. Immediately, we notice one thing: there is not one market system in America, but two. One of them, with which we are all familiar at firsthand, consists of the millions of small enterprises that make up the large stratum of the population known as "small-business men." Here are the stores we pass every day on the avenues, the columns of names in the yellow pages of the phone books.

There are roughly 14-million "small" businesses in America, counting every one from the newsstand through the farm (1.7-million farms) up to enterprises that employ several hundred people and count their dollar volume in tens of millions.* Among these 14-million business units, corporations number only about 2.0 million, but these 2.0-million corporations do nearly *six times* as much business as all the small proprietorships and partnerships. In turn, however, most of the 2.0-million corporations are small, even when measured by a small-business yardstick. Half do less than $100,000 a year in sales, with the result that the whole group of little corporations accounts for only 1 percent of all corporate sales.

Thus, in terms of sales (or assets), little business is little indeed. Yet, by virtue of its numbers, the small businesses of America are by no means unimportant in the national economic picture. Small business collectively employs roughly 40 percent of the American labor force. (This compares with 35 percent of the labor force that works for the "not-for-profit" sector —state, local, and federal government, hospitals, social-service agencies, clubs, etc.—and with 25 percent that works for big business.) Millions of small entrepreneurs constitute the very core of the American "middle class," and thus give a characteristic small-business view to much of American political and social life.

Yet it must be emphasized that even as a collectivity, the 14-million minibusinesses do not begin to match the economic power of a tiny number of giant enterprises at the other end of the scale. In the apt phrase of Robert Averitt, small business constitutes the Periphery, but the giants constitute the Center.[9] For here, in a few hundred large industrial corporations, is an economy within an economy, a "system" unto itself, with a third of all the tangible wealth of the nation.[10] All by itself, this very small core of corporations—500 at the most—accounts for two-thirds of all industrial sales, and

---

* Just to get an idea of scale: The 500th largest American industrial firm in 1977 (in term of sales) was McCormick (Md.), with sales of $355 million and assets of $207 million. At the other end of the list, the largest industrial corporation in terms of sales was General Motors, with a sales volume of $55 *billion*. Biggest in terms of assets was Exxon, with assets of $38 billion. This does not count AT&T, which is not classified as an "industrial" company, but which is the largest enterprise in the nation, by far, in terms of assets—$94 billion in 1977.

[9] Robert T. Averitt, *The Dual Economy* (New York: Norton, 1968).

[10] *Forbes*, May 1974.

TABLE 6·1

GIANT CORPORA-TIONS

RELATIVE SHARES OF LARGE CORPORATIONS IN VARIOUS SECTORS, 1972 *

Sector	All corporations		Corporations with assets of $250 million or more	
	Number	Total assets ($ billion)	Number	Percentage of assets in that sector
Mining	14,211	$ 30.5	22	47
Manufacturing	203,238	698.7	355	68
Transportation, communication, utilities	72,550	337.7	181	85
Finance, insurance, real estate	425.088	1,810.2	854	63
Wholesale and retail trade	586,228	241.8	60	24
All industrial divisions a	1,812,760	3,256.8	1,499	61

* NOTE: Statistics of later years do not show breakdown of corporations over $250 million.
SOURCE: *Statistical Abstract*, 1977, p. 498. (Data calculated from tax returns.)
a Including divisions not shown in table.

within that core there is an inner core that by itself produces the main flow of industrial production on which the economy rests.

Table 6–1 gives us a first overview of the strategic position of the giant corporation within various divisions of the economy.

The table speaks for itself. Note that the giant corporation is much more dominant in some sectors, such as transportation and communication, than in others, such as retail and wholesale trade. The Center and the Periphery stand out particularly in the latter sector, where we find over a half-million corporate enterprises (note that we are not even counting the millions of proprietorships and partnerships), but where 60 giant companies, such as Sears Roebuck, A&P, Safeway, and others, nonetheless control almost one-quarter of the total assets.

mergers These figures, however, do not give us a sense of the recent movement toward corporate concentration. The 1950s and 1960s saw a burst of merger activity comparable to the great merger movement of the late nineteenth century. Between 1951 and 1960, one-fifth of the top 1,000 corporations disappeared—absorbed within the remaining four-fifths. As a result of this and other growth, by 1971 the 100 largest manufacturing corporations owned 49.3 percent of the assets of all manufacturing corporations—*a larger percentage than the top 200 corporations had held in 1948!*

Moreover, the pace of this centralizing activity grew all through the 1960s. Between 1963 and 1966, the value of assets acquired by the big mining and manufacturing companies averaged $4 billion to $5 billion a year. This rate rose to $10 billion in 1967, then to $15 billion in 1968, and reached an all-time peak *rate* of $20 billion in the first quarter of 1969, before a break in the stock market brought mergers to an abrupt halt.[11]

Here is a trend that seems to confirm the worst fears of Berle and Means. Does the conclusion they feared also follow, for in *The Modern Corporation and Private Property* (p. 46), they wrote, "a society in which production is governed by blind market forces is being replaced by one in which production is carried on under the ultimate control of a handful of individuals." In the light of our historical study, we can rephrase that conclusion very simply. It means that the market as the basic control mechanism within capitalism is about to be replaced by another system, akin to a new economic feudalism. Is that the conclusion to which the statistics on corporate size now force us?

conglomerates and the marketplace

The answer is not a simple one. There is no question that a massive concentration of corporate power exists in America and that the degree of concentration within business as a whole is increasing. At the same time, rather surprisingly, the degree of concentration in the *marketplace*—an area of critical importance for the control mechanism of the capitalist society—does not seem to be getting significantly worse.

How can that seemingly contradictory state of affairs exist? How can corporations be getting bigger and not be increasingly monopolistic? The answer is that the marger wave of the 1960s that so dramatically boosted the figures for the national concentration of business wealth took place largely by the rise of so-called *conglomerates*—corporations that have grown by merging with other corporations not *within* a given market but in a *different* market. Consider the case of International Telephone & Telegraph. Originally a much smaller company wholly engaged in running foreign communications systems, ITT determined in 1961 to embark on a major acquisition and diversification program. During the next 7 years, it acquired 52 domestic and 55 foreign companies with combined assets of 1.5 billion. In 1969 alone, the directors approved an additional 22 domestic and 11 foreign acquisitions. As a result, by 1973 it had jumped from 34th to 9th in industrial size, with sales and assets of $10 billion each and 438,000 em-

---

[11] *Statistical Abstract,* 1970, pp. 476, 483. See also Federal Trade Commission, *Staff Report on Corporate Mergers,* October 1969, esp. pp. 184–98.

ployees—the 3rd largest private employer in the world. More important, whereas it had once been a "one-product" company, selling and operating telecommunications systems, in the 1970s ITT rented cars (Avis), operated motels and hotels (Sheraton), built homes (Levitt), baked bread (Continental), sold insurance, produced glass, made consumer loans, managed a mutual fund, and processed data—among other things.

We do not yet know what may be the long-term consequences of the rise of such giant, diversified companies. Many of them have been put together more with an eye to realizing the profits that could be had from exchanges of shares than with any careful consideration of operating efficiencies, which accounts for the fact that the merger movement declined sharply when the stock market weakened. Indeed, a number of conglomerates have already come unglued. Others may indeed prove to be efficient combinations of diverse activities that will enjoy the advantages of access to a central pool of capital and a topflight supermanagement. Still others may run afoul of antitrust laws and may be forced to dissolve. Or, having made the leap, a conglomerate may simply struggle to hold onto its place: ITT, for example, was down to the 11th biggest corporation within four years of reaching its 1973 peak.

stability of market shares But as matters now stand, it seems unlikely that the conglomerates will be adding to their size by buying up *competitors*. Hence, it is likely that the structure of the individual markets in which they operate will show no more change than they have in the past. And here, in the critical area of the marketplace, we discover a truly surprising long-run stability. *For more than half a century now, there has been no substantial increase in monopoly in the nation's markets, considered as a whole.* Going back to 1901, we find some industries—tobacco, chemicals, stone, clay and glass, transportation equipment—where industrial concentration has risen; but in others, no less important—food, textiles, pulp and paper, petroleum and coal products, rubber, machinery—concentration has fallen since 1901.

The same conclusion holds for more recent years. If we take the four largest companies in any industry between 1947 and 1972 (the latest year for which figures are available) and compare the value of their total shipments to the value of all shipments in the industry, we find a similar mixed trend. In a few instances, such as the automobile industry, where some early postwar competitors were shaken out, the concentration ratio has increased somewhat. In the majority of industries, however, the movement toward concentration was insubstantial; and in a considerable number, concentration actually declined.

Even more striking, the trend toward concentration of assets also seems to have stopped. In 1971, as we have seen, the top 100 corporations owned 48.9 percent of all corporate wealth. But since then their share has been steady or slightly declining—in 1976 and 1976, the last years for which we have data, it was down to 45 percent.

causes of stabiliza-tion: antitrust

What brought the great concentration movement to an end? We are not sure. In retrospect, the swift and frightening developments of the 1960s seem to have been the consequences of rapid economic growth and a period of "go-go" finance. At this writing, those influences have diminished, and with them, the reckless drive for concentration.

That suggests, of course, that the movement might begin again, if we enter a period of unrestrained optimism such as we had in the 1960s. Perhaps that is the case. But we must also take into account long term influences toward stabilization that exerted their effects indirectly and invisibly.

The first of these background reasons is *the restraining effect of antitrust legislation.* At the point at which we left our historical narrative, we had seen only the ineffectiveness of early antitrust legislation. But beginning in the 1930s under Franklin Roosevelt, a much stronger enforcement of the various antitrust laws began to gain favor. A vigorous campaign to block the drift toward concentration resulted in a number of suits brought against major corporations for restraint of trade. No less important was a change in the prevailing judicial view, which now construed much less narrowly the powers of the Constitution to impose social controls over business enterprise. In more recent years, new amendments to the antitrust acts and a growing stringency of Justice Department rulings have made the marriage of competitive firms increasingly difficult.

One result of these obstacles in the way of direct "concentration-affecting" mergers is that corporations have been forced to seek acquisitions in fields considerably removed from their original base of operations. This is one source of that trend toward conglomerates we noted above. What interests us here is that this process of diversification has put many large corporations into fields in which they are not the dominant companies by any means. One study has shown that in a thousand different product markets, the 100 biggest firms are not even among the four biggest sellers in almost half these markets.[12] By way of illustration, in 1965 the Radio Corporation of America acquired Random House, a book publisher. In its manufacturing activities, RCA is a large producer in a moderately concentrated field (the top four companies make just under half of all radios); in its broadcasting activities, as the owner of NBC, it is one of three great broadcasting networks; but as a book publisher it sails in a highly competitive race.

[12] A. D. H. Kaplan, *Big Enterprise in a Competitive System* (Washington, D.C.: Brookings, 1964), p. 286.

the new corporate executive A second reason for the stabilization within markets is more diffuse, but no less significant. It lies in a decisive *change in the character of business management.*

We have already noticed a certain change in the evolution of the great entrepreneur, from the production-oriented industrialist of the early nineteenth century to the sales- and strategy-oriented "captain of industry" of the late nineteenth. Yet throughout the first century of rapid corporate expansion, one characteristic marked both types of business leaders. Both were the direct owners of their enterprises. The men who ran the corporations were themselves the men who had put up the capital or who owned large blocks of stock in the enterprises. The Carnegie Steel Company, the Standard Oil Company, the Ford Motor Company were all extensions of the personalities of Carnegie, Rockefeller, and Ford. This personal direction of affairs was the case in the overwhelming majority of the other large and small enterprises of the day.

But with time, a significant change set in. As the original founders of the great businesses died, their stock was inherited by heirs who often did not have business ability and who receded into the background. In addition, the widening dispersion of stock ownership among more and more small investors made it unnecessary for any group to own an actual majority of the stock to exercise control over a company. In 1928, for example, the board of directors of US Steel (which included two of the largest stockholders in the company) held only 1.4 percent of the company's stock. In that year, the biggest stockholder in AT&T held but seven-tenths of 1 percent of the company's total stock, and the biggest shareowners of the Pennsylvania Railroad held less than 3 percent of the firm's stock.

The result was that the active direction of the big firms passed from owner-capitalists to a new group of "managers" who ruled the corporation by virtue of their expertise rather than because they owned it. The new management was different in many ways from its predecessors. In 1900, for example, half the top executives of the biggest corporations had followed paths to the top that could be described as "entrepreneurial" or "capitalist" —that is, half had built their own businesses or had risked their own capital as the means to business preeminence. By 1925, only a third of the top corporate executives had followed this path, and in 1960, *less than 3 percent* had done so. More and more, the route to success lay through professional skills, whether in law or engineering or science, or in the patient ascent of the corporate hierarchical ladder. Significantly, there was a visible change as well as a marked change in the educational background of the top corporate officials. As recently as the 1920s, a majority of the topmost corporate leaders had not gone to college; today over 85 percent have college degrees and 40 percent hold graduate degrees.[13]

[13] Mabel Newcomer, *The Big Business Executive* (New York: Columbia University Press, 1955), pp. 61–63; and Jay Gould, *The Technical Elite* (New York: Augustus Kelley, 1966), pp. 160–71.

The new management brought important changes in its wake. The affairs of big companies increasingly became matters to be handled in systematized, "professional" ways, rather than in the often highly personal, Haroun-al-Raschid mode of the founders. A certain bureaucratization thus crept into the conduct of business life, at the very time that the business community was waxing most vocal about the dangers of bureaucracy in government. More important, the new management now adopted a new strategy for corporate growth—or rather, abandoned an older one. Advances in technology, changes in product design, vigorous advertising, the wooing of businesses to be acquired in other fields—all these provided ample outlets for the managerial impulse toward expansion. But one mode of growth—the mode that the founders of the great enterprises had never hesitated to use—was now ruled out: Growth was no longer to be sought by the direct, head-on competition of one firm against another in terms of *price*.

oligopoly and market behavior

Thus, the evolution of a more "statesmanlike" attitude in business affairs brought a significant change in business tactics. But the change cannot be ascribed solely to a new outlook on the part of big-business. Behind that new outlook was *a change in the market environment*.

We call this new kind of market situation *oligopoly*, meaning a market shared by a few sellers. Note that it is not *monopoly*, which is a market entirely served by one seller. Neither is it "pure competition," such as we envisaged when we first looked into the theory of a market economy.

What is the essential difference? We cannot investigate it thoroughly in this book, but the main points of the contrast are not difficult to grasp. Classical competition implies a situation in which there are so many firms (of roughly the same order of size) that no one of them by itself can directly influence market prices. This is the case—more or less—within much of the Periphery. In oligopoly, by way of contrast, the numbers of firms are few enough (or the disparity in size among the few large ones and the host of smaller ones is so great) that the large firms cannot help affecting the market situation. Here is the typical situation at the Center. As a result, whereas in classical competition, firms must accept whatever prices the market thrusts upon them, in oligopolistic markets, prices can be "set," at least within limits, by the direct action of the leading firms.

In many of the most important industrial markets, as we have seen, it is oligopoly rather than pure competition that is the order of things today. In industry after industry, economies of large-scale production have brought about a situation in which a few large producers divide the market among themselves. Often these markets are dominated by one very large firm that serves as "price leader," raising or lowering its prices as general economic conditions warrant, and being followed up or down by everyone else in the field. US Steel in the steel industry, General Motors in the auto field, Corn

Products Refining in the cornstarch industry have more or less consistently "led" their industries in this fashion. By and large, as we would expect, these prices are considerably higher than the prices that a pure competitive market would enforce. General Motors, for instance, has traditionally "targeted" its prices to attain a 15 to 20 percent return after taxes, *calculating its costs on the assumption that it will use only 60 to 70 percent of its total plant capacity*. In fact, "target pricing" has come to be the established procedure for many leading manufacturing firms.[14]

adminis-
tered prices

Prices set by leading firms, rather than by the interplay of competition among many firms, are called *administered prices*. This does not mean that in each of these industries, firms do not vie with one another. On the contrary, if you ask a General Motors or a US Steel executive, he will tell you of vigorous competition. He may show you that Ford had edged out General Motors in such-and-such a line, or that Bethlehem Steel has captured some of US Steel's business. The point, however, is that *the competition among oligopolists typically utilizes every means except one: price cutting*. The tactics of lowering price to secure a rival's business is not regarded as "fair play," although once in a while it breaks out, just as it did in the days of cutthroat competition of the 1880s.* But what was common practice then is rare now. Competition among oligopolists today means winning business away from another by advertising, customer service, or product design—but not by "chiseling" on price. Everyone recognizes that it is to his advantage not to disturb the market. There have been few instances in steel, or oil, or automobiles, or chemicals, or cigarettes when out-and-out price "warfare" has taken the place of nonprice "competition."

challenge to
consumer
sovereignty

Our inquiry has led us from the emergence of the giant corporation to a consideration of the change in corporate tactics within industrial markets. Now we must stand back a pace and once again look at the operation of the market system as a whole, seeking an answer to the questions we posed at the outset. What is the consequence of the giant corporation for American society? What are its effects on the operation of a market economy?

[14] *Study of Administered Prices in the Steel Industry* and *Study of Administered Prices in the Automobile Industry*, Senate Report 1387, 85th Cong., 2nd sess.; see also R. F. Lanzillotti, "Pricing Objectives of Large Companies," *American Economic Review*, December 1958, pp. 921–40.

* On occasion, the administered prices in an oligopoly are maintained by out-and-out collusive agreement, which is strictly illegal. This was the case when General Electric, Westinghouse, and a number of smaller manufacturers were discovered in 1959 to be rigging prices and sharing the market for heavy electrical equipment. A number of top executives in the main concerns were sent to jail, heavy fines were imposed, and the purchasers of the equipment sued for triple damages. More frequently, however, oligopolistic prices are maintained simply by tacit consent.

The second question is easier to cope with than the first. We will remember that a distinguishing feature of the market system was that the *power of control was vested in the consumer.* There were two aspects of this power. First, a market society enabled consumers to have the ultimate decision as to the allocation of the factors of production. *Their* desires arranged the productive pattern of society, not the desires of society's rulers, its keepers of traditions, or its producers. Second, the market society assured the consumer that he would be able to buy the output of society at the lowest price compatible with a continued flow of production. While producers might wish to make exorbitant profits from consumers, they would be prevented from doing so by the pressure of competition from other producers.

Does the consumer still exercise this economic sovereignty? In a general sense he does. If the consumer does not choose to buy the goods produced by giant concerns, those concerns have no choice but to curtail the production of those goods. For example, in the mid-1950s, the Ford Motor Company poured nearly a quarter of a billion dollars into the production of a new car, the Edsel. The car was rejected by consumers, and after a few years its production was quietly discontinued. Familiar, too, is the effect of a swing in consumer tastes. From the mid-1950s on, imports of foreign sports and small cars rose steadily—from 57,000 vehicles in 1955 to 668,000 in 1959. With the exception of American Motors, the major car manufacturers insisted that the trend to compacts was only a fad and that Americans "wanted" bigger cars. But there was no brooking the contrary opinion of consumers themselves. Eventually, all the major manufacturers were *forced* into the production of small cars, and foreign manufacturers, who had specialized in small cars, increased their share of the US market from a mere 6 percent in the mid-1960s to 25 percent by the late 1970s.

What then is the difference between this state of affairs and that of the "ideal" market system? One major difference lies in the fact that the great corporations today do not merely "fill" the wants of consumers. They themselves help to *create* these wants by massive efforts to interest the public in buying the products they manufacture. In 1976, for example, business spent some $33 billion on advertising its products—an expenditure half as large as our total expenditures for public elementary and secondary education. By way of contrast, in 1867 we spend only $50 million on advertising; and in 1900, only $542 million. So it is that while consumers still move the factors of production to satisfy their "wants," these wants are themselves increasingly influenced by the producers. In contrast to the ideal market where producers hasten at the beck of an imperious consumer demand, in the new market, consumers are to some extent themselves at the beck of an imperious producer demand.

We might note, for instance, that no sooner was the first small Ford placed on the market than the company announced a "luxury" small car, and this example was quickly followed by other producers. It may very well be that consumers prefer a large spectrum of sizes and shapes of automobiles. But it is difficult to square the original image of serving the consumers' uninfluenced wants with the process by which new models are designed and touted. We shall have a further word to say about this at the conclusion of our chapter.

pressure on prices   The second main attribute of the ideal market was that consumers' interests were satisfied as cheaply as possible because prices were forced down to the average cost of producing goods. Is this still true?

We have already seen that prices in oligopolistic industries are considerably higher than they would be under competitive conditions. Yet they are not wholly without controls. If a direct price struggle is conspicuously lacking within oligopolistic industries, there are other pressures that nonetheless enforce a certain degree of price discipline.

One of these pressures has been called by John Kenneth Galbraith "countervailing power." [15] By this, Galbraith means that in an oligopolistic world the opposition of interests across the market provides some compensation for the absence of a contest of interests on each side of the market. Today, powerful corporate sellers often face equally powerful corporate *buyers*. The giant raw-materials producer who faces little or no competition within his industry must sell to the giant chemical or other processing plant; the giant steel mill to the giant auto firm; the giant canner to the giant supermarket chain. Not least important, the large firm no longer bargains with the individual employee, but with large and powerful unions. This kind of neutralization of economic power does not hold true in every market nor in every situation, but, Galbraith contends, it is true in enough markets and in enough situations to constitute a powerful restraining force on the unhindered exercise of oligopolistic power.

A second restraining force is the competition among different *products*. Even if all steel prices are kept at "administered" levels, steel as a whole must compete with aluminum. Nor does the competition end here. What we find, indeed, is an immense chain of interproduct competition—steel against aluminum, aluminum against glass, glass against plastics, plastics against wood, wood against concrete, concrete against steel. And this competition is without doubt effective. Note that automobile engines are now made of cast aluminum as well as of steel; that buildings are now sheathed in glass as well as brick or concrete; that cooking utensils are made of glass as well as of aluminum; that drinking "glasses" are often made of plastic.

Thus, prices are not *wholly* free from control. That does not mean that

[15] See John K. Galbraith, *American Capitalism, the Concept of Countervailing Power* (Boston: Houghton Mifflin, 1952), pp. 115ff.

they are therefore adequately controlled. Oligopoly does not mean *arbitrarily* high prices, but it does mean a price structure considerably higher than those a more competitive system might enjoy.

power and responsi- bility What can be done about the fortresses of power that have emerged in modern capitalism? Is there a way of imposing public responsibility on the labor union, the government office, the big corporation? As we shall see, the question is exceedingly difficult. Let us discover this for ourselves by examining four frequently encountered proposals for increasing the social responsibility of the giant corporation.

1. *Profit as social responsibility.*

The first suggestion is most prominently associated with the name of Prof. Milton Friedman, a philosophic conservative whose response to the question of what a corporation should do to discharge its social responsibility is very simple: *make money.*

The function of a business organization in society, argues Friedman, is to serve as an efficient agent of production, not as a locus of social improvement. It serves that productive function best by striving after profit—conforming, while doing so, to the basic rules and ethical norms of society. It is not up to business to "do good"; it is up to government to prevent it from doing bad.

Moreover, as soon as a businessman tries to apply any rules other than moneymaking, he takes into his own hands powers that rightfully belong to other parts of society, such as its political authorities. Friedman would even forbid corporations to give money to charities or universities. Their business, their responsibility to society, he insists, is *production.* Let the dividend receivers give away the money the corporations pay them, but do not let corporations become the active social-welfare agencies of society.[16]

The counterarguments to Friedman's position are not difficult to frame. They are two:

(1) Friedman assumes that stockholders' moral claims to the earnings of the vast semimonopolies they "own" are superior to claims of the consumers or workers from whose pockets these profits are plucked. This is at least a debatable point: Since the stockholders are *not* active entrepreneurs,

---

[16] Friedman, *Capitalism and Freedom*, Chap. 8. The late Prof. Frank Knight, a distinguished predecessor of Friedman's at the University of Chicago, would have carried the proposal further: Force corporations, he urged, to pay out to stockholders *all* their earnings every year! That would deprive them of the market power that stems from the very large "retained earnings" they do not distribute as dividends. Under Knight's proposal, a corporation would be under constant economic scrutiny from its stockholders, who would have to be persuaded to reinvest their earnings with the company if it were to grow.

they make little or no contribution to the profits of the corporation. Why, then, should their claim exceed a reasonable compensation for the risk of their money?

(2) Friedman assumes that the government, whose purpose is to set the rules and oversee the operations of business, acts *independently* of the corporations they regulate. But many studies show that the so-called regulatory agencies of the government usually act *on behalf of the big corporations* they "regulate," rather than on behalf of the consumer. For example, the Food and Drug Administration banned cyclamates as a dangerous food additive in 1969, *nineteen years* after the first warnings of their dangerous effects had been brought to its attention! In the long interim, it failed to act, largely because of its reluctance to incur the wrath (and political counterattack) of the industry it was supposedly "regulating." [17]

2. *The corporation as social arbiter.*

Quite a different approach to the problem of social responsibility has been widely espoused by many concerned corporate executives. This view recognizes that the corporation, by virtue of its immense size and strength, has power thrust upon it, whether it wishes to have it or not. The solution to this problem, as these men see it, is for corporate executives to act "professionally" as the arbiters of this power, doing their best to adjudicate equitably among the claims of the many constituencies to which they are responsible: labor, stockholders, customers, and the public at large. The executive of one of the largest enterprises in the nation said, two decades ago, "The manager is becoming a professional in the sense that like all professional men he has a responsibility to society as a whole." [18]

There is no doubt that many top corporate executives think of themselves as the referees among contending groups, and no doubt many of them use caution and forethought in exercising the power of decision. But the weaknesses of this argument are also not difficult to see. Unlike the case with other professions, there are neither criteria for "qualifying" as a corporate executive nor penalties for failing to accept social responsibilities. The executive of a corporation who fails to act responsibly may incur the opprobrium of the public, but the public has no way of removing him or her from office or reducing his or her salary.

Nor is there any clear guideline, even for the most scrupulous execu-

---

[17] See James S. Turner, "The Chemical Feast," in *The Report on the Food and Drug Administration*, eds. Ralph Nader and Summer Study Group (New York: Grossman, 1970), pp. 5–30. See also John C. Esposito, "Vanishing Air," in *The Ralph Nader Study Group Report on Air Pollution* (New York: Grossman, 1970); and Grant McConnell, *Private Power and American Democracy* (New York: Knopf, 1966).

[18] R. W. Davenport and *Fortune* editors, *U.S.A.: The Permanent Revolution* (Englewood Cliffs, N.J.: Prentice-Hall, 1951), p. 79. (The executive is Frank Abrams of Standard Oil, N.J.)

tive, defining the manner in which he is *supposed* to exercise his responsibility. Is his concern for the prevention of pollution to take precedence over his concern for turning in a good profit statement at the end of the year, or giving wage increases, or reducing the price of his product? Is the contribution of his company to charity or education supposed to represent *his* preferences, or those of his customers or workers? Has Xerox a right to help the cause of public broadcasting; Exxon to help finance Harlem Academy (a private school aimed at assisting Harlem youths to go on to college); the makers of firearms to help support the National Rifle Association?

These are questions to which there are no answers. But they begin to indicate the complexity of the issue of "social responsibility" and the problems implicit in allowing these extremely important *social* decisions to be made by private individuals who are in no way publicly accountable for their actions.

3. *Dissolution of monopoly.*

A third approach to the problem of responsibility takes yet another tack. It suggests that the power of big business be curbed by dividing large corporations into several much smaller units. A number of studies have shown that the largest *plant* size needed for industrial efficiency is far smaller (in terms of financial assets) than the giant firms typical of the *Fortune* list of the top 500 industrial corporations (or for that matter of the next 500). Hence, a number of economists have suggested that a very strict application of antitrust legislation should be applied, not only to prohibit mergers but to separate a huge enterprise such as General Motors into its natural constituent units: a Cadillac Company, an Oldsmobile Company, a Chevrolet Company, and so on.

One major problem stands in the way of this frontal attack on corporate power. It is that size and social responsibility are by no means clearly correlated. Professor Galbraith has wryly remarked that the showpiece firms of the economy are the very ones that the Department of Justice suspects of antitrust practices. The other side of that coin is that small, competitive industry is typically beset by low research and development programs, antilabor practices, and a general absence of the kinds of amenities we associate with "big business."

Moreover, there is no reason to believe that smaller firms would be more pollution-conscious (indeed, owing to competitive pressures, they might be less inclined to minimize pollution) or that they would be more conscientious in advertising, racial nondiscrimination, and other practices. In other words, the loss of *political* power, which might well accompany the fractioning of the largest firms, is apt to be offset by a rise in certain forms of economic ruthlessness or even antisocial behavior.

Competition, it has been remarked more than once, is a social condition to which all parties in an enterprise economy pay homage, but that only economists take seriously. Business and labor both spend much of their energies trying to avoid competition or to minimize it, and the attempt to intensify competition by breaking up large firms into smaller ones might bring about worse problems than it alleviates.

4. Nationalization.

Then why not nationalize the large firms? The thought comes as rank heresy to a nation that has been accustomed to equating nationalization with socialism. Yet Germany, France, England, Sweden, Italy, and a host of other capitalistic nations have nationalized industries ranging from oil refineries to airlines, from automobile production to the output of coal and electricity. Hence, Professor Galbraith has suggested that we should nationalize the giant armaments producers who are wholly dependent on the Pentagon, in order to bring such firms under public control.

But would nationalization achieve its purpose of assuring social responsibility? We have seen the Pentagon prevent one of its "ward" companies, Lockheed Aircraft, from suffering the fate of an ordinary inefficient firm by rescuing it from bankruptcy with special contracts and "loans." Outright nationalization would only cement this union of political and economic power by making Lockheed a part of the Pentagon and thus making it even more difficult to put pressure on it to perform responsibly.

Or take the Tennessee Valley Authority, perhaps the most famous American public enterprise: until recently, it has been notorious for the environmental devastation it has wrought by its strip-mining operations. So, too, the Atomic Energy Commission, which operates "nationalized" plants, has been severely criticized for its careless supervision of radioactive processes, and the Post Office has been converted into a semi-autonomous agency, having proved a disaster as a "nationalized" industry.

The problem is that nationalization not only removes the affected enterprise *entirely* from the pressures of the market, but almost inevitably brings it under the political shelter of the government, which further removes the venture from any effective criticism. Experience in the socialist world (to which we will turn in Chapter 10), as well as in Europe, where a number of industries have been nationalized, suggests that nationalization may be a necessary step to rescue a sick industry, but that it is no guarantee of the good operation of a potentially healthy one.

remaining possibilities   All these difficulties make it clear that the problem of social responsibility will not be easy to solve (or for that matter, even to *define*), no matter what step we choose, from Professor Friedman's laissez-faire to Galbraith's nationalization. And for each of these problems with regard to the corporation, we could easily construct counterparts that have to do with the control over labor unions or over the government itself.

What, then, is to be done? A number of lines of action suggest themselves. One is the widening of the *legal responsibility* of the corporation to include areas of responsibility for which it now has little or no accountability. Environmental damage is one of these; consumer protection is another. (The suits filed against various oil companies for their spills and against the producers of the thalidomide sleeping pills are important first steps in this direction.) Ralph Nader has further suggested that a top corporate official be legally charged with seeing to it that his company complies with the law in full, and that the top officers of noncomplying companies be suspended, as is the case in certain violations of SEC regulations. He also strongly advocates the federal, rather than state, incorporation of big companies—a step that would greatly facilitate the establishment of tough national standards of corporate responsibility.

A second step would be a widening of *public accountability through disclosure*—the so-called fishbowl method of regulation. Corporations could be required to report to public agencies their expenditures for pollution control, for political lobbying, and so on. Corporate tax returns could be opened to public scrutiny. Unions and corporations both could be required to make public disclosure of their race practices, with regard to hiring or admission, advancement, and rates of pay. Public responsibility for advertising, with formal proofs submitted to back all claims, is yet another means of securing better accountability to the public.

Still another course of action would be to appoint *public members* to boards of directors of large companies or to executive organs of large unions and to charge these members with protecting the consumers' interest and with reporting behavior that seemed contrary to the public interest. Worker-members of boards of directors might also serve such a useful purpose (there are such members in Germany). The mobilization of the votes of concerned stockholders is still another way of bringing social pressure to bear.

Finally, there is the corrective action of dedicated private individuals such as Ralph Nader, who rose to fame on his exposé of the safety practices of the auto industry, and who has since turned his guns on pollution and other irresponsibilities of big business, and on poor performance in the federal bureaucracy. Such public pressure is necessarily sporadic and usually short-lived, but it has been a powerful source of social change.

advan-
tages of
bigness

Last, there is the other side of the coin: there are some advantages that bigness brings ,some social gains that require large-scale enterprise to be realized.

One of these is *research and development*. The momentum of capitalism depends to a large degree on the continuous "creative destruction" (as economist Joseph Schumpeter called it by which the products of society are winnowed and replaced by new products. That process of winnowing and replacement in turn depends to a large degree on the ability of companies to invest large sums in experiments, in laboratory tests, and in pure and applied research. Only big companies can absorb the financial costs of doing so.

A second advantage of bigness lies in the *amenities offered to employees* and the consideration shown to consumers by a significant number of big companies. The best labor practices, the best record of consumer-mindedness is to be found among the largest firms, not among the smaller corporations. And the reason is not that big business is inherently more social-minded. It is that big business, by virtue of its large and relatively secure profits, can afford to indulge in enlightened employee practices and in solicitous relations with consumers. As John Kenneth Galbraith, so often an acerbic critic of the big corporation, has written: "The showpieces [of the economy] are, with rare exceptions, the industries which are dominated by a handful of large firms. The foreign visitor, brought to the United States . . . visits the same firms as do the attorneys of the Justice Department in their search for monopoly." [19]

power:
the
unresolved
problem

How shall we summarize this complex situation? No single, simple judgment can be passed on the consequences of business size. Rather, it may help if we stand aside and view bigness in a historical perspective.

But then it can be seen that mass organizations seem an inescapable concomitant of our age of high technology and increasing social interdependence. The roots of this fact were discussed earlier, and its broader consequences will be seen later. Here we should note that, depending on our interests, we stress different aspects of this universal phenomenon. To some, who fear the continued growth of very large-scale business, the most significant aspect is that we have not managed to control business power. To others, concerned over the emergence of larger labor unions, it is labor power that most dangerously eludes effective control. And to still others, who are most worried by the growth of big government, it is the growth of public power that is the main problem.

What is common among these concerns is the awareness that very large, only half-controlled organizations have come to dominate much of the market system. But the problem is bigger than that. For if we look to the nonmarket systems, we see the growth of socialist ministries of production and administration that display much of the same bureaucratic indifference and mixed political and economic power as do our corporations, unions, and

[19] John Kenneth Galbraith, *American Capitalism* (Boston: Houghton Mifflin, 1952) p. 96.

government agencies, together with the same uncertainty about how to reconcile their power with their conception of the public good.

This is a problem that we will examine in Chapter 12. There we will also see that the market system, for all its problems, has certain advantages that go a long way toward redressing the balance in historical perspective. The market system has huge strengths in bringing about the *efficient operation* of an economic society, and these strengths may be more important *at certain stages of historical development* than the weaknesses into which we have been looking.

In other words, in a final appraisal of the market system—and of capitalist society that depends on a market mechanism—it is a historical perspective that we require more than any narrow calculus of pluses and minuses. For that, let us return to our narrative.

6	*Key Concepts and Key Words*

Concentration 1. A combination of aggressive entrepreneurship and the economies of scale typical of industrial technology brought about a *concentration of economic power* in many markets in the late nineteenth and early twentieth centuries.

Merger 2. The emergence of large firms with massive capital structures led to "cutthroat" competition that was exceedingly dangerous for the firms concerned. Hence there were *many attempts to stabilize the competitive struggle* by means of pools, trusts, holding companies, and mergers.

Antitrust 3. As the great trusts and combines rose to power, there was a "countervailing" thrust of political *antitrust legislation,* culminating in the Sherman Anti-Trust Act (1890), later in the Clayton Anti-Trust Act (1914), and in subsequent amendments designed to make mergers more difficult.

Internal growth 4. None of these laws prohibited or interfered with *internal growth.* As a result, large businesses continued to expand. A famous survey by Berle and Means in 1933 predicted that if the rate of growth of the top 200 nonfinancial corporations continued, they would soon own virtually the entire economy.

Conglomerates 5. This prediction has been partly borne out, especially in the rise of the *conglomerates*—enormous diversified corporations—that dramatically increased the concentration of all manufacturing wealth held by the top 100 corporations during the 1960s. At the same time, the very diversification of these enterprises has precluded any marked change in concentration within industrial markets.

Monopoly 6. This stability within markets can be traced to several causes:
  • More effective *antitrust* legislation.
  • The *diffusion of corporate growth* into new, competitive markets.

Bureaucrati-zation

- The *bureaucratization* of business management.
- The rise of *more stable market structures.*

Oligopoly

7. We call the new market structures *oligopoly,* meaning few sellers. *The outstanding difference between oligopoly and traditional competition is that oligopolistic firms can set the levels of their prices more or less at their own discretion, whereas competitive firms have no alternative but to meet the "going" price of the market.*

Stability of market structures

8. The effect of oligopoly is twofold. First, it greatly *reduces the role of price competition.* Second, it opens the consumer to the *influence of advertising.*

9. The shift of power from consumer to producer is not total. Consumer tastes, however influenced, cannot be shaped at will or ignored. And *competition among products* still exercises an important restraint on firms.

Power

10. Power is a difficult problem of modern society. A market system finds an important rationale in the idea of *consumer sovereignty,* in which power is fragmented into the households that constitute the sources of demand (and of factor supply). But it is clear that in modern society, huge units of business, labor, and government have greatly reduced, although not entirely eliminated, consumer sovereignty.

Consumer sovereignty

11. A number of proposals have been advanced for assuring the responsible social conduct of large corporations. These include: (1) strict attention to *profit making only;* (2) *"professional"* standards of conduct and self-conscious attention to social needs; (3) *breakup of big business;* and (4) *nationalization.*

Corporate responsibility

12. Each of these proposals has its weaknesses. (1) The abdication of social responsibility by business assumes that stockholders have a "right" to profits and that government will in fact supervise, and not protect, big business. (2) The professionalization of corporate management ignores the absence of any professional standards for management and the essential arbitrariness of corporate decisions in the social area. (3) The breakup of big business assumes that smaller, more competitive business is also more socially responsible, which is doubtful; and (4) nationalization ignores the sorry record of many state-owned enterprises.

13. There remain as means of improving corporate (or union or government) performance the development of new *legal responsibilities* for business and labor, new areas of *public accountability, public representation* on executive boards, and the important power of *private investigation and publicity.*

14. The overall problem of power remains recalcitrant, not only in a market society but in all societies. This is a problem to which we will return in our subsequent investigation of the historical trajectory of the market system itself.

1. Can you name the chief corporate executives of these top industrial firms in the United States: General Motors, Exxon, Ford, General Electric, Socony, US Steel, Chrysler, Texaco, Gulf, Western Electric? How many names of leading businessmen do you know? What does this suggest as to the character of business leadership today as contrasted with the 1890s?

2. Why does heavy overhead cost lead to "cutthreat competition"? Why is this kind of competition dangerous?

3. Suppose Congress decided to foster a return to classical competition in the United States. What changes would have to be wrought in the American business scene? Do you think this is a practical possibility?

4. Compare the situations of a farmer selling fruit on a roadside stand and an executive of a large auto company selling a new model. How much latitude does each have in pricing his product?

5. Do you believe that tastes are ever created by advertising? Have your own been?

6. What do you consider to be the most desirable characteristic of bigness in business? The most undesirable?

7. Suppose you wanted to measure concentration in an industry. What attributes of the firms in that industry would interest you: their respective sales? their assets? their number of employees? Might different measures give different concentration ratios?

8. What are the important differences between "pure" competition and oligopoly as regards the position of the consumer? the producer? On net balance, which do you think is preferable? Why?

9. Do you think businesses should be more socially responsible? How would you go about achieving a higher level of social responsibility in the following areas: (1) truth in advertising; (2) absence of political interference with government; (3) colorblind hiring and promotion; (4) high levels of antipollution performance? What measures would you propose for numbers 2 and 3 with regard to labor unions? How would you bring government agencies to a higher level of social responsibility?

10. Do you think corporations have a right to back right-wing groups? left-wing groups? center-wing groups? modern art? old-fashioned art? universities? sports groups? political parties? How do you justify your answers?

11. Do you think it would help to nationalize the big arms companies? Could you imagine a situation in which you would favor the nationalizaton of any company? How about the ralroads, if they were about to go bankrupt and leave the nation stranded? How about GM if it defied a government regulation

with regard to producing a pollution-free vehicle? How about a textile company that admitted to racial discrimination in its advancement policies?

12. What relation do you see between the growth of power in all areas of the society and the development of modern technology? Discuss with relation to the automobile, the airplane, nuclear power, the computer.

7 *The Great Depression*

In the preceding chapter we concentrated on important aspects of the developing industrial economy—the swift rise in productivity, the impact of mass production, the thickening texture of the market. But we purposely ignored one effect of technology that, in retrospect, towers over the others. This effect was the tremendous impetus that technology gave to the process of economic growth.

In Chapter 4, "The Industrial Revolution," we commented on the importance of technology for growth. Prior to the Industrial Revolution, a chart of the well-being of the average person in Europe would have shown a distressingly horizontal profile, rising in some years or even centuries, falling in others, perhaps tilted slightly upward as a whole, but certainly displaying nothing like a steady year-by-year increase in the output of goods and services available per capita. Even with the initial introduction of the new technology we noted that the standard of living did not immediately improve. But starting in the third quarter of the nineteenth century, the accumulations of capital and the accretion of expertise began to display their hidden powers. In nearly every industrializing country, and most dramatically in the United States, the profile of economic well-being now began to show that steady and regular improvement that has become the very hallmark of modern economic times.

Figure 7–1 shows us the general path of this growth in the United States from the 1870s, when the process was in full swing, to 1929, when it reached a dramatic peak, to which we will shortly return. If we draw a line through the irregularly upward-moving graph to express the average rate of growth, taking good years and bad together, we find it to be about 3.5 percent (with all price changes eliminated), which means that the total volume of output was doubling about every 22 years. Since the number of people was also doubling, although more slowly, per capita shares in this mounting volume of goods obviously grew more slowly. Roughly, we can estimate that individuals improved their lot at a rate of about 1½ to 2 percent a year, doubling their real incomes every 40 years on the average.

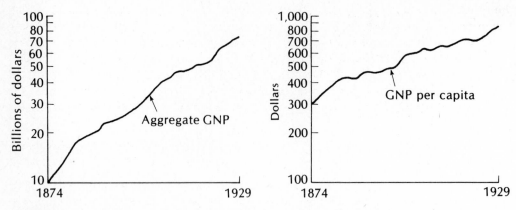

FIGURE 7 · 1   REAL GNP (1929 PRICES) AGGREGATE AND PER CAPITA

There is no doubt that the period as a whole was one of unprecedented progress and improvement. How strange then that it should have ended in the greatest disaster in the history of the market system—one that very nearly spelled the end of capitalism and that permanently altered the system in ways that we must now learn about.

America in 1929

We in America today are nearer to the final triumph over poverty than ever before in the history of any land. The poorhouse is vanishing from among us. We have not yet reached the goal, but, given a chance . . . we shall soon with the help of God be in sight of the day when poverty will be banished from this nation.

Thus spoke Herbert Hoover in November 1928, and indeed by 1929 the American economy had shown extraordinary progress. Population had grown from 76 million in 1900 to over 121 million, while ten years had been added to the expectation of life at birth for whites and thirteen for non-whites. To hold and feed and sustain its growing numbers, the nation had built up two new cities to a million each, five to over half a million, nearly 1,500 from rural to urban classification; $75-billion worth of homes, $9-billion worth of new farm structures; over $30-billion worth of new industrial equipment. Meanwhile, there were jobs for 48-million people—all save 3.2 percent of the labor force in 1929. Furthermore, these job holders had seen average weekly hours of work in manufacturing drop from nearly 60 in 1900 to 44. Average hourly earnings rose from 20 cents in 1909 to 56 cents, while consumer prices lagged sufficiently behind to allow a rise in real wages of some 10 to 20 percent. It was not surprising, then, that an atmosphere of optimism gripped America in 1929 and that President Hoover's official words only reflected an informal sentiment throughout the nation.

the stock market boom Certainly few Americans suspected that a major economic calamity might be just around the corner. On the contrary, most people were concerned with quite another prospect of the American economy, and a highly attractive one. This was the great stock market boom—a boom that by 1929 had pulled perhaps 10,000,000 people into "the market," where they had the pleasure of watching their money painlessly and effortlessly grow. As Frederick Lewis Allen, the social historian of the Twenties, described it:

> The rich man's chauffeur drove with his ears laid back to catch the news of an impending move in Bethlehem Steel; he held fifty shares himself on a twenty point margin. The window cleaner at the broker's office paused to watch the ticker, for he was thinking of converting his laboriously accumulated savings into a few shares of Simmons. Edwin Lefevre (an articulate reporter on the market at this time who could claim considerable personal experience) told of a broker's valet who made nearly a quarter of a million in the market, of a trained nurse who cleaned up thirty thousand following the tips given her by her grateful patients; and of a Wyoming cattleman, thirty miles from the nearest railroad, who bought or sold a thousand shares a day.[1]

It was, of course, admittedly speculative, and yet the risks seemed eminently justified. Someone who had put $1,000 each year, from 1921 on, into a group of representative stocks would have found himself worth over $6,000 in 1925, almost $9,000 in 1926, well over $11,000 in 1927, and an incredible $20,000 in 1928. And that was just the beginning: during June and July of 1929, industrial stock averages went up nearly as much as they had during the entire year of 1928, which had been, in its time, a year of unprecedented rise. By August 1929, the three months' summer spurt had already outdistanced the entire 1928 rise. In those three months alone, an investor who had bought 100 shares of Westinghouse would have almost doubled his money; even a buyer of staid AT&T would have been richer by a third. It seemed that everyone had but to beg or borrow money to buy shares in order to get rich.

the great crash What pricked the bubble? No one knows exactly what final event was to blame. But when the boom did break, it was as if an enormous dam had suddenly crumbled. All the frenzy that had stretched out over two years in sending stocks up was concentrated in a few incredible weeks beating them down. On Tuesday, October 29, 1929, an avalanche of selling crushed the exchanges. On occasion there were *no* offers to buy stock at all—just to sell it. Goldman Sachs, a much-sought-after investment trust, lost almost half its quoted value on this single day. By the end of the trading session (the

[1] *Only Yesterday* (New York: Bantam, 1946), p. 349.

ticker, lagging behind, stretched out the agony two and a half hours longer than the actual market transactions), 16,410,000 shares of stock had been dumped. In a single day, the rise in values of the entire preceding year had been wiped out. A few weeks later, $30 billion of "wealth" had vanished in thin air. Millions who had counted their paper gains and thought themselves well off discovered they were poor.

The great crash is in itself a fascinating chapter in the "madness of crowds." At first it seemed unconnected with anything bigger. In fact, the early weeks after the crash were regularly marked with expressions of confidence: the general cliché of the day was that things were "fundamentally sound." Yet things were *not* fundamentally sound. The terrifying crash ushered in the much more terrifying depression.

the Great
Depression

Frederick Lewis Allen wrote:

It was an oddly invisible phenomenon, this Great Depression. If one observed closely, one might note that there were fewer people on the streets than in former years, that there were many untenanted shops, that beggars and panhandlers were much in evidence; one might see breadlines here and there, and "Hoovervilles" in vacant lots at the edge of town (groups of tar-paper shacks inhabited by homeless people); railroad trains were shorter, with fewer Pullmans; and there were many factory chimneys out of which no smoke was coming. But otherwise there was little to see. Great numbers of people were sitting home, trying to keep warm.[2]

However invisible to the casual observer, the depression was far from being a mere figment of the imagination. To begin with, gross national product—the measure of the nation's total output—fell precipitously from $104 billion in 1929 to $56 billion in 1933. Almost one dollar's worth of final output out of every two simply disappeared. As a result, unemployment soared. In 1929, the unemployed had numbered 1.5 million. By 1933, the number had risen eightfold until *one person out of every four in the entire labor force was without a job.* In the nation as a whole, residential construction fell by 90 percent; there were virtually no houses built. Nine million savings accounts were lost as banks closed their doors. Eighty-five thousand businesses failed. In Pennsylvania in 1932, it was reported by the state Department of Labor that wages had fallen to 5 cents an hour in sawmills, 6 cents in brick and tile manufacturing, 7.5 cents in general contracting. In Tennessee, women in mills were paid as little as $2.39 for a 50-hour week. In Kentucky, miners ate the weeds that cows ate; in West Virginia, people began to rob stores for food. In California, a child starved to death and was discovered to have been living on refuse.[3]

---

[2] *The Big Change* (New York: Harper, 1952), p. 248.
[3] Arthur Schlesinger, Jr., *The Crisis of the Old Order* (Boston: Houghton Mifflin, 1957), pp. 249–50.

causes of the depression: speculation

How did this tragedy come about?

An immediate, precipitating cause was, of course, the speculative fever that had engulfed the economy by 1929. The mania was not just confined to Wall Street. Throughout the nation, a get-rich-quick philosophy had destroyed normal business and banking caution. Foreign bonds of the most dubious validity were eagerly (and sometimes ruthlessly) pushed by the banks into investors' hands or, worse folly, put into their own portfolios.* In addition, huge pyramided structures of investment trusts and holding companies erected a house of cards atop the operating base of enterprise. For instance, Georgia Power & Light Company was controlled by the Seaboard Public Service Corporation, which was controlled by the Middle West Utilities Company, which was controlled by Insull Utility Investments, Inc., which was controlled by the Corporation Securities Company of Chicago (which was controlled, in turn, by Insull Utility Investments, which presumably *it* controlled). Of these companies, only one—Georgia Power—actually produced electricity. The rest produced only profits and speculative opportunities. And the Insull empire was only one of *twelve* holding companies that owned 75 percent of all the utility operating plants in the country.

All these manipulative activities helped to pave the way for the depression. When the stock market finally crashed, it brought down with it an immense flimsy structure of credit. Individual investors who had borrowed to the hilt to buy securities had their stock sold out from under them to meet their indebtedness to brokers. Banks and financial institutions, loaded with dubious foreign bonds, were suddenly insolvent. Meanwhile, to compound the terrible panic, the monetary authorities pursued policies that unwittingly weakened the banking system still further.[4]

weakness on the farm

In the vulnerability of an economy bound up with a rickety and speculative financial superstructure, we have located one reason for the Great Depression—or, more specifically, one reason why the Wall Street crash pulled down with it so much business activity. But we have far from exhausted the explanations for the depression itself. For the crash, after all, might have been no worse than many previous speculative disasters. Why was it protracted into a chronic and deep-rooted ailment?

The question turns our attention away from the spectacular misfor-

---

* Many of these deals were unsavory to the point of malfeasance. The son of the President of Peru, for instance, was paid $450,000 by the securities affiliate of the National City Bank for his services in connection with a $50-million bond issue, which the bank's affiliate then floated for Peru. The President's son's "services" consisted almost entirely of an agreement not to block the deal. Eventually, of course, the bonds went into default. (John K. Galbraith, *The Great Crash, 1929.* Boston: Houghton Mifflin, 1955, p. 186.)

[4] See Milton Friedman and Anna Schwartz, *The Great Contraction* (Princeton, N.J.: Princeton University Press, 1965).

tunes of 1929 to a consideration of the state of the economy as a whole in the years preceding the collapse. We have already characterized the first quarter of the twentieth century as a time of unprecedented expansion. Could it be, however, that behind the overall figures of rising output and incomes there were concealed pockets of trouble?

There is no question that one such worrisome sector existed. This was the farm sector, especially the all-important grains. All through the 1920s, the farmer was the "sick man" of the American economy. Each year saw more farmers going into tenantry, until by 1929 four out of ten farmers in the nation were no longer independent operators. Each year the farmer seemed to fall further behind the city dweller in terms of relative well-being. In 1910, the income per worker on the farm had been not quite 40 percent of that of the nonfarm worker; by 1930, it was just under 30 percent.

Part of this trouble on the farm, without question, stemmed from the difficult heritage of the past. Beset now by drought, now by the exploitation of powerful railroad and storage combines, now by his own penchant for land speculation, the farmer was proverbially an ailing member of the economy. In addition, American farmers had been traditionally careless of the earth, indifferent to the technology of agriculture. Looking at the average individual farmer, one would have said that he was poor because he was unproductive. Between 1910 and 1920, for instance, while nonfarm output per worker rose by nearly 20 percent, output per farm worker actually fell. Between 1920 and 1930, farm productivity improved somewhat, but not nearly so fast as productivity off the farm. For the great majority of the nation's agricultural producers, the trouble appeared to be that they could not grow or raise enough to make a decent living.

inelastic
demand   If we had looked at farming as a whole, however, a very different answer would have suggested itself. Suppose that farm productivity *had* kept pace with that of the nation. Would farm income as a whole have risen? The answer is disconcerting. The *demand* for farm products was quite unlike that for manufactured products generally. In the manufacturing sector, when productivity rose and costs accordingly fell, the cheaper prices of manufactured goods attracted vast new markets, as with the Ford car. Not so with farm products, however. When food prices fell, people did not tend to increase their actual consumption very greatly. Increases in overall farm output resulted in much lower prices but not in larger cash receipts for the farmer. Faced with what is called an *inelastic demand*—a demand that does not respond in proportion to price changes, sellers are *worse* off than they were before a flood of output.

That is very much what happened during the 1920s. From 1915 to 1920, the farmer prospered because World War I greatly increased the demand for his product. Prices for farm output rose, and his cash receipts rose as well; in fact, they more than doubled. But when European farms resumed their output following the war, the American farmers' crops simply glutted the market. Although prices fell precipitously (40 percent in the single year 1920–1921), the purchases of farm products did not respond in anything like equal measure. As a result, the cash receipts of the farmer toppled almost as fast as prices. Meanwhile, his taxes were up by some 70 percent, and his mortgage payments and his cost of living in general had approximately doubled. Matters improved somewhat during the later 1920s, but not enough to bring the crop farmers back to substantial prosperity.

There is a lesson here in economics as well as history. Had farmers constituted an oligopolistic market, the decline in farm income might have been limited. A few producers, facing an inelastic demand for their products, can see the sense in mutually curtailing output. Rather than flooding a market that does not want their product, they can agree, tacitly or otherwise, to hold back production to some amount that the market will absorb at a reasonable price. But the individual farmer is about as far from an oligopolist as one can imagine. When the price for his crop falls, it gains the individual farmer nothing to decrease his output. On the contrary, in his highly competitive situation, the best that he can do is to rush to sell as much as he can before things get worse—thereby unwittingly *making* things worse.

As its core, the trouble with the farm sector was that the market mechanism in this particular case did not yield a satisfactory result.* That might not have been so serious, had it not been for another development: While agriculture remained static and stagnant, the manufacturing sector was growing by leaps and bounds. Yet its growth was undermined because a fifth of the nation—the agricultural sector—was unable to match the growing volume of production with a growing volume of purchasing power. As the farmers' buying power lagged, it pulled down the demand for tractors, cars, gasoline and electric motors, and manufactured consumers' goods, generally. Weakness on the farm was thus symptomatic of a weakness throughout the economy, a failure of purchasing power across the whole lower stratum of the nation to keep up with the tempo of national industrial production.

---

* In theory, there is a cure for situations in which the producers of one commodity are undercompensated relative to other pursuits: Producers will leave the undercompensated field for more lucrative occupations. Indeed, the American farmer tried this cure. It has been estimated that 20 farmers left the soil to seek city work for every urban worker who came to the land. Unfortunately, the cure did not work fast enough. While the agricultural sector steadily diminished in relative size, it could not shrink its absolute numbers significantly. From 1910 to 1930, approximately 10-million farmers remained "locked" on the farm, perhaps half of them barely contributing to national output beyond their own meager livelihoods.

Most economists of the 1920s, as we have said, would have agreed that there was a source of potential trouble on the farm. Had we suggested that there might be another potential breeding ground for trouble in the factory or the mine, however, few would have given their assent. Most people's eyes, during the 1920s, were fixed on only one aspect of the industrial sector—production—and here there was surely little reason for complaint.

Yet had scrutiny penetrated a bit deeper, very serious signs might well have been spotted in this presumably most buoyant section of the economy. For while production was steadily rising, *employment* was not. In manufacturing, for example, physical output in 1929 was up 49 percent over 1920, while employment was precisely unchanged. In mining, output was up 43 percent, while employment had shrunk some 12 percent. In transportation and in the utility industry, again output was higher—slightly in transportation, spectacularly in utility's electrical output—and again employment had actually declined.

Overall employment had not, of course, declined. It was significantly up in construction, in trade and finance, in the service industries, and in government. But note that all these employment-absorbing industries were characterized by one common denominator: They were all relatively devoid of technological advance. Or to put it the other way around, all the employment-static or declining industries were singularly characterized by rapid technological advance. In other words, pressing against the overall upward tendency of the economy was an undertow of *technological displacement.*

Heretofore in our frequent consideration of technology, we have never stopped to inquire what its effects might be on employment. Rather, we have implicitly assumed those effects to be positive, as we dwelt on the capacity of industrial technology to increase output. Yet it is not difficult to see that technology need not always be favorable for employment. When a new invention creates a new industry, such as the automobile, it is clear that its employment-creating effect can be enormous. Yet, even in such an instance there is an undertow, albeit a small one, as the growing automobile industry crowds out the old carriage industry. When we turn to inventions that do not create new *demands* but merely make an established industry more productive, it is clear that the initial impact of technical change can generate serious unemployment.

Technologically displaced workers may be reabsorbed eventually, particularly if the economy is growing rapidly. We will return to this problem later on in the chapter, but now we want to examine still further the effect of rapid technological change in the "displacing industries" themselves during the 1920s. And here we see an interesting fact. As production soared and employment sagged, the output per man-hour rose rapidly; in fact, between 1920 and 1929, it increased over 30 percent in transportation, over

40 percent in mining, and over 60 percent in manufacturing.* This much larger flow of production per hour meant that wages *could have* been raised substantially or prices cut sharply. But this is not what we find to have been the case. Only on the unionized railroads did wage rates rise (by about 5 percent). In mining, hourly earnings fell by nearly 20 percent, and in manufacturing they remained steady. Since the hours of work per week were also declining, the average annual earnings of employees in these industries were far from keeping pace with the rise in their productivity. In mining, average yearly earnings fell from $1,700 to $1,481. In transportation and manufacturing, yearly earnings fell from 1920 through 1922 and did not regain 1920 levels until 1928 and 1929.

Thus, the gains from higher productivity were not passed along to the industrial worker in terms of higher wages. Were they passed along via lower prices? Yes, to some extent. The overall cost of living between 1920 and 1929 fell by about 15 percent. Part of this reduction, as we have seen was due to falling food prices. Nonfood goods fell sharply in price from 1920 postwar peaks to 1921; thereafter they, too, declined about 15 percent up to 1929, but the fall was not enough to distribute all the gains from industrial technology. How do we know this? Because the *profits* of large manufacturing corporations soared between 1920 and 1929. From 1916 through 1925, profits for these companies had averaged around $730-odd million a year; from 1926 through 1929, they averaged $1,400 million. Indeed, in the year 1929, profits were triple those of 1920.[5]

maldis-tribution of income   Now we can generalize from what we have just discovered about the trend of wages and profits to state one further reason for the sudden weakness that overcame the economy, beginning in 1929. Income was distributed in such a way as to make the system vulnerable to economic shocks.

This does *not* mean that somehow the American economy was failing to generate "enough" purchasing power to buy its own output. An economy always creates enough *potential* buying power to purchase what it has produced.

There can, however, be a very serious *maldistribution* of the income payments arising from production. For not all the proceeds arising from production may be placed in the hands of people who will *exercise* their purchasing power. Incomes paid out to the lower-paid strata of the labor force do, indeed, return to the stream of purchasing power, for the working-man tends to spend his wages quickly. But incomes that take the form of profits, or business accruals, or as very high individual compensations may not quickly turn over as purchasing power. Profits or high incomes may be

---

* These productivity indexes cannot be computed from our previous output and employment figures, since weekly hours changed. For the original figures, see *Historical Statistics*, Series W.

[5] *Historical Statistics*, V, 236.

TABLE 7·1

**TOP
INCOMES**

	Percentage shares of total income received by the top 1 percent and top 5 percent of total population *		
Year	Top 1 percent	Top 5 percent
1919	12.2	24.3
1923	13.1	27.1
1929	18.9	33.5

* The table shows the "disposable income variant"; i.e., income after payment of taxes and receipt of capital gains.
SOURCE: *Historical Statistics*, G135–6.

saved. They may eventually return to the great stream of purchasing demand, but income that is saved does not "automatically" return via the route of consumption expenditure. Instead, it must find a different route—the route of investment, of capital building.

Returning to the economy in 1929, we can now see as well what was perhaps the deepest-seated reason for its vulnerability: the fact that its income payments were not going in sufficient volume to those who would surely spend them. We have already understood why farmers and workingmen, who were indeed possessed of a "limitless" desire to consume, were pinched in their *ability* to buy. Now we must complete the picture by seeing how the failure to distribute the gains of productivity to the lower-income groups swelled the incomes of those who were potential *non*spenders.

What we see here is an extraordinary, and steadily worsening, concentration of incomes. By 1929, the 15,000 families or individuals at the apex of the national pyramid, with incomes of $100,000 or more each, probably received as much income as 5- to 6-million families at the bottom of the pyramid. And more was involved here than just a matter of moral equity. It meant that the prosperity of the Twenties—and for the majority of the nation, it *was* a prosperity of hitherto unequalled extent—in fact covered over an economic situation of grave potential weakness. For *if* the nation's ongoing momentum should be checked, in this lopsided distribution of purchasing power lay a serious problem. So long as the high profits and salaries and dividends continued to be returned to the income stream, all was well. But what if they should not be?

*critical role
of capital
formation* The question brings us to a critical relationship that has gradually been emerging throughout these pages as the central dynamic process in determining the level of activity in a market society. The relationship is that between the savings that a society desires to make, on the one hand, and its opportunities for profitable investment, on the other. We cannot explain the

main events of the Great Depression unless we have a general grasp of the central economic problem of a market society.

Actually, we have already understood half the savings–investment relationship. In our chapter on the Industrial Revolution, we saw that saving was an indispensable prerequisite for capital formation. Now we must complete our understanding by adding the next step in the growth process. *Unless we make large enough capital expenditures to absorb our saving, we will not be able to keep the economy moving forward.* If saving is essential for investment, investment is essential for prosperity.

Indeed, because investment expenditure is the way we return savings to the income flow, we can see that the rate at which we add to our stock of capital equipment will have a deep effect on our overall economic well-being. When spending for investment is sluggish, bad times are upon us. When spending for capital formation quickens, good times are again at hand. In other words, *the rate of capital formation is really the key to prosperity or recession.*

That does not yet tell us why the rate of capital expenditure should fluctuate. But a moment's reflection makes the answer clear enough. Spending for consumption purposes tends to be a reliable and steady process. Most consumer goods are quickly used up and must be replaced. The desire to maintain a given standard of living is not subject to sudden shifts or changes. As consumers, we are all to a considerable extent creatures of habit.

investment and profit expectations Not so with capital expenditures. Unlike consumer goods, most capital goods are durable, and their replacement can therefore easily be postponed. Again in contrast to consumer goods, capital goods are not bought out of habit or for personal enjoyment. They are bought only because they are expected to yield a *profit* when put to use. We commonly hear it said that a new store, a new machine, or an additional stock of inventory must "pay for itself." And so it must. New investment increases output and that additional output must have a profitable sale. If for any reason a profit is not anticipated, the investment will not be made.

This enables us to see that the *expectation* of profit (which may be greater or less than profits actually being realized at the moment) plays a crucial role in the rate of capital formation. But why—and this is the last and obviously the key question—should a profit *not* be expected from a new investment good?

The answers all bring us back to our point of departure in the early 1930s. One answer may be that a speculative collapse, such as the great crash, destroys "confidence" or impairs financial integrity and leads to a period of retrenchment while financial affairs are put in order. Another reason may be that costs shoot up and monetary troubles impede the boom:

The banks may become loaned up and money for new capital projects may suddenly become "tight" and dear. Still another reason may be that consumption expenditures are sluggish, owing perhaps to a maldistribution of income, such as that of the late 1920s, thereby discouraging plant expansion. Or the rate of population growth or of family formation may decline, bringing a slowdown in the demand for housing. Or the boom may simply die a natural death—that is, the wave of technological advance on which it rode may peter out, the great investments needed to build up a tremendous industry may be completed, and no second wave of equal capital-attracting magnitude may immediately rise to take its place.

effects of falling investment

Many of these reasons, as we have seen, served to bring capital formation to a halt in the Great Depression. The crash itself, with its terrible blow to confidence and to the solvency of banks and holding companies, the weakness of the agricultural sector, the drag of technological displacement, and the maldistribution of income all combined to bring about a virtual cessation of economic growth. The figures in Table 7–2 for gross private domestic investment—the proper nomenclature for private capital formation—tell their own grim story.

Thus, the Great Depression can be characterized essentially as a tremendous and long-lasting collapse in the rate of capital formation. In housing, in manufacturing plant and equipment, in commercial building, in the accumulation of inventories, a paralysis afflicted the economy. Between 1929 and 1933, investment-goods output shrank by 88 percent in real terms— that is, after allowances for price changes. Although the capital-goods industries employed only one-tenth of the total labor force in 1929, by 1933 one-third of total unemployment had been caused by the shrinkage of these critical industries. Here is a major key to the depression.

multiplier effect

But the trouble did not end there. When savings are not returned to active purchasing power because of inadequate investment, the fall in buying begins to spread. Let us say that a steelworker is laid off because of the

TABLE 7 · 2

GROSS PRIVATE DOMESTIC INVESTMENT

Year	Residential nonfarm construction	Other construction	Producers' durable equipment	Change in inventories
	Billions of current dollars			
1929	$3.6	$5.1	$5.9	$+1.7
1932	.6	1.2	1.6	−2.6

slump in building. He will certainly pare his family's budget to the bone. But this in turn will create a further loss in income for the businesses where the steelworker's family ordinarily spent its income. Others will lose their jobs or have their wages reduced. In this way a kind of snowball effect, or to use the proper term, a *multiplier effect,* is brought about.

This helps us understand the mechanism of the Great Depression. As capital expenditures fell during the early 1930s, they pulled down consumption expenditures with them; and because of the multiplier effect, by an even larger amount than the fall in investment. From 1929 to 1933, consumption declined from $79 to $49 billion, nearly twice as large a drop as the absolute fall in investment. And the fall of consumption, in turn, pulled down still further the flow of capital expenditures.

To be sure, the process works the other way around, as well. When capital expenditures again begin to mount, consumption expenditures typically climb by an even larger amount. For example, President Truman pointed out in a radio address in 1949 that $1 billion of new public expenditures, which gave initial income to some 315,000 people, also added to the incomes of some 700,000 more. In expansion as well as in contraction, there is a typical *cumulative* pattern to economic activity, as success breeds further success, and failure breeds further failure.

Our brief excursion into theory of economic fluctuations comes to an end at this point. But the understanding we have gained enables us to see the Great Depression not only as an historical phenomenon, but as an instance of a more endemic problem of a market society. We have seen how that society paved the way for the Great Depression by its malfunctions in the 1920s. Now let us follow the struggles of the economy in the 1930s as it sought to escape from the deepest and most destructive depression it had ever known.

7	*Key Concepts and Key Words*

Growth

1. The outstanding economic fact of the hundred years prior to 1929 was the long trend of *economic growth*—a trend that doubled per capita incomes in the United States roughly every forty years and that brought US prosperity in 1929 to unprecedented heights.

Depression

2. The long trend of growth came to a disastrous stop—for nearly a decade—with the advent of the *Great Depression.* The causes of the depression were many:

Credit structure

Technological unemployment

- A *speculative and shaky credit structure* that was demolished by the *stock market crash* of 1929, and by *inept monetary policy.*

- A *steady deterioration of farm purchasing power* aggravated by the inelastic demand for farm products.

Distribution of income
- A considerable undertow of *technological unemployment.*
- A bad and *worsening distribution of income.*

Capital formation

3. The joint effect of these causes was a tremendous *collapse in capital formation.* Between 1929 and 1933, investment (in real terms) declined by 88 percent.

National income

4. A *fall in investment is a prime cause of a fall in national income,* because investment is the route over which savings return to the flow of national spending. When investment fails to return savings, recession begins.

Investment spending

5. Investment is thus a critical element in determining the level of prosperity. It is however, a highly volatile element, since *investment spending depends on expected profits.* When expectations are not optimistic, new capital will not be built.

Multiplier effect

6. A relatively small decline in investment spending can spread through the economy. This is called the *multiplier effect.*

---

7   Questions

1. Discuss the causes of the Great Depression in terms of what you know about the economy today. Do you think another Great Depression is possible? Another stock market crash?

2. Among the families you know, how many work for companies that provide goods or services for capital formation—that is, for investment purposes rather than for consumption?

3. Suppose that you were in business and intended to build a plant to turn out a promising new item—say, a pencil that would last twice as long as present kinds. What sorts of developments might discourage you from making this investment? How much would your final decision hinge on what you anticipated for the future, compared with what you knew to be the situation today?

4. How can the money you put into a savings bank get back into someone's hands as his or her income? the money you put into a newly formed business? the money you put into insurance?

5. If your income (or your parents') were suddenly reduced to half, by how much would your expenditures fall? What sorts of businesses would be hit by your reduced spending? Would they in turn curtail their expenditures?

6. Why is investment so critical in determining the level of prosperity?

8

The Evolution of Guided Capitalism

"This nation asks for action, and action now. . . . We must act and act quickly."

The words are from the inaugural address of the incoming president, Franklin Delano Roosevelt. It is hard today to reconstruct the urgency, the sense of desperation, against which the words were addressed on March 4, 1933. A few hours before the actual inauguration ceremony, every bank in America had locked its doors. The monetary system was at the point of collapse. Nearly thirteen million Americans were without work. A veterans' march on Washington, 15,000 strong, in the previous year had been dispersed with tear gas, tanks, and bayonets. On the farms, mortgage-lifting parties, at which a noose was tactfully displayed, served as powerful deterrents to any representatives of insurance companies or banks who might be thinking of bidding on foreclosed land. Meanwhile, a parade of business leaders before the Senate Finance Committee had produced a depressing sense of impotence. Said the president of a great railroad, "The only way to beat the depression is to hit the bottom and then slowly build up." "I have no solution," said the president of one of New York's biggest banks. "I have no remedy in mind," testified the president of US Steel. "Above all we must balance the budget," urged a long string of experts.[1] The crisis was a deep and genuine one; it is doubtful if the United States has ever stood closer to economic collapse and social violence.

the New Deal   The new president's response was immediate and vigorous: In the three months after Roosevelt's inauguration, writes Arthur Schlesinger, "Congress and the country were subjected to a presidential barrage of ideas and programs unlike anything known to American history." This was the famous Hundred Days of the New Deal—the days in which, half by design,

[1] Arthur Schlesinger, Jr., *The Crisis of the Old Order* (Boston: Houghton Mifflin, 1957), pp. 457–58.

half by accident, the foundation was laid for a new pattern of government relationship to the private economy, a pattern that was to spell a major change in the organization of American capitalism.

We begin to trace its general outline in the main measures of the Hundred Days. In all, some fifteen major bills were passed: the Emergency Banking Act, which reopened the banks under what amounted to government supervision; * the establishment of the Civilian Conservation Corps to absorb at least some of the young unemployed; the Federal Emergency Relief Act to supplement the exhausted relief facilities of states and cities; the Emergency Farm Mortgage Act, which loaned four times as much to farmers in seven months as all federal loans in the previous four years; the Tennessee Valley Authority Act, setting up TVA, a wholly new venture into government enterprise; the Glass-Steagall Banking Act, divorcing commercial banks from their stock- and bond-floating activities and guaranteeing bank deposits; the first of the Securities Acts aimed at curbing stock speculation and reckless corporate pyramiding.

The Hundred Days only inaugurated the New Deal; it did not by any means complete it. Social Security, housing legislation, the National Recovery Act, the dissolution of public-utility holding companies, the establishment of a Federal Housing Authority were yet to be passed. So was the Wagner Act. Indeed, it would not be until 1938 that the New Deal would be "completed" with the passage of the Fair Labor Standard Acts, establishing minimum wages and maximum hours and banning child employment for interstate commerce.

It would take us beyond the boundaries of our survey of general economic history to investigate the content of each of these important pieces of legislation, but we can gain an overall view of the New Deal by summarizing its achievements against the backdrop of the problems and issues of economic history that we have already encountered. Then we can see that the New Deal is important as marking a genuine change in the development of the market economy itself. With its advent we begin to trace the evolution of a new kind of capitalism, different in significant ways from that which we have heretofore studied. We must understand the nature of this evolution if we are to bring our survey of general economic history to its contemporary terminus in our own society.

the farm problem   One general problem that confronted the New Deal we have noted earlier, in the preceding chapter. It was the severe misfunction of the market mechanism in agriculture.

The problem, we will remember, arose in large part from two causes:

---

* Some idea of the desperation of the times can be gained from the fact that the act was passed by the House of Representatives, *sight unseen!*

the nature of the inelastic demand for farm products, and the highly com-petitive, "atomistic" structure of the agricultural market itself. The New Deal could not alter the first cause, the inelasticity of demand, for this arose from the nature of the consumers' desire for food. But it could change the condition of supply that hurled itself, self-destructively, against an unyield-ing demand. Hence, one of the earliest pieces of New Deal legislation—the Agricultural Adjustment Act—sought to establish machinery by which farmers, as a group, could accomplish what they could not as competitive individuals: curtailment of output.

The curtailment was sought by offering payments to farmers who agreed to cut back their acreage or in other ways hold down their output. In the first year of the act, there was no time to cut back acreage, so that every fourth row of growing cotton had to be plowed under, and six million pigs were slaughtered. In a nation still hungry and ill-clad, such a spectacle of waste aroused sardonic and bitter comment. And yet, if the program re-flected an appalling inability of a society to handle its distribution problem, its attack on overproduction was not without results. In both 1934 and 1935, more than thirty million acres were taken out of production in return for government payments of $1.1 billion. Farm prices rose as a result. Wheat, which had slumped to 38¢ a bushel in 1932, rose to $1.02 in 1936. Cotton doubled in price, hog prices tripled, and the net income of the American farmer climbed from the fearful low of $2.5 billion in 1932 to $5 billion in 1936.

We need not here retrace the many later developments in the agricul-tural programs of the New Deal and its successors. Suffice it rather to make the point that the *central* idea of the AAA has remained. Farmers' incomes no longer reflect the extreme fluctuations characteristic of an inelastic de-mand, but are cushioned by government payments earned by adhering to some form of crop limitation. The uncontrolled competitive struggle to market crops has given way to a continuing effort to achieve a balance between supply and demand by limiting supply itself.

farm
results   Has the idea worked well? It might have, but for one thing. Belatedly, technology caught up with American agriculture. Starting in the years before World War II and continuing thereafter with accelerating effect, productivity on the farm began to soar—in fact, it rose faster than produc-tivity in industry. Hence, despite the limitation of *acreage,* the actual output of *crops* increased steadily: between 1940 and the late 1960s, for instance, the amount of harvested acreage declined by 15 percent, but the yield per acre increased by *more than 70 percent.* The result was a flood of output, huge quantities of which had to be purchased and stored by the government under its support programs. Only the gradual distribution of these surpluses to the underdeveloped lands during the 1960s, and the emergence of a

world food shortage in the 1970s, prevented the surplus problem from becoming a permanent national embarrassment.*

Thus, the attempt to solve the farm problem has been but a mixed success. It has not, for instance, succeeded in much improving the economic status of the million and a half least-productive small farmers. Yet, without doubt, agriculture, as an income-producing activity, has benefited substantially—especially for the million-odd successful farmers who produce 90 percent of our marketed farm products. Between 1940 and the end of the 1970s, the farm-operator families enjoying the use of electricity increased from 33 percent to virtually 100 percent; those owning refrigerators increased from 15 percent to more than 95 percent. In the West, Midwest, and Northeast, the independent farm operator is today, as he was never before, at a close parity to the urban middle class in terms of living standards.

the attempt to control markets

Our primary interest, however, is not to assess the relative success or failure of the farm programs from early New Deal days to the present. It is rather to note that all the programs spelled a fundamental change in the role of the government in a market society. *The essence of that change was that the government sought to alter the structure of certain markets to allow the competitive process to produce socially acceptable results.*

For it was not only in the agricultural sector that the government tried to ameliorate the functioning of the competitive process. In the industrial sector as well, a new policy of active intervention tried to bring about a better working of the economic mechanism.

In industry as in agriculture, during the first years of acute economic distress, intervention mainly took the form of an attempt to limit supply. Under the provisions of the National Industrial Recovery Act (NIRA), passed in 1933, business was permitted to make sweeping price-and-production agreements (in return for wage agreements designed to better the incomes of the poorest paid). In other words, recovery was aimed at by legalizing the partial oligopolization of business.

The NIRA was greeted with great enthusiasm, and nearly 800 industrial "codes" were elaborated under it. But as the demoralized markets of the early 1930s regained some degree of orderliness, a new source of complaint arose. Smaller producers within many industries claimed that the

---

* Actually, technology had been catching up with—and creating problems for—the farmer for a long time. One of the reasons for the overproduction of the 1920s was that we were steadily cutting back on the acreage needed to sustain horses and mules, as tractors came into general use. Before World War I, we used to devote over a quarter of our cropland to sustaining draft animals. After 1940, this fell to just over 10 percent. Much of the land not needed for animals went into production for the market, thereby adding its load of straw to the camel's back. I am indebted to Professor Eldon Weeks for this point.

codes favored the large producer. By the time the experiment was declared unconstitutional by the Supreme Court in 1935, it had already become apparent that the problem was not too much competition, but too little.

There arose a radical shift in policy signaled by the vigorous prosecution of the antitrust laws, a development we traced in Chapter 6. Yet, although the angle of attack had changed completely, the objective was much the same: *to make the market work.*

To what extent can the government make markets work? The answer, as we have seen, is far from clear-cut. Against the powerful forces of oligopoly on the one hand, and the self-defeating competition of "atomistic" industries on the other, the market-shaping powers of government may well prove to be inadequate. But in the formulation of the aim itself is evidence of a profoundly important change in the philosophy of the market society. No longer does laissez-faire constitute the ideal relationship between government and economy. *Slowly there has arisen the conception of active public intervention to ensure the orderly operation of the system.*

countering
the
depression

But the market system had broken down in a much more important way than was revealed in the farm glut, or even in the troubles of the manufacturing sector. Its real collapse in the 1930s was its inability to solve the basic production problem itself—its inability to put together human beings, capital, and land, in order to produce a satisfactory level of output for the nation.

It is curious that the Roosevelt administration had little clear idea of how to remedy this situation when it first took office. Neither, as we have seen, did the business community. Indeed, for nearly everyone, economists included, the only "remedy" for the depression was thought to be a balanced budget for the government.

Yet there were emergencies to be faced that could not be deferred, even if they unbalanced the budget. Many of the unemployed were literally at the brink of starvation, and the resources of private, state, and local charities were in most instances exhausted. President Roosevelt, unlike his predecessor, did not believe that the receipt of federal relief would "demoralize" the unemployed any more than the receipt of federal loans from the Reconstruction Finance Corporation had "demoralized" business. By May of the inaugural year, a relief organization had been established; and a year later, nearly one out of every seven Americans was receiving relief. In nine states, one out of five families—in one state one out of three families—was dependent on public support. Not that relief did much more than keep these unfortunate families from starvation—the average grant per family was less than $25 per month—but it did provide an economic floor, no matter how rickety.

The immediate aims of relief were humanitarian. Shortly, however, they were followed by thoughts of the *useful* possibilities of relief expenditures. Soon the great bulk of relief spending was being paid for public works of various sorts: schools, roads, parks, hospitals, slum clearance—and even federal art, theater, and writing projects.

As the public-works program grew, however, the finances of the federal government took a turn for the worse, until, by the mid-1930s, it was clear that something like a chronic deficit of $2 to $3 billion a year had been achieved. Each year the government spent more than it took in through taxes—not only for relief, but for conservation, farm subsidies, veterans' bonuses, public housing, aid to the states. To meet its bills, it borrowed the necessary money from the public through the sale of government bonds to private individuals, to corporations, and to the commercial banks. Obviously, as the total amount of bonds outstanding grew each year, so did the total debt of the nation. In 1929, the national debt totaled $16.9 billion. By 1935, it had risen to $28.7 billion, and each year it steadily rose: to $36 billion in 1937, to $40 billion in 1939, to $42 billion in 1940.

the **At first, the heavy spending of the federal government was greeted with**
economy wary acceptance by the business and banking communities as a necessary
fails to temporary expedient. Before long, however, even within the administration
respond itself, the mounting deficit was regarded with considerable misgivings. The recurrent excess of government expenditure over tax receipts was thereupon apologized for as "pump priming"—as an injection of government fuel which would, so to speak, start up the stalled motor of private expenditures, making further injections unnecessary. Thus, a few billions of government spending, it was hoped, would set into motion an upward spiral of spending and job expansion by the business sector.

But the upward spiral did not materialize. After 1933, helped by government spending, *consumption* expenditures began to rise, but private capital expenditures lagged behind. Although they, too, improved after 1933, by 1938 they were still 40 percent below 1929.

Why did private investment fail to rise? The answer lies partly in the fact that the very government deficits that were supposed to cure the depression only frightened business into a condition of economic paralysis that prolonged it. Coupled with the reform legislation of the New Deal, the new presence of government's large-scale economic activity caused business to lose its former "confidence." The businessman felt uncomfortable and ill at ease in a changing economic and political climate and was in no mood to plan ahead boldly for the future. The general outlook stressed caution rather than promise; cycles rather than growth; safety rather than gain. And then, behind the psychological factors, real forces were also at work. A much slower rate of population growth in the 1930s depressed the important housing market. Even more serious, no major industry-creating technological breakthrough, comparable to the railway or the automobile, held sufficient promise of profitable growth to tempt private capital into a major capital-building boom of its own.

Thus, for many reasons, the new federal expenditures did not prime the pump. Private investment did not spontaneously rise to take over its traditional propulsive function, now "temporarily" carried out by the government. This did not mean, however, that the economic influence of government was therefore relegated to a minor role. On the contrary, the failure of pump priming—conceived as an emergency measure—caused a widening in the conception of the government's role. Government now began to be envisioned as a *permanent stabilizing and growth-promoting agency for the market economy as a whole.*

compensa-
tory
government
spending

The idea was slow in taking form and did not, in fact, receive its full-dress theoretical exposition until the middle 1930s.° As is often the case with new ideas, it seemed at first complicated and difficult, and even among professional economists its basic concepts were the subject of murky discussion for a number of years. Yet in retrospect, it appears as a very simple argument.

The key to prosperity or depression, it had become increasingly evident, lay in the *total volume of expenditure* that a market society laid out for its goods and services. When that volume was high, employment and incomes were high; when it declined, output and employment declined as well. And what determined the volume of expenditure? As we have seen, the stream of consumption spending tended to be a passive factor, rising when individuals' incomes rose and diminishing when they fell. The volatile item, as both history and theory made clear, was the stream of capital expenditure.

From this starting point, it is not difficult to take the next step. If lagging private capital expenditures were responsible for lagging employment and output, why could not the government step in to make up whatever deficiencies arose from private expenditure? There had always been, after all, a fairly regular flow of public expenditure, much of it for capital-creating purposes, such as roads or schools. Why could not this flow of public spending be deliberately enlarged when the occasion demanded, to maintain the needed total volume of expenditure? True, this required the government to borrow and spend and thereby increase its debt. But did not much private capital spending also result in corporate debts? And why could not the debt, itself, be handled like corporate debts, which were never

---

° The most influential book setting forth the concept—albeit in highly technical terms—was John Maynard Keynes' *General Theory of Employment, Interest and Money,* published in 1936. Few books have roused such controversy or left so permanent a mark.

"paid off" in the aggregate but refunded, with new bond issues being sold to take the place of those coming due?

To the economists of the Roosevelt administration, the answers to these questions seemed plain enough. The government not only could, but should, use its spending powers as an economic instrumentality for securing full employment. By this, they did not have in a mind a "radical" revision of capitalism. Rather, they envisaged the evolution of a new form of *guided* capitalism—a market society in which the all-important levels of employment and output would no longer be left to the vagaries of the market but would be protected against decline and stimulated toward growth by public action.

fears of government intervention

This was not how matters appeared to many members of the nation, however, and especially to the business community. They saw government spending as inherently "wasteful," and the mounting debt as evidence that we would spend ourselves into "bankruptcy." Beneath these arguments there lurked a deeper suspicion, a suspicion that government spending, whatever the protestations to the contrary, was the entering wedge for socialism or worse.

The controversy raged through 1940. But in a sense, it was an empty debate. At its peak, the annual deficit never touched $4 billion, and federal government purchases never contributed more than 6 percent to gross national product. Judged by the importance of government in the economy, probably no industrial nation in the world was *less* socialist than the United States. Yet if the fears of the conservatives were hardly realistic, neither were the hopes of the liberals. For in the prevailing atmosphere of distrust, the remedy of government spending could never be more than halfheartedly applied. Deficit spending in the 1930s was a holding operation and not an operation of growth. By 1939, although conditions had improved considerably over the levels of 1932, there were still 9.5-million people—17 percent of the labor force—without work.

impact of the war

In the end, it was not theory that settled the history of compensatory government spending, but history that settled the theory. With the outbreak of World War II came a tremendous forced expansion in government outlays. Year by year, spending for war purposes rose, until in 1944 federal expenditures totaled just over $100 billion, and with this unprecedented rise in expenditure came an equally swift rise in GNP. By 1945, our gross national product had risen by 70 percent in real terms over 1939, and unemployment had dwindled to the vanishing point. The demonstration that public spending could indeed impel the economy forward—indeed, could lift it beyond all previously imagined bounds—was unmistakable. So was the fact that a government could easily carry an enormously much larger debt, a debt that now towered over $250 billion, provided that its gross national product was also much larger.

And with the war had come a marked change in attitude both toward the government and toward the economy in general. After four years of unprecedented effort, the American people looked to massive government action with a more accustomed eye; so, too, after four years of record output, they looked back upon the days of mass unemployment with a new feeling of shame. Perhaps most important of all, they looked ahead to the postwar period with considerable trepidation. Virtually every economist, contemplating the huge cutback in spending consequent upon a termination of hostilities, feared the rise of a vast new army of the unemployed. Even the most conservative opinion was uneasy at the political possibilities of such a return to the 1930s.

The upshot of the change in attitude was the passage of the Employment Act of 1946, one of the truly historic pieces of American economic legislation. The act recognized (although in carefully circumspect terms) that it was "the continuing policy and responsibility of the Federal Government . . . to provide maximum employment, production, and purchasing power." It was, as we shall see, one thing to write such an act and another thing to implement it; but without question, the Employment Act marked the end of an era. The idea that the best thing the government could do to promote recovery was to do nothing, the belief that a balanced budget was in all cases the goal for government fiscal policy, and, beyond that, the trust in the blind forces of the market as inherently conducive to prosperity—all these once firmly held ideas of the past had been abandoned. The debate within capitalism was no longer whether or not government should undertake the responsibility for the overall functioning of the market system; only the specific means were questioned: how best to achieve that end.

aftermath
of the war   The war ended in 1945; within a year, federal spending dropped by $40 billion, and the nation waited tensely for the expected fall in employment, incomes, and prices.

Instead, it found itself confronting the least anticipated of all eventualities: a rousing inflationary boom. It is true that unemployment doubled, rising to two million, but this was still less than 4 percent of the labor force. Meanwhile, the number of people at work showed a steady rise: 54-million jobs in 1945; 57 million in 1946; 60 million in 1947; 63 million in 1950. Industrial production, after a brief postwar dip, was buoyant; by 1953, it would surpass its wartime peak with no sign of more than a momentary turndown. Most striking of all was what happened to prices. Year by year, the cost of living rose: up a third between 1945 and 1948, up another 10 percent between 1948 and 1952, up still another 7 percent from then to

1957. In all, the purchasing power of the dollar declined by more than a third in the first twelve postwar years.

We will come back to study inflation in our next chapter which focuses on our current problems. First, let us fill in some more vital background before we turn to the issues of the 1980s. For out of the confrontatation with the problem of inflation, there emerged for the first time a general consensus on the nature of the mechanisms government was entitled to use in seeking to affect the overall operation of the system.

INSTRUMENTS OF POLICY

A full understanding of these mechanisms requires a study of technical economics. But it is not difficult to grasp the three basic devices of control.

The first was *monetary control*, mainly centered in the Federal Reserve banking system. By easing or tightening the reserve requirements that all banks had to maintain behind their deposits, the Federal Reserve was able to encourage or discourage lending, the source of much economic activity. In addition, by buying or selling government bonds, the Federal Reserve was able to make the whole banking system relatively flushed with funds when these were needed, or relatively short of funds when money seemed in excess supply.

The second was *tax adjustment*. The pressure of consumer buying during the postwar boom served as a reminder of the fact that the largest fraction of the volume of total expenditure was always consumption spending. By raising or lowering taxes, particularly income taxes, the government could quickly increase or diminish this broad flow of purchasing power.

The third was *the federal budget*. By the 1950s, the great debate over the virtues of a balanced government budget had virtually come to an end. Among academic groups and in a widening circle of business leaders, the budget was recognized as a tool for regulating total national expenditure. In inflationary times, a budget surplus would serve to "mop up" part of the inflationary purchasing flow. In depressed times, a budget deficit (covered by borrowing) was a mechanism for generating a desired increase in that flow.

The idea of monetary controls was not new, but the general consensus on the use of taxes and budgets as deliberate instruments of economic policy to counter boom and recession *was* new.* Once again, as in the case with

---

* In economic circles, there is a continuing debate between "monetarist" and "fiscal" views; the first emphasizing the importance of monetary controls, the second giving priority to tax and budgetary policy. Nonetheless, a large measure of agreement exists as to the usefulness of the main control mechanisms. The debate is largely about which mechanisms are the most effective.

government spending, it was not the force of theoretical argument that had won this historic agreement. Rather, it was the fact of historic change that had placed theory in a new light. For essentially, what commended the new means of influence over the market system were profound changes in the structure of that system. Let us see what those changes were.

redistribu-
tion of
income

In our concentration on the functional problems of the economy in its years of depression, war, and inflation, we have omitted one very significant development. This was a marked movement away from the extreme inequalities of reward that had so vividly marked the capitalism of the past.

In part, this was brought about by a decline in unemployment, in part by aiding lower income groups through the support of trade unions, through the enactment of minimum wage floors, and through the passage of welfare legislation. The change was not entirely due to public policy, however. The occupational shifts that we noted at the commencement of our previous chapter also played a powerful role, as workers shifted out of low-paid agricultural and unskilled labor into the semiskilled and skilled categories of the factory.

However varied the causes, the results were striking. Beginning with the New Deal, then receiving an even stronger impetus from the war, stiffer tax schedules and stricter enforcement had borne down upon the relative affluence of upper income groups. Table 8–1 gives us some idea of the change.

What had happened was quite extraordinary. The share of income going to the top 1 percent had been cut by over 60 percent. That going to the top 5 percent had been cut by more than half.

To be sure, we must exercise a great deal of caution in interpreting these figures. Without question, they give evidence of a substantial improvement in the relative distribution of income in the United States since the lopsided days of the late 1920s. However we must not therefore leap to the

TABLE 8·1

RELATIVE AFFLUENCE

	Percentage shares of total income received by top 1 percent and top 5 percent of total population			
	1929	1941	1946	1970
Top 1% (after tax)	19.1%	9.9%	7.7%	n.a.
Top 5% (before tax)	30.0	24.0	21.3	14.4

SOURCE: *Historical Statistics*, G135, 105 (1929, 1941, 1946). *Statistical Abstract*, 1973, p. 330.

TABLE 8·2

SHARE OF
TOTAL
INCOME
BY FAMILY
UNITS

Income rank	Percentage of total income	
	1960	1976 a
All families	100.0	100.0
Lowest fifth	4.8	5.4
Second fifth	12.2	11.8
Third fifth	17.8	17.6
Fourth fifth	24.0	24.1
Highest fifth	41.3	41.1
Top 5 percent	15.9	15.6

a The income (before taxes) boundaries of each fifth in 1976 were: lowest fifth—under $7,441; second fifth—$7,441–$12,400; third fifth—$12,400–$17,300; fourth fifth—$17,300–$23,923; highest fifth—$23,923 and over; top 5 percent—$37,047 and over. Income includes wages and salaries, proprietors' income, interest, rent, dividends, and money transfer payments. Figures in 1976 Dollars.
NOTE: Detail may not add to totals because of rounding.
SOURCE: *Statistical Abstract*, 1977, p. 443.

conclusion that the existing distribution is "fair." Table 8–2 shows us the share of money income received by family units in 1960 and 1976. Note that there has been no large-scale change over the last sixteen years, and that the top 20 percent of families get almost eight times as much income as the bottom 20 percent.

middle-
class
America

Finally, Figure 8–1 shows the expected change in income distribution in the 1980s. If present trends continue, about one-third of all families will be in income brackets of $25,000 and up (in constant 1978 dollars), compared with one-quarter today; and the share in the $10,000-and-less brackets will fall from a third to a quarter. By 1990 some 60 percent of all families are likely to have incomes of over $15,000 of 1978 purchasing power.

These present and projected realities go a long way toward explaining the predominantly "middle-class" viewpoint of American society (and may help explain as well our indifference to the plight of those who fail in the competitive struggle for incomes). If we look at the extent and size of the "tax bite," as shown in Table 8–3, we can also understand the source of the powerful trend of sentiment against government taxing and spending that has emerged in recent years. When the New Deal first instituted its programs for social betterment, it was just "the rich" who paid income taxes. By the mid-1970s, it was more or less everybody.

Projected Percentage Distribution of Households Based on 1978 Dollars

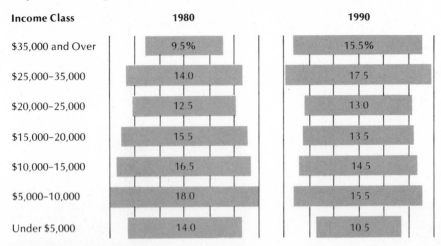

Income Class	1980	1990
$35,000 and Over	9.5%	15.5%
$25,000–35,000	14.0	17.5
$20,000–25,000	12.5	13.0
$15,000–20,000	15.5	13.5
$10,000–15,000	16.5	14.5
$5,000–10,000	18.0	15.5
Under $5,000	14.0	10.5

Source: Conference Board Nov. 1978

FIGURE 8 · 1   THE CHANGING INCOME PYRAMID

the growth of government impact

But we must return to our main theme—the evolution of a new form of "guided" capitalism. For the change in the distribution of income is important not alone because of its social and political significance, but because of its economic effects. The widening and deepening tax bite shown in Table 8–3 means that a much larger number of families is affected by a change in taxes, up or down. *This gives far greater leverage to government tax policy, as a means of stimulating or holding back the economy, than it had in the 1920s.*

A second change is of even greater consequence. This is the emergence of the public sector as a major component of the economy—a component larger in size, and more powerful in its impact, than the sector of private

TABLE 8 · 3

IMPACT OF INDIVIDUAL INCOME TAXES

Year	Number of individual returns (millions)	Income tax liability of median family ($)
1929	2.5	$ 17
1940	7.4	101
1975	82.2	2020

SOURCE: *Statistical Abstract,* 1977, p. 259; *Historical Statistics,* Series Y 292, 299, 303, 307.

TABLE 8 · 4

GROWTH OF GOVERNMENT DEMAND

Year	Gross national product	Government purchases: Federal	Government purchases: State and local	Total government purchases as percentage of GNP
		Billions of current dollars		
1929	103.1	1.3	7.2	8.2
1939	90.5	5.1	8.2	14.4
1949	256.5	20.1	17.7	14.7
1959	483.7	53.7	43.3	20.0
1969	930.3	98.8	111.2	22.4
1978	2106.6	154.0	280.2	20.6

SOURCE: *Historical Statistics*, Series F 1–5; 1978 (prelim.), US Department of Commerce.

business investment. Table 8–4 shows us the change in ten-year jumps over the entire period.

The magnitude of the shift can be summed up very simply. *In 1929, all government buying accounted for less than a tenth of gross national product. By the end of the 1970s, government purchasing has risen to exceed a fifth of GNP.*

Two matters require our attention, however, before we go on. The first is the composition of government demand for output. Notice that state and local government is usually a much larger source of demand than the federal government. This is because most public services, such as education, sanitation, police and fire protection, and the like are bought at state and local levels. The importance of state and local government as a source of purchasing would be even more striking if we eliminated defense spending from the figures. This would reduce federal purchasing by about two-thirds, while not affecting state and local spending at all.

Second, we must understand that the impact of the federal budget is much larger than appears in Table 8–4, where we only see the goods and services that government buys. The federal budget also includes "transfer payments," which do not buy goods and services, but which directly affect the incomes of millions of households. The largest category of transfer payments is Social Security, but a very considerable amount of transfers also goes as "grants-in-aid" to states and localities to support programs of various kinds, and for interest payments on the national debt. If we add these transfer payments to government purchases, the impact of the federal budget is much increased. In 1979, for example, the federal government bought an estimated $154 billions of goods and services, but it disbursed an estimated additional $290 billions in transfers of all kinds.

As a result, total federal expenditures alone amount to almost a quarter of GNP, and if we add net state and local purchases, the impact of all government spending rises to about one-third of GNP.

As we shall see in our last chapter, this does not make the United States an unusually government-oriented economy. On the contrary, compared with other capitalist nations in the world, we have a relatively modest public sector, and the impact of public spending is less than in nations such as West Germany, France, Netherlands and many others.* *What we have described, in other words, is a change that can be seen in every capitalist nation—a change in government's role within the market system.* Partly the outcome of a rising sense of public responsibility for individual well-being, partly the result of the urbanized, industrialized environment that besets us, a large and powerful public sector has emerged within every capitalist economy. The movement that we have traced within the United States as a consequence of the New Deal is part of a worldwide transformation of laissez-faire capitalism into guided capitalism.

a new economic era? Does the rise of guided capitalism mean that economic catastrophes such as the Great Depression cannot recur? The answer is a cautious "Yes." The reason for the caution is that we know from the experience of the 1970s that capitalism can still be subjected to wracking crises. As we will see, some of these problems, above all inflation, could bring very serious disorders in their wake.

What is different is that these crises are unlikely to unleash the terrible social and economic consequences of the past. A stock market crash, for example, will not cause widespread bankruptcies because the government does not allow stocks to be owned on thin "margins" of borrowed money. A severe squeeze on credit may imperil many businesses, or even bring the downfall of a great bank or corporation, but it will not wipe out the savings of millions of households because bank accounts are now insured by the government while they were not in the 1930s. Unemployment and sagging production may impose human and economic costs, but the human cost will be substantially lessened by unemployment insurance, and the economic cost will not again mount up simply because of government inaction.

Thus there are new and important ways of guarding against another Great Depression. Economists and businessmen alike think that the new institutions and new understandings that are outlined in this chapter can prevent a fall in production from developing a sickening downward momentum. Very large problems remain, as we shall see in our next chapter; but "another 1929" is not likely to be among them.

* See p. 289.

Key Concepts and Key Words

New Deal

1. *The New Deal* was a major effort to reverse the downward spiral of the Great Depression. A many-pronged attack, it sought both to correct the failures of the economy and to strengthen its workings.

2. The New Deal *interfered with the structure of markets* to a greater extent than had been tried by an American government before. Not only agricultural, but many industrial markets were regulated in an effort to bring about an orderly economic recovery. Although many of these efforts failed or were declared unconstitutional, the heritage of the New Deal has been a new concept of *government intervention* and an effective end to the philosophy of laissez-faire.

Pump priming

3. The most important of the New Deal policies was the deliberate initiation of *government spending*, first for relief, then for public works, as a means of stimulating private investment—so-called priming of the pump. Owing to the small scale of the public spending and the prevailing business attitude of fear and suspicion of government intervention, the pump priming did not work.

Compensatory government spending

4. Out of the New Deal experience evolved a new conception of how the economy operated, and of how government might counteract depression. The key was now recognized to be the *total volume of expenditure.* And the new conception urged that whenever private expenditure was insufficient to maintain full employment, the government should add *compensatory spending* of its own.

Employment Act of 1946

5. The war provided convincing evidence that public expenditure could indeed bring about a high level of employment and output. After the war, the *Employment Act of 1946* recognized the role of the government in promoting "maximum employment."

Fiscal policy

6. Postwar experience brought inflation, rather than the generally expected recession. But the period also saw the formulation of a general consensus on the tools of the *New Economics:*

Monetary controls
Federal budget

• *Monetary controls* to encourage or discourage private spending.
• *Tax adjustments* to induce or to dampen consumer and business spending.
• The use of the *federal budget* as a balance wheel in the economy.

Public sector

7. These new tools were made more workable by a considerable *redistribution of income* that had taken place and by *the enlargement of the public sector.*

Guided capitalism

8. By no means a cure for all economic ills, *guided capitalism*, nonetheless, holds the promise of an end to the terrible depressions of the past.

1. What do you think is the prevailing attitude of big business to government today? of small business? farmers? students?

2. "Even if the Hoover administration had wanted to take a more active role in combating the depression, it would have been difficult in those times for it to do so." Why?

3. Do you consider inflation to be as dangerous a condition as depression?

4. The farm problem will always be difficult to solve as long as agriculture is a highly competitive industry, faced with an inelastic demand and with a technology that continuously increases productivity. Explain why.

5. Do you think that all government spending is wasteful? some? all private spending? some? How does one measure "waste"?

6. In what ways has history provided the testing ground for the theory of government spending? Was World War II such a test? Was it conclusive? What would invalidate the theory that government spending can properly supplement private investment to cure a depression?

9 Problems of the 1980s

Our journey through history has brought us to the present. We have watched the emergence of the basic market system that underpins our economic society, and we have followed the development of that system into the complex institutional reality of contemporary American capitalism. Now we are ready to turn to the issues of the 1980s—issues that seem likely to persist for many years, even though (as we have mentioned in our Introduction) they may be displaced in the headlines by new problems before the next edition of this book is readied for the press.

inflation There is no doubt where to begin in our survey. The great issue of the 1980s, towering over all others, is the problem of inflation. What can we say about this central preoccupation of our time?

HISTORICAL PERSPECTIVE

Inflation is both a very old problem and a very new one. If we look back over history, we discover many inflationary periods. Diocletian tried (in vain) to curb a Roman inflation in the fourth century A.D.; between 1150 and 1325, the cost of living in medieval Europe rose fourfold; between 1520 and 1650, prices again rose between 200 and 400 percent, largely as a result of gold pouring into Europe from the newly opened mines of the New World. In the years following the Civil War, the South experienced a ferocious inflation, while prices in the North doubled; during World War I, prices in the United States doubled again.

Let us focus more closely on the U.S. experience up to 1950 (Figure 9-1). Two things should be noted about this chart. *First, wars are regularly accompanied by inflation.* The reasons are obvious enough. War greatly increases the volume of public expenditure, but governments do not curb

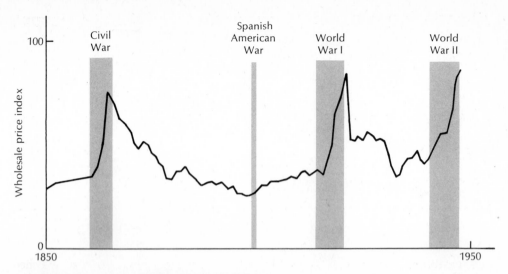

FIGURE 9·1   INFLATION IN PERSPECTIVE

private spending by an equal amount through taxation. Invariably, wars are largely financed by borrowing, and the supply of money and the total amount of spending, public and private, rises rapidly.

Second, inflations have always been relatively short-lived in the past. Notice that prices fell during the periods 1866 to 1900 and 1925 to 1933, and that the long secular trend, although generally tilted upward, is marked with long valleys as well as sharp peaks.

RECENT INFLATIONARY EXPERIENCE

Now examine Figure 9–2, which shows the record of United States price changes since 1950. Once again we notice that the outbreak of war has brought price rises. This is because the financing of the Korean and Vietnam wars, exactly as in the preceding, larger wars, did not sufficiently curtail private spending. But in a vital regard, contemporary experience is different from that of the past. The peaks of inflationary rises have not been followed by long gradual declines. Instead, inflation seems to have become a chronic element in the economic situation, a lingering fever that has defied economic ice packs and economic antibiotics.

WORLDWIDE INFLATION

One further fact of great significance should be noted. *It is that inflation has been a worldwide experience.* It has ravaged underdeveloped countries, where prices have often risen by 20 to 50 percent per year. And it has

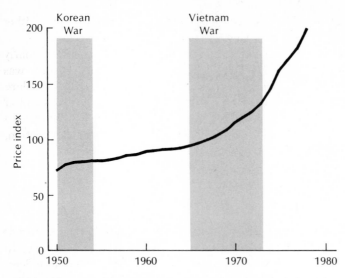

FIGURE 9·2   CONSUMER PRICES SINCE 1950

appeared in every industrialized nation, *even though these nations did not participate in the Korean or Indochinese wars.* As Table 9–1 shows, the United States inflationary problem, on the whole, has been much *less* severe than the European or Japanese experience. In other words, contemporary inflation seems to be a new kind of economic problem that has appeared—and resisted attempts to remedy—in all industrialized nations.

TABLE 9·1

WORLDWIDE
INFLATION

PRICE RISES IN INDUSTRIALIZED COUNTRIES

	Average annual percentage		
	1959–69	1969–72	1973–78 *
U.S.	2.2	4.5	9.3
Canada	2.4	3.7	10.9
France	3.7	5.8	12.8
Italy	3.6	5.1	22.8
Japan	5.0	6.1	14.0
U.K.	3.4	7.6	22.0
W. Germany	2.4	4.9	5.2

* Preliminary figures.

What is the source of this worldwide inflationary outburst? There is neither a single nor a simple answer to the problem. For one thing, a number of individual factors have contributed to the rise in prices. The peculiarly inflationary financing of the Vietnam War was one of these. Another was the OPEC oil crisis of 1973. Still another was a worldwide harvest failure in that year. But these causes seemed to trigger the inflationary potential of the world, rather than to bear full responsibility for it. If we are to explain a phenomenon as widespread and as persistent as global inflation, we must look for changes of great depth and breadth.

What could these background reasons be?

1. *The shift to services.*

One striking fact that we notice in all industrialized nations is the movement of an ever larger fraction of their work forces into the service industries. In the United States today, over 60 percent of the labor force works in offices, shops, classrooms, and municipal, state, and federal buildings, producing the "services" that are ever more in demand in a highly urbanized, high-consumption society.

This movement has a powerful inflationary result. Productivity in the service sector tends to grow much more slowly than in the industrial or agricultural sectors. But wages in the service sector tend to stay abreast of the wage levels set by the great industrial unions. Professor William Baumol has suggested that this major fact of life has inflationary repercussions that must be taken into account.

2. *Increasing power in the marketplace.*

One of the most striking differences between modern inflations and those of the past is that in former days, inflationary peaks were followed by long, slow, deflationary declines, as prices and money wages both fell, particularly in times of recession. It was not unusual in the early years of this century for a large company to announce an across-the-board wage cut. Indeed, that happened frequently during the Great Depression. Certainly, prices frequently declined, partly as a result of technological advance, partly through the sporadic outbreak of cutthroat competition.

All that seems a part of the past beyond recall. Since World War II, most prices and wages in every nation have shown a "ratchet" tendency. They can go up, but they rarely or never come down. This characteristic is probably due to the increasing presence of oligopolistic market structures, to stronger trade unions, and to a business climate in which wage cuts and price wars are no longer regarded as legitimate economic policies. These changes may have salutary social consequences, but they undoubtedly add to our inflationary propensities.

3. *The expansionist influence of governments.*

A third change is equally visible throughout the Western world and Japan. It is the much larger role played by the public sector in generating demand. This change has taken place because governments in all capitalist nations are today charged with responsibilities they never had before—responsibilities to promote growth to the maximum possible extent and to provide adequate levels of social welfare. The result of this change has been an expansionist tendency within the economy, created partly by a high, and upward trending, flow of government spending; and partly by the altered environment of a government-supported socioeconomic system.

To be sure, governments must often use their powers to curb inflation, and may rein in monetary and fiscal programs, and even deliberately create recessions. But these tendencies are short-lived. The political pressures for expansion and social welfare have been, at least until recently, greater than those for stability or recession.

4. *A new social climate.*

A last suggestion is closely related to the previous one. It is a change in the social climate, a change whose roots also lie in the new role of government. In addition to playing a much enlarged economic role, government today is committed to underpinning the *social* surety of its citizens in ways that represent a sharp break from the past. Old age retirement, unemployment benefits, welfare allowances, and health insurance (in most nations) have greatly lessened the extreme risks to which most individuals were subject in the era of laissez-faire capitalism.

With the change in social setting has come a new attitude about one's proper role in society. The age of passive submission, of grateful acceptance of whatever jobs or incomes society offered, has given way to an age of ambitious impatience, of an expectation of "entitlement". A policeman in New York City in the 1920s did not think that he had a "right" to earn as much as a young lawyer, or even as much as a Detroit automobile worker. A policeman in New York or any other large city today does not recognize those older traditional pecking orders: he considers that he is worth exactly as much as he can get.

Such attitudes are not to be deplored. They are expressions of a democratization of social life, of the disappearance of older views which implied that "humbler" occupations should "know their place." But we must also recognize the consequences of this change. The old pecking order had a profoundly settling influence on economic behavior. The new free-for-all has a profoundly unsettling one. The higher expectations that follow from the much greater security of individuals is another element in our society that adds to its upward-tilting instability.

inflationary
propensity

All these changes exert their influence in a common direction. The vulnerability to depression so characteristic of capitalism in its early and middle periods seems to have been replaced by a vulnerability to inflation that is the chronic problem of capitalism in its mature or latest period.

That does not mean, of course, that we cannot have recessions or depressions, any more than the depressions of early or middle capitalism meant that there would never be periods of rising prices. But the latent tendency of the system in our times seems to be inflationary. Capitalist economies have become unstable *upwards* rather than downwards. Just as the older, unsupported capitalism typically reacted to blows by going into a cumulative depression, the new capitalism appears to react to blows by displaying its tendency to go into cumulative inflation.

WHY IS INFLATION SUCH A PROBLEM?

All this poses an interesting problem. For looking back over the decade that ended in the late 1970s, inflation does not seem to have created much social damage. Working people actually *gained* over the ten-year span, although they were injured by rising prices in the last few years. The most vulnerable groups in the nation—those on Social Security and on welfare—came out ahead of inflation because of upward adjustments in their benefits. Social Security receivers in particular were protected by being *indexed* into the level of prices (that is, by automatic cost-of-living adjustments). Only the propertied groups suffered—rent incomes, for example, have steadily fallen as a share of GNP, and corporate profits have been adversely affected. On the other hand, interest payments are up—good news for millions of bond holders.

Why, then, all the fuss? Why is inflation not a politically popular process?

1. *Erosion of money assets.*

There are a number of reasons. *The first is that inflation bears heavily on the value of money assets.* We have seen that inflation's effect on income is two-sided—raising some incomes while lowering others. But its effect on money wealth is one-sided. Everyone loses. Real assets such as houses may gain in value—indeed, inflation typically sets off booms in real estate values or in the values of commodities.

But money-wealth depreciates. Savings accounts, life insurance policies, government bonds, and all other assets of fixed money value lose some of their worth as prices rise. This deals a severe blow to millions of middle-class families who impotently watch their savings melt away. It also holds out the threat of a potential "flight" from money into goods—a flight that could wreck the economic system as completely as the worst depression.

2. Bankruptcies.

A second worry is that inflation will cause widespread bankruptcies and business failures. The steady erosion of the value of money makes it necessary for banks to charge ever higher interest rates, if they are to get enough back to warrant a loan in the first place. And the expectation of rising prices makes it tempting for borrowers to pay higher interest, because they will be paying off the loan in cheaper dollars. Therefore interest rates soar.

This makes doing business very expensive for industries such as housing or utilities that depend heavily on borrowed funds to finance their operations. Inflation thus pushes some firms toward insolvency. If the insolvencies are large enough they can cause serious damage to a bank that has such a firm as a depositor, and if a bank is in deep trouble, it can spread that trouble by calling in loans or by defaulting on its obligations. In the mid-1970s the country narrowly missed a major financial crisis when a large New York bank failed for just these reasons. In other words, inflation can bring business failure just as depression can.

3. The tendency to accelerate.

Third, and perhaps most dangerous, is the tendency of inflations to accelerate. Looking back at Table 9–1, we see a dismaying fact. The inflation rates of all nations rise from period to period. Toward the end of the time span (1973–1978) they were rising very fast. In some cases these last, very high rates have subsequently been reduced, but there is no mistaking the accelerating tendency that we can see in the table as a whole.

Why do inflations accelerate? The reason is that continuously rising prices directly generate further price rises through their effects on behavior. When firms or households *expect* prices to rise, they tend to buy more than they need, trying to stock up while prices are still "low." But the very act of rushing in to buy, when it is generalized to all firms or households, serves to send prices up. Thus the prophecy of higher prices fulfills itself— and actors on the marketplace repeat their hopeless, but dangerous, activities. As a result, the rise in price quickens. Not everyone can march in the front rank in a parade, but the pace of a parade can change from a walk to a run if everyone tries to move up to the front rank.

controlling inflation

So there are reasons enough to fear inflation. The question is "Can we stop it?"

The answer is "Yes—at a price." Certainly we would know how to cope with inflation if a war were to break out tomorrow, threatening a runaway of the price level. We would then freeze all prices and impose heavy taxation to mop up all excess incomes. Many problems might follow in the wake of such a policy, but inflation would not be one of them.

problem of controls   Then why do we not impose controls? The answer is that they are administratively clumsy, hard to enforce, and almost invariably evaded in one way or another. A wage-and-price freeze always catches someone at a disadvantage: a union that was just about to sign an advantageous but perhaps deserved contract, a store whose prices were at "sale" levels on the day that the freeze was announced, a business whose costs increase as a result of a rise in the prices of imported goods. Thus, price controls lead to endless adjustment and adjudication. Moreover, unless there is a general sentiment of patriotic "pulling together" (as during World War II or the Korean War, when controls were fairly successful in repressing inflation), controls tend to lead to black or gray markets or to downgrading the quality of the "same" goods that are sold at fixed prices.

Not surprisingly, efforts to control wages tend to be more successful than efforts to control prices. This is because the government has an ally to help it enforce its wage regulations—namely, employers. Employers know what their employees make and have an interest in keeping wages within the legal limits. Consumers, on the other hand, usually do not know what products cost and cannot demand that stores refrain from marking up items.

As a result, when controls are imposed, they tend to work fairly well for a short period of time on the wage side, while prices continue to creep upward. After a certain point, consumer resentment explodes in the form of demands from workers that their wage restraints be loosened. In nation after nation, this process has been repeated.

tax problems   It is just as hard to curb inflation from the demand side rather than from the supply side, by imposing severe taxes that will bring the expansion of purchasing power to a halt.

The problem here is obvious enough. Bringing the expansion of incomes to a halt means imposing severe taxes on the middle levels of American society where the bulk of purchasing power is concentrated. Unfortunately for anti-inflationary policy, increasing taxes on this group is political dynamite.* Perhaps a truly effective tax increase could be imposed on the middle and upper middle class, if receivers of very large incomes were taxed at least as severely. This means closing the loopholes that have been stubbornly and successfully defended for many years.

---

* This is particularly the case because one of the effects of inflation is to raise people's money incomes, thereby pushing them into higher tax brackets. It is not a coincidence that the growth of sentiment against taxation has gathered force after a long period of inflation.

It is a hard fact of political life that no government in any Western nation, including the most socially progressive, such as Sweden, has succeeded in winning the political support necessary to impose a fully effective anti-inflation tax program. Perhaps people prefer inflation and relatively lower taxes to price stability and very high taxes. If this is the case, there is nothing the economist can do—except warn that inflation is likely to go on.

the
recession
approach

Because controls and taxation are so unpopular, governments have relied mainly on another means of curbing inflation—inducing mild recessions in the hope that they will cause the "overheated" economy to cool down.

Unfortunately, mild recessions are difficult to control. The tight money policies and more stringent government budgets by which such recessions are engineered tend to exert their impact unevenly. Big businesses, with strong cash reserves, may make their way through the recession relatively unhurt, while small businesses, unable to get bank credit, collapse right and left. This quickly leads to an outcry to let up on small business, to which Congress cannot help but respond.

At the same time, an effort to cut back "wasteful" government spending soon brings the realization that it is not easy to change the institutional structures of federal, state, and local governments. The choice is often between "wasteful" (i.e. expensive) programs, or no programs at all. If the choice is made for no programs, the community soon begins to feel the impact of fewer police or firemen or teachers, insufficient prison space or correction officers, slow-moving courts, ill-repaired streets, inadequate state or national recreational facilities, and the like. Cutting taxes is always popular, but living with the results is not likely to be so popular.

Thus the recession approach, although "milder" than controls or heavier taxation, also has its shortcomings. So far, at least, it has not worked. *The result of recession-inducing policy has been to cut growth, but not to cut inflation.* Instead we have the worst of both worlds—stagnation plus continued inflation, the modern disease of "stagflation."

inflation as
a way of
life

Does this mean that inflation has become a chronic fact of life, incurable except at levels of unemployment that would be socially disastrous, or by the imposition of severe and unpopular wage, price, and income controls?

It seems so. All efforts to find a middle ground, where a moderate amount of inflation could be combined with a moderate degree of recession have failed. In Europe this has led to inflation rates that have reached above 20 percent per year; in the United States to inflation rates in double digits (over 10 percent), combined with unemployment rates at around 6 percent. What is still more discouraging, this situation has not been static, but deteriorating. Inflation rates have continued to show their accelerating tendencies.

Thus one country after another has been forced to try more vigorous means. In the United States the Carter administration in 1978 deliberately risked a severe recession in order to bring inflation under control. We do not yet know whether this recession can be prevented from becoming a depression, or whether Congress can withstand the cries of anguish that the recession will cause, or whether the recession, even if it is severe, will stop inflation.

For that we will have to wait and see. What seems certain is that we will have to turn to controls and heavier taxes if the present course does not work. No one welcomes such a difficult and intrusive role of government. But if inflation continues, despite our efforts to cure it, the taste of the necessary medicine will become much less unpalatable.

problem of unemploy- ment

More than once in our study of economics, we have come up against the problem of unemployment. And no wonder. Unemployment bulks large in our study because it is a problem peculiarly associated with market systems. In tradition-run economies, we do not encounter unemployment in the same form as we do in a market system. Peasants or nomadic tribesmen or serfs may be very unproductive, extremely poor, or reduced to idleness because their institutions exclude them from land or from the ownership of animals or other wealth, but unemployment in these societies is a static condition that results from existing institutions. We do not find periods of high and low unemployment in these societies (good and bad harvests perhaps excepted), but a more or less unchanged proportion of workers to the total population. So, too, in command societies, the labor force may be poorly allocated or underutilized, but here again, unemployment appears as a fault of the planning mechanism, not as a result of the malfunction of the market machinery.

By way of contrast, the single most important social task that a market system entrusts to its "machinery" is that of finding acceptable work for the members of the society. It is also a task that the market does not perform altogether satisfactorily. From time to time, as we know, severe depressions have wracked market systems, causing unemployment to rise to heights that not only inflicted great damage on people who were unable to find work, but threatened the political and social stability of the system.

the focus of unemploy- ment

It seems unlikely that we will ever again suffer the 25 percent unemployment of the Great Depression. We have learned that government spending —a means of generating demand unthinkable in the early 1930s—can pump up a depressed economy and restore high employment. The experience of

World War II was decisive on that point; thus it is doubtful that we will again tolerate the trauma of mass unemployment.

But unemployment can be a cruel and difficult problem, even if it does not reach mass proportions. All during the 1970s the unemployment rate ran at a level of about 4 to 7 percent, rising as the decade went along. Even 7 per cent unemployment would not be a terrible social burden, if it were equally shared by all members of the work force; it would amount to about two weeks of joblessness per person.

But unemployment is never equally shared. Typically it affects and afflicts some groups much more severely than others. Women suffer unemployment rates that are 30 to 40 percent higher than those of men. Blacks have twice the joblessness of whites. Teenagers experience four and five times the unemployment of adults.

Therefore even "mild" unemployment can hit with terrible force against particular groups, or sometimes against particular regions. The social damage of unemployment is more narrowly focused than it was during the Great Depression, and it is mitigated by a system of unemployment benefits and welfare support that was unknown in that earlier period. Nevertheless the social costs of unemployment are high, measured not only in terms of lost purchasing power, but in the social unrest and political disaffection that being without work can generate. Inflation may be the problem that worries people most, but unemployment is the problem that wounds them most.

combatting unemploy- ment

How effectively can we combat the problem of unemployment? Because unemployment has more than one cause, there is more than one answer to the question. Let us look at the range of policies and solutions open to us.

1. *Increasing demand.*

As a general rule, anything that increases the total demand of society is apt to increase employment. This is particularly true when unemployment tends to be widespread, both in geographic location and industrial distribution. *The expansion of GNP, whether by the stimulation of private investment or consumer spending or government expenditure or net exports, is generally the single most reliable means of creating more jobs.*

There is, however, a problem. Or rather, three problems.

First, *increasing total demand may well increase the rate of inflation.* Therefore, we cannot easily use the general spending approach except when unemployment is high and widely shared, as during a major recession. Once we begin to climb out of recession, additional spending jacks up prices more noticeably than it cures unemployment. The perceived benefits of spending begin to wane, and the perceived costs of spending (inflation) increase. Thus massive spending programs have limited usefulness in eliminating unemployment.

Second, *spending programs may not create jobs for the particular groups who are most seriously affected by unemployment.* A typical problem of our times is the bunching of joblessness in city ghettos. But a program of spending—or a private expansion of demand—will not reach into the ghetto, where industry does not usually recruit its work force. Special training programs, or highly concentrated programs designed for particular regions or particular social groups, are then required.

Third, *spending programs require public support and approval.* At the start of the 1980s, we find ourselves in a period when the public's willingness to support public spending is clearly on the decline. The tax cost of public expenditures seems much greater for many middle class citizens than the benefits that they will derive from additional spending. Thus a problem of political disapproval must be overcome, before even relatively small economic programs are likely to become available as anti-unemployment measures.

2. *Remedying structural unemployment.*

As we have just seen, not all unemployment is due to insufficient demand. Some can be traced to "structural" causes—to a lack of "fit" between the existing labor force and the existing job opportunities.

A sharp debate has raged in the United States concerning the importance of structural reasons (as contrasted with a general deficiency of demand) in accounting for the present level of unemployment. Many observers have pointed out that the unemployed are typically grouped into certain disprivileged categories: race, sex, age, lack of training, and unfortunate georgraphic location. The aged and the young, the black and the unskilled, and the Massachusetts textile worker are not quickly pulled into employment by a general expansion of demand. The broad stream of purchasing power passes most of them by and does not reintegrate them into the mainstream of the economy. Hence stress is increasingly placed on measures to assist labor mobility, so that the unemployed can move from distressed to expansive areas, and on the retraining of men for those jobs offered by a technologically fast-moving society.

Retraining is, unfortunately, much easier when it is applied to relatively few persons than when it is proposed as a general public policy affecting large numbers of unemployed. Then the question arises, For what jobs shall the unemployed be trained? *Unless we very clearly know the shape of future demand, the risk is that a retraining program will prepare workers for jobs that may no longer exist when the workers are ready for them.* And unless the *level* of future demand is high, even a foresighted program will not effectively solve the unemployment problem.

Most economists would suggest a combination of measures to combat structural unemployment. One of them is *a much more effective job-finding system* than we now have—a computerized "job bank" has been proposed. Another is *a more generous program of unemployment benefits* to give people time to look for work they want, rather than forcing them to settle for work they can do. *Training schools* are very valuable, especially if they are connected with a program of *public demand,* so that trainees know that jobs exist. A survey made by the Urban Coalition in 34 cities has estimated that over a million potential new jobs exist in the public sector—in education, welfare administration, environment control, library services, police and fire protection, hospital and sanitation improvement, and so on.

3. *Using the government as employer of last resort.*

Finally, we can effectively limit the problem of unemployment by formally adopting the policy of using the public sector as "employer of last resort."

This proposal, recently incorporated in rather vague language, in the Humphrey-Hawkins bill, does not mean the use of the public sector as a kind of vast "work relief" program. On the contrary, the purpose is to use public employment primarily as a positive force in establishing a higher quality of life, an objective that will require a substantial expansion of much public-service activity along the lines mentioned above in the proposals of the Urban Coalition. Only as a secondary objective is "the employer of last resort" to provide jobs for those who fail to find satisfactory work in the private sector or in the current career lines of public services.

the US and European experience

As evidence of what can be done by a more vigorous attack on unemployment, using many of these techniques, the performance of the United States in recent years can be compared with that of various European nations.

The lesson of Table 9–3 is clear. A tendency to generate unemployment

TABLE 9·3

UNEMPLOY-
MENT
RATES

Selected Countries, 1960–1974			
Country	Highest	Lowest	Average
United States	6.7	3.5	4.9
Canada	7.1	3.9	5.4
Japan	1.7	1.1	1.3
France	3.0	1.6	2.3
West Germany	2.1	0.3	0.8
Italy	4.3	2.7	3.6
United Kingdom	5.3	1.2	3.2
Sweden	2.7	1.2	1.9

may be an unavoidable consequence of a market system, *but it is not an irremediable evil. It is possible to run a capitalist system at high levels of employment—very likely paying the price of a considerable degree of inflation.*

A critic might retort that low unemployment was achieved in many European countries because they used "guest workers"—Greeks and Yugoslavs and Turks—who were sent home when the economy sagged. This is partly true, although it does not apply to Japan. There is general agreement, nonetheless, that European economies have achieved much lower unemployment rates than we, by establishing efficient labor exchanges, or by generous policies that have enabled workers to move to high employment areas. The prize example is Switzerland which boasted of less than 1 percent unemployment *or inflation* in 1978!

The problem, then, is to bring about the political changes in the United States that may be the prerequisite for introducing the kinds of employment programs that have proved their worth in capitalism abroad. That may involve a very difficult problem of public education and persuasion, but it is a problem different from a defeatist admission that the economic system itself cannot be made to work adequately.

the military subeconomy Now let us turn to another aspect of our economic troubles. It is that perhaps 6 percent of the total output of the American economy consists of military goods and services—missiles, bombs, planes, tanks, payrolls of the armed forces, military subsidies to foreign nations, and the like. The "perhaps" refers to the fact that we cannot give a very precise estimate of total military spending, because its full extent is only now being revealed. In 1971, for example, the Senate Foreign Relations Committee discovered that direct and indirect military assistance to foreign nations totalled $6.9 billion, whereas the item for Military Assistance in the president's budget message to Congress listed it at only $625 million. It was discovered as well that under the Food for Peace program, $691 million had been transferred to foreign nations *for the purchase of arms;* that the United States had spent $1.5 billion in supporting South Vietnamese currency, of which $680 million was lost because of an overevaluation of that currency; and that the Pentagon had a surplus weapons stock worth $17 billion.[1]

After listening to three days of testimony with regard to the hitherto undisclosed flow of military assistance abroad, a senator said, "Most of us in Washington have seen a lot of mismanagement in government programs. But military assistance is the first program I have come across that appears to be characterized by unmanagement. . . . In some respects, the United

[1] Joint Subcommittee on Economy in Government (January 1971).

States has been transformed from an 'arsenal of democracy' to a gigantic discount supermarket with no check-out counters, no store managers—only clerks who blithely deliver to foreign governments of practically any political persuasion whatever they happen to see and like."

the
Department
of Defense

If there is much that we do not yet know about the extent of our military economy, what we do know is sobering enough. The Department of Defense (DOD) is the largest planned economy outside the Soviet Union. Its property—plant and equipment, land, inventories of war, and other commodities—amounts to about 8 percent of the assets of the entire American economy. It owns 39-million acres of land, roughly an area the size of Hawaii. It rules over a population of 4 million—direct employees or soldiers —and spends an "official" budget of well over $100 billion, a budget three-quarters as large as the entire gross national product of Great Britain.

This makes DOD richer than any small nation in the world and, of course, incomparably more powerful. That part of its assets represented by nuclear explosives alone gives it the equivalent of six tons of TNT for every living inhabitant of the globe, to which must be added the awesome military power of its "conventional" weapons. The conventional explosives dropped in Indochina *before* the extension of the war to Laos amounted to well over 3-million tons, or 50 percent *more* than the total bomb tonnage dropped on all nations in both the European and Pacific theatres during World War II.

The DOD system embraces both people and industry. In the late 1970s, the people included, first, some 3-million soldiers deployed in more than 2,000 bases or locations abroad and at home, plus another million civilians located within the United States and abroad. No less important are some 5-million civilian workers who are employed in "defense-oriented" production. This does not include still further millions who owe their livelihood to the civilian services they render to the military.

Meanwhile, the sale of US arms abroad has become a major US export. During the last half of the decade of the 1970s, arms exports averaged around $9 billion per year. What would be the effect of a major contraction in defense spending is a problem we will have to defer for later consideration, but no one denies that such a major contraction—*unless counteracted by vigorous expansion of civilian spending*—could plunge this country into a severe depression.

This is not to say, of course, that the United States does not need a strong defense capability today. But there is no question that the Pentagon subeconomy—some would say "substate"—has become a major element in, and a major problem for, American capitalism. Indeed, the questions it raises are central: How important is this subeconomy to our economic vitality? How difficult would it be to reduce? Can our economy get along without a military subsector?

military
dependency

Let us begin by reviewing a few important facts.

At the height of the Vietnam War in 1968, more than 10 percent of our labor force was employed in defense-related work. As the Vietnam War gradually decelerated, this percentage fell to about 5 percent. Defense expenditures, meanwhile, dropped from their peak of nearly $77 billion to a low of $71 billion in 1971, after which they began an upward march toward the $120-billion level at the end of the 1970s. (In real terms, of course, the rise was less, but still considerable.)

These global figures do not, however, give a clear picture of the strategic position of defense spending within the economy. For the problem is that war-related spending and employment are not distributed evenly across the system, but are bunched in special areas and industries. In a survey made in 1967, the Defense Department found that 72 employment areas depended on war output for 12 percent or more of their employment, and that four-fifths of these areas were communities with labor forces of less than 50,000. This concentration of defense activity was still a fact of economic life in the late 1970s. The impact of a cutback on these middle-sized communities can be devastating.

In addition, defense employment is concentrated among special skills as well as in a nucleus of defense-oriented companies. In the late 1960s, about one scientist or engineer out of every five in private industry was employed on a defense-related job. Thirty-eight percent of all physicists depended on war work. Twenty-five percent of all sheet-metal workers, the same proportion of patternmakers, and 54 percent of all airplane mechanics worked on defense projects. These proportions have declined, but "defense" is still a major employer of these skills. A number of observers have remarked that this concentration of talent not only accelerates the development of costly military technology, but retards the development of civilian technology.

Finally, there is a core of companies dependent on military spending for its very existence. These are not usually the largest companies in the economy (for whom, on the average, defense receipts amount to about 10 percent of total revenues), but the second echelon of corporations: Of 30 companies with assets in the $150-million to $1-billion range, 6 depended on war spending for *half* their incomes, 7 depended on it for a quarter of theirs.

Thus, a cutback in defense spending will be felt very sharply in particular areas where there may be no other jobs available, or among occupational groups who have no alternative employment at equivalent pay, or in companies that are "captives" of the DOD. Such companies and areas naturally lobby hard for defense expenditure on which their livelihood depends. So do their representatives in Congress. It is this interweaving of economic and political interests that makes the problem of defense cutbacks so difficult.

conversion *possibilities* Yet a cutback is not economically impossible. What is needed is a program of retraining, relocation, income support, and conversion aid that will cushion the inevitable shock of a decline in military spending. In 1971, the National Urban Coalition estimated that we would need to spend about $4 billion over two years to move and retrain the bulk of the personnel who would be displaced if we cut our military budget by one third. In 1980, that estimate would probably have to be doubled.

Nonetheless, the sum is not large compared with the saving in real wealth that would thereby be affected. *What is crucial, economically, is that the decline in war-related spending be offset by increases in peace-related spending, to be sure that the overall level of demand would remain high enough to act as a magnet, attracting the displaced workers to other jobs.* The Coalition therefore proposed a broad-scale attack on many social problems that would raise total (local, state, and federal) government expenditures on goods and services by over 50 percent, to assure that the conversion would in fact be a smooth one.

Could such a vast conversion actually be carried out? There is no insuperable *economic* problem posed by conversion. After World War II, defense spending fell from 37.5 percent of GNP to 6.6 percent in the short space of two years. During this period, 10 million men and women were demobilized from the armed forces and added to the labor force. Yet unemployment from 1947 to 1949 rose only from 3.6 percent of the labor force to 5.5 percent. Clearly, the problem today appears much less formidable than it was then.

But there is a difference between the two periods. Post–World War II conversion was greatly facilitated by the presence of a huge pent-up civilian demand. Today there is no evidence of unfilled consumer needs. Thus, unless we are willing to undertake an ambitious program of public spending or tax cuts, the conversion will almost certainly generate severe unemployment—and consequently political pressures to maintain military spending.

A substantial cutback in military spending therefore seems very unlikely as we enter the 1980s. We shall have to live with a military substate for a long time. The problem will be to insure that it remains just that—an internal economy under the control of its civil host. The condition of liberty, it has been wisely said, is eternal vigilance.

problem of *economic* *growth* Inflation, unemployment, military dependency are all obvious problems for the American economy. But until a very few years ago, no one would have listed growth as a problem. On the contrary, growth was regarded as the greatest single benefit of the system. As Adam Smith's "growth model" made clear, the natural workings of the system brought a stream of benefits in the form of rising material wealth. To question the usefulness of more wealth seemed irresponsible.

negative
externalities

But today we are not so certain that more growth, from our present levels of output, is an unequivocally "good thing." More and more, we are becoming aware of the unpleasant or even harmful side effects of production that economists call "negative externalities." Here are a few examples:

ITEM: *Annual throwaway list:*

214-million tons of carbon monoxide, sulfur oxides, hydrocarbons, particulates, and nitrous oxides (over a ton per American)
55-billion tin cans (275 for each of us)
20-billion bottles (100 apiece)
65-billion metal and plastic bottle caps (325 each)
7-million cars (our annual output has to go *somewhere* after 100,000 miles or so)
10-million tons of steel and iron scrap (an average of 1,000 pounds each)
150-million tons of garbage and trash (4.1 pounds per person daily)
3-billion tons of tailings, mine debris, and waste (4 tons for each of us, each day)

ITEM: On several occasions in recent years inhabitants of Los Angeles and St. Louis have been warned against indulging in any kind of exercise, including jogging, golf, and so on, because deep breathing was dangerous.

ITEM: Nitrates and phosphates in fertilizers and detergents cause water-pollution problems that are beyond the control of present technology. The use of these chemicals is estimated to increase by tenfold before the year 2000. Professor Barry Commoner, ecologist, predicts a major agricultural crisis in the United States from this source alone within 50 years.

ITEM: It is estimated that by the year 2000, there will be, at any time, some 3,000 six-ton trucks in transit carrying dangerous radioactive wastes to burial sites.

ITEM: With 6 percent of the world's population, the United States annually consumes about 40 percent of the world's output of raw materials and discharges into the environment about the same percentage of the world's waste products. Thus, each American is roughly the equivalent of seven Asians or Africans or South Americans in his ecological disturbance. There are, in round numbers, some 2.5 billion inhabitants of Asia, Africa, and South America. What does this imply for the long-run chances of economic development in those areas? What does it imply about the long-run acceptable levels of economic "development" in the United States? [2]

[2] See Paul and Anne Ehrlich, *Population, Resources, Environment* (San Francisco: Freeman, 1970), *passim*.

Clearly, here is a situation in which something must "give." Will it be the chance for economic development for the world's peoples, or will it be our profligate use of resources?

These negative externalities shed light on a very important problem. Because of growth, we are often said to be twice as "rich" as our parents, four times as rich as our grandparents, and incalculably richer than our distant forbears. But no one would say that we were two or four times happier, or more content, or more fulfilled as individuals than they. Why not? More and more we ask if growth is not a two-sided process, bringing additional material wealth on the one hand, but also bringing unpleasant or dangerous side effects on the other.

It has become clear, then, that "growth" in itself is not enough to improve our general quality of life, for the growth may take place in the wrong things or in the wrong places. We are piling up mountains of toothpaste while we ignore the possibility of providing dental care to those who cannot afford it. We are "growing" in terms of military output, but not in low-cost housing. As John Kenneth Galbraith has put it, we are becoming a society of "private affluence and public squalor," because we have failed to exert a proper guiding influence over the kind of growth that the unsupervised market process brings about.

the exponential problem

Finally, our growth process has brought us to consider a crucial question for our future. It is whether a continuation of the growth trend of the past will not ultimately "bankrupt" us—not in monetary terms, but in terms of the ability of our planet to sustain our voracious use of its resources or to absorb the waste products that are one unwanted result of our ravenous material appetites.

Here the sobering aspect of the problem lies in the fact that growth is an *exponential process*. Today global industrial output is rising at about 7 percent a year, thereby doubling every 10 years. If we project this rate of growth for another fifty years, it follows that the rate of use of resources would have doubled *five times* (assuming that today's technology of industrial production is essentially unchanged). Thus, 50 years hence we would need 32 times as large a volume of material inputs as today. A century hence, when output would have doubled ten times, we would need over a thousand times the present volume of output—and this gargantuan volume of extraction would still be relentlessly doubling.

the technological factor

Does this mean that we will run out of resources? We do not know. We are constantly making resources, learning to use less-concentrated forms of minerals, and finding wholly new materials, such as plastics. Thus, we may be able to expand our supply of resources exponentially, along with our use of them.

All this, however, requires the appropriate technology. It is one thing to "mine the seas and melt the rocks" on paper, and another to move and refine the millions of tons of water and earth in fact. Where will we get the energy to undertake these huge labors? It is one thing to run a nuclear fusion plant on paper; another to bring it on-stream. (No controllable fusion process yet exists, except in the most advanced laboratories.)

Thus we are essentially engaged in a race between technology and the exponentially rising demands for raw materials. Technology enters this race in many ways. It may enable us to recycle existing wastes, so that we do not need to extract as much new materials. It may enable us to get more usable resources from a given quantity of raw materials. It may open up new modes of production that enable us to shift production techniques away from materials that are becoming scarce (and therefore expensive), to those that remain abundant and therefore cheap. It gives us new sources of energy that enable us to use materials that are now too "low-grade" for economic production.

One primary question in estimating the "limits" to growth is therefore the rate at which we will develop the appropriate technology. Unfortunately, the link between research and development and economically usable technology is not clearly understood. We do not really know whether we will find an appropriate technology to permit us, for example, to run a vast private-automobile fleet in the year 2000, or whether we will be able to turn out high-quality steels in the volume that will support industrialization on a global scale fifty years hence. More important, we do not know if a technology that permitted us to "mine the seas and melt the rocks" will be perfected—or whether such a technology would be compatible with other ecological and environmental considerations. Some scientists are concerned that our enormous consumption of energy will affect the climate of various parts of the earth, altering weather patterns and eventually overheating the atmosphere.

visible limits to growth

Is it possible to assign some sort of timetable to the growth problem? Inevitably there is a large measure of uncertainty attached to projections into the future that are so dependent on technological change. But there are three warning signals, now visible, that can give us some rough and ready estimates.

1. An impending energy crunch.

Sooner or later, we will exhaust the available reservoirs of one finite resource—petroleum. How soon? That depends on two factors. One of them is the extent of present and probable reserves. The other is our rate of use of oil. Both these parameters of the problems are shrouded with uncertainty. Only a short time ago economists felt that within another 20 to 30 years oil would become a "scarce" resource—scarce in the sense that its price would be set by demand rather than by the cartel policies of OPEC.[3] That scenario may very possibly take place ahead of schedule.

This means that well before the year 2000, we will have to change our industrial production and consumption habits substantially. The world's automobile fleet (which may be much larger by then) will have to be designed to use far less gasoline, or to run on some alternate fuel. The heating apparatus for the world will have to adapt to coal or solar energy. The use of oil in utility and other industrial processes must make way for coal or nuclear sources.

All this can be done, of course. But such a giant change-over is almost certain to require a reduction in our rate of industrial expansion. Moreover the pollution problems implicit in a much heavier reliance on coal, and the problems of disposal of radioactive wastes that are inseparable from a move toward nuclear fuel, both entail enormous costs for making growth safe.

From the energy side, then, are indications that growth will become more expensive and more dangerous well before the year 2000.

2. The investment problem.

Earlier we mentioned that continued growth at existing rates would require enormous expansions in the provision of resources. Nobel prize winning economist Wassily Leontief has projected that it would require four times as much food output and five times as much mineral output to sustain growth at present growth rates until the year 2000.[4]

The question is not whether the planet can provide us this wealth, but the cost at which it will do so. According to the Leontief report it will require tremendous expenditures for irrigation and fertilizer, for mining and refining and transportation equipment, to achieve these goals. For the less-developed nations, investment expenditures would rise to as much as 40 percent of gross national product. An investment effort of this magnitude would tax the capacities of even the most industrialized nations, where investment rarely amounts to as much as twenty-five percent of gross national product. To mount such an investment program in a poor nation would probably be impossible, except perhaps under the rigid control of a semi-military economy.

In Chapter 12 we shall look again at the dilemmas this poses for the

---

[3] See Andrew Flower, "World Oil Production," *Scientific American,* March, 1978.
[4] *The Future of the World Economy,* (New York: Oxford Univ. Press, 1977), pp. 4, 5.

poor nations. Here it is sufficient to recognize another constraint on growth likely to exert its braking effect before the year 2000.

3. *The scale of technological intervention.*

Last, we have the problem of the fragility of the biosphere—that thin film of green and blue organic chemistry on which all life depends.

It is sobering to examine the severity of our present intrusion into this life-supporting film. Recently, for example, scientists anxiously have debated whether fluorocarbons—the gas propellants for such products as hair sprays and deodorants—might not change the filtration properties of the atmosphere in ways that were inimical to health. What was astonishing about this debate was not the complex findings about the interaction of fluorocarbons and the atmosphere. It *was that the tonnage of such gasses was sufficiently large so that the threat of global contamination had to be considered as a realistic possibility.*

There are many more such examples of the scale of our technological incursion into the biosphere. We have mentioned in passing the danger of changing the pattern of climate as a consequence of the release of industrial heat. A related problem is the "greenhouse" effect that results from the release of carbon dioxide into the atmosphere during combustion. The carbon dioxide acts as an invisible trap for reflected solar heat, like the glass in a greenhouse, threatening to raise temperatures disastrously within a generation or two. And then there is the problem of disposing safely of nuclear wastes—not just for a year or two, but for a hundred thousand years during which they will continue to give off dangerous radio-active rays.[5]

summing up the risks

We do not possess enough information to project the degree of risk of any one of these dangers very accurately. But the cluster of so many dangers of this kind strongly suggests that our present scale of industrial activity is already threatening to encroach on the life support capabilities of the biosphere, and that the encroachment of a doubled or trebeled scale of industrial activity would be extremely hazardous, perhaps even fatal.

This, too, gives us reason to believe that the pace of growth will have to be much reduced, and will certainly have to be much more carefully monitored and supervised before the arrival of the next century.

global inequality

Two problems must be squarely faced if we contemplate the consequences of a slowdown in growth. The first has to do with the unequal distribution of income (and resources) among the nations of the world. As we will

---

[5] See William Baumol and Wallace Oates, *Economics, Environmental Policy and the Quality of Life* (Englewood Cliffs, N.J.: Prentice-Hall, 1975), pp. 64–70.

see in Chapter 12, the underdeveloped nations today enjoy standards of living that are far below even the poorest levels in the advanced countries. Thus the prospect of an enforced slowdown in the rate of industrial output raises the specter of *an international struggle for resources,* as the poor countries attempt to build up the framework of modern industrial structures, and the developed nations continue along their present course.

The question of an impending limit to industrial growth therefore poses a major economic problem for international relations. How are the remaining easily available resources of the world to be shared? As the advanced nations continue to build up their industrial systems, will they leave the underdeveloped regions on a permanently lower level of well-being? Our analysis poses this fundamental question, but cannot answer it.

stationary capitalism?   Second, we must ask whether a very slow rate of industrial growth—not to mention a zero or negative rate—is compatible with capitalism. As economists from Adam Smith through Karl Marx down to the present day have pointed out, such a "stationary state" would pose very great difficulties for a capitalist system. As expansion ceased, competition among enterprises would lead to a falling rate of profit. This would directly undercut the main source of income of the capitalist class. Worse, the cessation of net investment might set in motion a downward spiral of incomes and employment that would plunge capitalism into severe depression.

Could capitalism be rescued from this fate by a much larger volume of public spending that would not add to environmental danger? Could it give up industrial expansion in exchange for programs of education, the arts, greatly improved care for the old and the very young? Could it manage the political problem of income distribution in a situation in which the growth of material output was very small, or in which material output per capita actually fell because of the demands of the underdeveloped countries?

Once again, we do not know. The impending environmental pressures surely indicate that major changes will be needed to make the economic system of the still distant future compatible with environmental constraints. Whether capitalism can make that adjustment—or whether industrial socialism can make it better—are questions that our analysis raises, but cannot answer.

a spaceship economy   What is certain, however, is that *all* industrial systems, socialist as well as capitalist, will sooner or later have to change their attitudes toward growth.

For in the long run there is no alternative to viewing the earth itself as a spaceship (in Kenneth Boulding's phrase) to whose ultimately finite carrying capacity its passengers must adjust their ways. From this point of view, production itself suddenly appears as a "throughput," beginning with the raw material of the environment and ending with the converted material of the production process, which is returned to the environment by way of emissions, residuals, and so on. In managing this throughput, the task of producers is not to maximize "growth," but to do as little damage to the environment as possible during the inescapable process of transformation by which man lives. If "growth" enters man's calculations in this period of rationally controlled production, it can be only insofar as he can extract more and more "utility" from less and less material input; that is, as he learns to economize on the use of the environment by recycling his wastes and by avoiding the disturbance of delicate ecological systems.

Such a spaceship economy is probably still some distance off, although by no means so far away that our children or grandchildren may not encounter its problems. Much depends on the rate at which the Third World grows in population and productivity and on the technological means of lessening pollution in the advanced countries. Not least, a true Spaceship Earth would require a feeling of international amity sufficiently great so that the industrialized peoples of the world would willingly acquiesce in global production ceilings that penalized them much more severely than it did their poorer sister nations.

These longer perspectives begin to make us aware of the complexity of the problem of growth. Growth is desperately needed by a world that is, in most nations, still desperately poor. Yet, growth is already beginning to threaten a world that is running out of "environment." If growth inevitably brings environmental danger, we shall be faced with a cruel choice indeed. Today we have only begun to recognize the problems of pollution-generating growth, and we are engaged in devising remedies for these problems on a national basis. Ahead lies the much more formidable problem of a world in which growth may encounter ecological barriers on a worldwide scale, bringing the need for new political and economic arrangements for which we have no precedent. The true Age of Spaceship Earth is still some distance in the future, but for the first time the passengers on the craft are aware of its limitations.

<table>
<tr><td>9</td><td>Key Concepts and Key Words</td></tr>
</table>

Inflation	1. Inflation is an ancient phenomenon, often associated with wars, but usually followed by periods of declining prices. *The features of modern inflation are that it has been experienced in all industrialized nations*, whether or not involved in war, *and that it has not shown the traditional peaks and valleys.*
Inflation causes	2. Behind the worldwide phenomenon of inflation we can discern a number of structural shifts. They are: a marked increase in the proportion of low-productivity service sector jobs; much greater organized power of labor and

Latent upward instability

business; expansionary government economic policies; and a social climate of "entitlement" that leads to a "free-for-all" in place of the old established pecking order. The result is a new kind of upward capitalist instability, manifested in a tendency toward inflation rather than depression.

Costs of inflation

3. The costs of inflation are of two kinds. One is redistributional. Thanks to Congressional action in "indexing" social security payments, inflation has not severely damaged the main body of pensioners in the economy. The other cost is the effect on the system's viability. Inflation always erodes the value of money wealth, and threatens a panicky flight from money. It also brings higher interest rates which can cause bankruptcies in important business areas. And inflation tends to accelerate, threatening a disastrous runaway.

Controls

4. Mild controls have not been very successful in curbing inflation. Severe controls—wage and price curbs or drastic taxation—are clumsy and unpopular. The outlook is therefore for a continuation of inflation—worse, of stagflation (slow growth plus continued inflation)—until the public is prepared to accept the very harsh medicine that may be needed to bring it under control.

Unemployment

5. Unemployment is another major problem of our time. We do not seem to be faced with the massive joblessness of the Great Depression, but even "mild" unemployment creates very severe problems for those affected, and damages the social fabric of society.

Remedies for unemployment Increasing demand and its problems

6. The remedies for unemployment are as varied as its forms. The single most powerful remedy is to increase demand. However, increasing demand can also increase inflation. Further, it may not reach the groups who are most affected by unemployment. And finally, it requires a degree of public support that is not evident in the United States at this writing.

Structural unemployment and government as employer of last resort

7. Structural unemployment requires much more carefully structured programs. Without an assurance as to jobs that will be filled, it is difficult to mount such a program. This implies the need for a work-creating program using the government as employer of last resort. Only a limited degree of support exists for such a large-scale public employment program today. Finally, we should recognize that a number of capitalist nations have tackled the unemployment problem more successfully than we.

Military subeconomy

Conversion

8. The military subeconomy is a huge "sector" that absorbs about 6 percent of output and provides about 6 percent of employment. Its importance is much larger, however, in particular industrial fields or geographic areas.
Conversion to a less armament-dependent economy requires the substitution of civil output and employment for military output and employment. This is a problem whose major difficulty is political rather than economic.

Side effects of growth

9. Economic growth has traditionally been regarded as an unequivocal gain. Today it is increasingly recognized that growth can bring adverse effects as well as good ones. These adverse side effects include such things as pollution, congestion, and other dangers and inconveniences that result from increasing output.

Exponential growth

10. A serious problem is posed by the exponential growth of output: We may "run out of" needed minerals or food or energy, or we may overload the absorptive capacity of the earth. *The central issue here is the outcome of a race between technology and environmental constraints.* We cannot predict the result of this race.

Limits to growth

Energy Investment

Biosphere

11. No one can place a definite timetable on the growth potential before us. But there are three "visible" barriers to be reckoned with. Most experts agree that the price of energy will rise sharply within the next 20–25 years mainly as a consequence of the exhaustion of oil. There is also widespread agreement that the scale of investment needed to continue our present rate of growth will force a scaling down of expansion within that same time frame. And the dangers of a technological disruption of the biosphere are already at hand. Together these warnings suggest that growth will have to be slowed down or strictly monitored before the year 2000.

International distribution

Stationary state

12. Slow industrial growth will bring severe problems for the international distribution of wealth and may pose major problems for capitalism as a stationary state.

9	*Questions*

1. What explanations can we give for inflation?

2. What kind of event might give rise to a hyperinflation in the United States? Might a defeat in war trigger such an event? a victory? If we were to experience a runaway inflation, what measures would you counsel?

3. Suppose that you could add up the costs of unemployment in terms of income lost. Suppose that you could add up the losses incurred just by those groups who are left behind in inflation (forget about the "winners"). Suppose further that the losses imposed by inflation were greater than those imposed by unemployment. Does this mean that inflation is necessarily a worse economic disaster than unemployment? Must personal values enter into such a calculation? (If you simply compare amounts, is this also a value judgment?)

4. Why have measures to control inflation been so unsatisfactory? Why are price controls more difficult to monitor than wage controls?

5. Unemployment among the black population in many cities in the late 1960s was worse than it was during the Great Depression. What steps would you propose to remedy this situation?

6. Do you believe that there exists general support for large public employment-generating programs? Why, or why not? What sorts of programs would you propose?

7. How would you encourage private enterprise to create as many jobs as possible?

8. Do you consider military spending to be a net gain or loss for the nation? How would you justify both answers to this question?

9. What do you think is the reason for the failure of Congress or the public to bring about a high degree of efficiency in military spending?

10. How would you go about measuring the amount of iron ore "available"? At what level of concentration would you draw the line?

11. What policies do you think should be followed to avoid a severe environmental threat to industrial society?

12. Do you think that *global* growth control is a realistic goal today? If not, what do you foresee as the long-run scenario of world economics and politics?

II THE CHALLENGE TO THE MARKET SYSTEM

10

The Drift of European Economic History

In the last several chapters, we focused our narrative of economic history on the rise of modern capitalism in America, and on its current problems. But our initial narrative is not yet complete. For the central subject of our early pages was not just the rise of American capitalism, but the emergence of the market system itself, and in describing its development in America, we have by no means described it everywhere. That will be our task in this final section of our book. We must follow the fortunes of the market first in Europe and Russia, and then in the underdeveloped world. Then we will hazard a concluding generalization about the market system in the long evolution of economic society.

trials of capitalism abroad

One thing is immediately apparent when we direct our eyes away from America to the continents of the east, west, and south. It is that the trajectory of economic evolution there has been utterly different from that in the United States. No doubt we recall that when we left the European scene in the early 1800s, capitalism was fast becoming the dominant form of economic society. England was the very cradle of industrial capitalism itself; elsewhere on the Continent, if capitalism was not already established, it was clearly waiting in the wings for the last remnants of feudalism to disappear. Moreover, had we looked abroad from America at any time in the nineteenth century, our expectations would have been fully justified. By then, all of Europe was unquestionably capitalist in orientation. And not only Europe. By the end of the nineteenth century, capitalism had reached out to touch most of the other continents of the world. In Asia and Africa, the main European nations had established colonies or spheres of influence that projected the imprint of capitalism into these societies, many of which had barely awakened from an age-long slumber of ancient ways. In South America, as well, capitalism was clearly the main fertilizing influence. Even in reactionary Russia—the last of the great European powers to abolish the legal fetters of feudalism—by the early 1900s, capitalism had succeeded in creating a small but active nucleus from which further growth seemed assured.

Yet what do we find today? To our astonishment, the seemingly unopposed evolution of the world into a capitalist market system has not taken place. In Europe, its original birthplace, capitalism continues to be the dominant economic system; and yet we find that socialist parties either hold power or constitute the main opposition in England, France, Belgium, the Netherlands, Italy, Sweden, Norway, Denmark, Germany, and Austria. In Russia, the nucleus of capitalism has been entirely swept away by a communist society. In the huge continents of the east and south—in Asia and Africa and South America—we find that the original organizing impetus of capitalism has given way, in many of the most important nations, to a noncapitalist framework of economic organization. China is more communist than communist Russia. India proclaims herself a socialist state. So do Burma, Sri Lanka, Guinea, Syria. Only in South America do we find socialism largely absent from the official ideologies of political economy; and even there, the example of Cuba, the ill-fated regime in Chile, and rumblings elsewhere hardly make it possible to anticipate the kind of capitalist development that we would have expected fifty years ago.

What happened outside America to abort the seemingly assured development of capitalism? A full answer to such a question would require much more than a book in itself, but we can begin to grasp the main picture of evolutionary trends if we follow, first, the factors that caused capitalism in Europe to take on a form different from that in America. From Europe it is not so long a jump, geographically or historically, to Russia; and from Russia we can turn with increased understanding to the so-called underdeveloped world.

European capitalism: feudal heritage   What are the reasons behind the turn of events in Europe? They must be sought, to begin with, not in the economic tendencies of European capitalism but in the social and political background whence those tendencies emerged.

Certainly the social background was significantly different from that of America. In the New World, capitalism developed with a population that had, to a large degree, spiritually and physically shed the feudal encumbrances of the Old World; but in that Old World, many of the social outlooks and habitudes of the past lingered on. An awareness of class position—and more than that, an explicit recognition of class hostility—was as conspicuous by its presence in Europe as by its absence in America. In Vienna, in 1847, writes one social historian:

At the top were the nobles who considered themselves the only group worth noticing. The human race starts with barons, said one of them. Then there were the big businessmen who wanted to buy their way into the human race; the little businessmen; the proud but poor intellectuals; the students who were still poorer and still prouder; and the workers who were poor and had always been very, very humble.[1]

The result was a totally different climate for the development of an economic society. Capitalism in America, building on a new and vigorous foundation, was, from the beginning, a system of social consensus. Capitalism in Europe, building on a feudal base, was deeply tinged with class conflict. It was without effort that American capitalism secured the loyal support of its "lower orders"; but in Europe, by the time of the revolutions of 1848, those lower orders had already turned their backs on capitalism as a vehicle for their hopes and beliefs.

national rivalries
Second, and no less important in explaining the divergence of American and European economic evolution, was the profound difference between the political complexion of the two continents. In America, save only for the terrible crisis of the Civil War, a single national purpose fused the continent; in Europe, a historic division of languages, customs, and mutually suspicious nationalities again and again prevented just such a fusion.

Accordingly, American capitalism came of age in an environment in which political unity permitted the unhindered growth of an enormous unobstructed market, while in Europe a jigsaw puzzle of national boundaries forced industrial growth to take place in cramped quarters and in an atmosphere of continued national rivalry. It is curious to note that whereas Europe was considered "wealthier" than America all through the nineteenth century, American productivity in many fields began to outstrip that of Europe from at least the 1850s, and perhaps much earlier. For instance, at the Paris Exposition of 1854, an American threshing machine was twice as productive as its nearest (English) rival and eleven times as productive as its least (Belgian) competitive model.[2]

These advantages of geographic space, richness of resources, and political unity were widened by subsequent developments in European industry. Not surprisingly, European producers, like those in America, sought to limit the destructive impact of industrial competition, and for this purpose they turned to *cartels*—contractual (rather than merely voluntary) agreements to share markets or fix prices. Unlike the case in America, however, this self-protective movement received the blessing, overt or tacit, of European governments. Although "anticartel" laws existed in many European coun-

[1] Priscilla Robertson, *Revolutions of 1848* (New York: Harper, Torchbooks, 1960), p. 194.

[2] Thomas Cochran and William Miller, *The Age of Enterprise,* rev. ed. (New York: Harper, Torchbooks, 1961), p. 58.

tries, these laws were almost never enforced; by 1914, there were more than 100 international cartels, representing the most varied industries, in which most European nations participated.*

Cartelization was undoubtedly good for the profit statements of the cartelized firms, but it was hardly conducive to growth—either for those firms or new ones. By establishing carefully delineated and protected "preserves," the cartel system rewarded unaggressive behavior rather than economic daring; and together with the ever-present problem of cramping national frontiers, it drove European producers into a typical high-cost, high-profit-margin, low-volume pattern rather than into the American pattern of very large plants with very high efficiencies. The difference in economic scale is dramatically illustrated by steel. In 1885, Great Britain led the world in the production of steel; fourteen years later, her entire output was less than that of the Carnegie Steel Company alone.

the lag in productivity As a result, by the early twentieth century, European productivity lagged very seriously behind American. A study by Professor Taussig in 1918 showed that the daily output of coal per underground worker was 4.68 tons in the United States, as contrasted with 1.9 tons in Great Britain, 1.4 tons in Prussia, and 0.91 tons in France. In 1905, the output of bricks per person employed was 141,000 in the United States and 40,000 in Germany; US pig-iron production was 84.5 tons per worker in 1909, compared with only 39 tons in Great Britain in 1907.[3] Parts of these differences were attributable to geological differentials, but these, too, were made worse by restrictive business practices. The result was a steady falling behind in Europe as the twentieth century went on.

The divergence was strikingly noticeable in per capita incomes. In 1911, for example, when per capita income in the United States was $368, the corresponding figure for Great Britain was $250, for Germany $178, for France $161, for Italy $108. By 1928, American per capita income was $541 (in unchanged dollar values), while that of the United Kingdom was only $293; of Germany, $199; of France, $188; and of Italy, $96.[4] While American per capita incomes had grown by nearly 46 percent, English and French per capita incomes had increased only one-third as rapidly. German incomes rose only about one-quarter as fast, and Italian per capita incomes had actually declined.

---

* In 1939, an estimated 109 cartels also had American participation, since American companies were not prohibited by antitrust laws from joining international restrictive agreements.

[3] Heinrich E. Friedlaender and Jacob Oser, *Economic History of Modern Europe* (Englewood Cliffs, N.J.: Prentice-Hall, 1953), p. 224.

[4] Friedlaender and Oser, *Economic History of Modern Europe,* p. 522.

Still another consequence followed from the division of European industry and agriculture into national compartments. To a far greater extent than in America, it made the development of European capitalism subject to the expansion of international trade.

The division of the European continent into many national units made international trade a continuous and critical preoccupation of economic life abroad. For instance, a study has shown that in 1913, when manufactured imports provided but 3.6 percent of United States consumption of manufactured goods, they provided 9 percent of Germany's, 14 percent of England's, 21 percent of Sweden's.[5] Perhaps even more striking is the degree to which some nations in Europe depended on international trade for the foodstuffs on which they lived: In the five years preceding World War I, for instance, England produced less than 20 percent of the wheat she consumed and barely over 55 percent of the meat.[6] We find the same dependence on foreign trade in the export side of the picture. Whereas the United States in 1913 exported a mere fifteenth of its national product, France and Germany exported a fifth, and Britain exported nearly a quarter.

Thus, to a far greater degree than America, Europe lived by foreign trade. Here we see clearly the advantage to America of its enormous unbroken market over the fragmented national markets of Europe. All the gains from trade that were realized in the swift rise of American productivity were denied to Europe. To put it differently, in America, the division of labor was permitted to attain whatever degree of efficiency technology made possible, for in the end, virtually all products entered into a single vast market where they could be exchanged against one another. In Europe, where the need for, and the potential benefits of, a far-reaching division of labor were no less pressing, a tangle of national barriers prevented the optimal specialization of effort from taking place.

Instead, what was visible in Europe was a struggle between the need for international trade as a primary means for advancing productivity, and the retarding hand of national suspicions, rivalries, and distrust. A striking example was provided as recently as the early 1950s by the great cluster of European steel and coal industry near the German-Belgian-Luxembourg borders. Here, in a triangle 250 miles on a side, was gathered 90 percent of European steelmaking capacity in a kind of European Pittsburgh. But this natural geographic division of labor had to contend with political barriers that largely vitiated its physical productivity. Typically, German coal mines in the Ruhr sold their output to French steelmakers at prices 30 percent higher than to German plants; while, in turn, French iron-ore producers charged far higher prices in Germany than at home. As a result, while

[5] *Der Deutsche Aussenhandel* (Berlin: 1932), II, 23.
[6] Friedlaender and Oser, *Economic History of Modern Europe*, p. 206.

American steel production soared 300 percent between 1913 and 1950, the output of Europe's steel triangle rose but 3 percent during the same period.

breakdown of international trade

Our example itself poses a question, however. Prior to 1913, as we have. seen, something like a great international division of labor did, in fact, characterize the European market, albeit to nothing like the extent seen in America. By 1913, we will remember, a very considerable flow of international trade was enhancing European productivity, despite the hindrances of cartels and national divisiveness. It was only the beginning of a truly free and unhampered international market, but at least it *was* a beginning.

What brought this promising achievement to an end? Initially, it was the shock of World War I, with its violent sundering of European trade channels and its no less destructive aftermath of punitive reparations, war debts, and monetary troubles. In a sense, Europe never recovered from its World War I experience. The slow drift toward national economic separatism, at the expense of international economic cooperation, now accelerated fatefully. Tariffs and quotas multiplied to place new handicaps before the growth of international trade.

Then came the depression of 1929 as the final blow. As the depression spread contagiously, nation ofter nation sought to quarantine itself by erecting still further barriers against economic contacts with other countries. Starting in 1929, an ever-tightening contraction of trade began to strangle economic life around the world. For 53 grim months following January 1929, the volume of world trade was lower each month than in the preceding month. Between the late 1920s and the mid-1930s, manufactured imports (in constant prices) fell by a third in Germany, by nearly 40 percent in Italy, by almost 50 percent in France. As international trade collapsed, so did Europe's chance for economic growth. For two long decades, there followed a period of stagnation that earned for Europe the name of the "tired continent."

European socialism

Against this background of economic malfunction, it is easier to understand the growing insecurity that afflicted European capitalism. During the 1930s, serious rumblings were already heard. In England, the Socialist Labour Party had clearly displaced the middle-class Liberals as the Opposition. In France, a mildly socialist "Popular Front" government came to the fore, albeit insecurely. Even in Italy and Germany, the fascist dictators repeatedly declared their sympathy with "socialist" objectives—and whereas their declarations may have been no more than a sop to the masses, it was certainly indicative of the sentiments the masses wanted to hear.

Note that the socialist movements were not communistic—that is, they were pledged strongly to democratic political principles and envisaged a "takeover" through education and persuasion rather than by revolution and coercion. In addition, the socialists sought to convert only the strategic centers of production into public enterprises, rather than to "socialize" all of industry and agriculture. Thus, socialism was always a much more evolutionary program than communism. Nevertheless, to the European conservatives of the 1930s, the socialist leaders appeared every bit as dangerous as did the socialists' bitterest enemies, the communists.

By the end of World War II, socialist ideas were clearly ascendant throughout most of Europe. Even before the war was concluded, the Labour Party swept into office in England and rapidly nationalized the Bank of England, the coal and electricity industries, much of the transportation and communications industries, and finally steel. As the first postwar governments were formed, it was evident that a socialist spectrum extended across Europe from Scandinavia through the Lowlands and France to Italy (where the communists came within an ace of gaining power). To many observers, it seemed as if capitalism in Europe had come to the end of its rope.

RECOVERY OF EUROPEAN CAPITALISM

welfare capitalism Yet, European capitalism did not come to an end. Instead, beginning in the late 1940s and early 1950s, it embarked on what is unquestionably its period of strongest economic growth. Indeed, a comparison not only with the past but with United States performance during the same period shows the remarkable change that had come over the Continent.

Note, in Table 10–1, that the nations of Europe not only doubled and tripled their pre-World War I rates of per capita growth, but actually outstripped the contemporary performance of the United States economy by a margin almost as large.

TABLE 10 · 1

COMPARA-TIVE GROWTH RATES

	AVERAGE ANNUAL RATES OF PER CAPITA INCREASE				
	France	Germany	Italy	U.K.	U.S.
Pre–World War I (1870–1913)	1.4	1.8	0.7	1.3	2.2
Post–World War II (1948–1962)	3.4	6.8	5.6	2.4	1.8 (1950–64)

SOURCE: M. M. Postan, *An Economic History of Western Europe* (London: Methuen, 1967), p. 17.

To bring about such results, important changes obviously must have taken place in these economic societies. One of them, it is hardly surprising to learn, was political. The postwar socialist governments quickly showed that they were not revolutionary but reform-minded administrations. Once in power, they quickly instituted a number of welfare and social-planning measures, such as public health facilities, family benefits and allowances, improved social security, and the like; but they did not engage in sweeping changes. Hence, when many of the socialist governments, facing the exigencies of the postwar period, were voted out again, they bequeathed to the conservatives the framework of a welfare state, *which the conservatives accepted*. Harking back to one of the traditional weaknesses of European capitalism, we can say that this represented a conservative attempt to create a social-service state that would mend the historic antagonism of the lower classes. As a result, we find today that in most European states, welfare expenditures form a considerably higher proportion of government expenditures than they do in the United States. Social Security expenditures in most European Community countries run 50 to 100 percent higher than in our own.

The second reason was even more important. This was the rise of a movement within the conservative ranks to overcome a still more dangerous heritage of the past—the national division of markets. This great step toward creating a full-scale continental market for European producers is called the European Economic Community—or more familiarly, the Common Market.

the Common Market

To some extent, the Common Market was born out of the vital impetus given to postwar European production by the so-called Marshall Plan, under which Europe received some $12 billion in direct grants and loans from the United States to rebuild its war-shattered industry. Despite Marshall Plan aid, it soon became apparent that Europe's upward climb would necessarily be limited if production were once again restrained by cartels and national protectionism. To forestall a return to the stagnation of the prewar period, a few farsighted and courageous statesmen, primary among them Jean Monnet and Robert Schumann, proposed a truly daring plan for the abolition of Europe's traditional economic barriers.

The plan as it took shape called for the creation of a *supranational* (not merely an international) organization to integrate the steel and coal production of France, Germany, Italy, Belgium, Luxembourg, and the Netherlands. The new Coal and Steel Community was to have a High Authority with power to eliminate all customs duties on coal and steel products among members of the Community, to outlaw all discriminatory pricing and trade practices, to approve or disapprove all mergers, to order the dissolution of cartels, and to provide social and welfare services for all Community miners and steelworkers. The Authority was to be given direct power to inspect books, levy fines, and enforce its decrees—and, still more remarkable, it was to be responsible not to any single member government but to a multinational parliament and a multinational court, both to be created as part of the Community. A Council of Ministers was to act as a *national* advisory and permissory body, but even here, action could be taken by majority vote, so that no single nation (or even two nations) could block a decision desired by the Community as a whole.

By the fall of 1952, the Coal and Steel Community was a reality, and it lost no time going about its business. At mid-1954, customs duties and discriminatory pricing within the coal and steel "triangle" had been virtually eliminated, and roughly 40 percent more coal and steel was being shipped across national boundaries than had been shipped prior to the etablishment of the Community. Cartels and secret agreements still remained, but the restrictive influence on production was much less than it was formerly.

The success of the Coal and Steel Community led, in 1957, to the next two organizations: Euratom, a supranational atomic power agency, and the Common Market itself, an organization that was to do for commodities in general what the Coal and Steel Community had done for its products. Under the Common Market treaty, a definite schedule of tariff cuts was laid down, envisaging within slightly more than a decade an entirely unimpeded continental market for Common Market members, with a single "external" tariff vis-à-vis the world. In addition, there was to be a single agricultural policy and, perhaps most imaginative, full freedom for the intermember mobility of both capital and labor.

recent advances   The Common Market is still in the process of achieving some of these goals, although it is well ahead of its timetable. Prior to the great oil crisis of 1973, however, it led to a remarkable increase in European trade and production. Trade among member countries grew from $6.8 billion in 1958 to $110 billion in 1975. Table 10–2 shows, during the decade of the 1950s, the Common Market's growth was almost twice that of the United States; and although the pace of expansion has slowed somewhat abroad and quickened

TABLE 10 · 2

AVERAGE ANNUAL GROWTH IN REAL GNP

	1950–1960	1965–1975
Common Market	5.9%	3.5%
United States	3.2	2.6

SOURCE: OECD; *Basic Statistics of the Community.*

at home in recent years, it is clear that the doldrums of the European past are well behind us.

European
standard
of living

These figures indicate that something dramatic has happened to Europe as a consequence of its postwar surge. The laggard and limping economies of the early twentieth century have given way to economies that in many ways match, and in some ways surpass, the United States in terms of productivity, amenities, and standards of living. For the first time, the style of life of the European middle and working classes has begun to resemble that of America. Although ownership of assets such as cars and TV sets is still only about half that of the US, doctors and pharmacists and hospital beds per capita exceed the US. And average per capita incomes are higher in several European nations than in America.°

socialism
and modern
European
capitalism

Thus after its time of trial, European capitalism has achieved a high degree of economic success in the decades of the 1950s and 1960s. It is true that socialist parties continue to constitute a strong political movement in Europe, but the thrust of these programs is no longer directed mainly toward nationalization or other fundamental economic changes, but aims instead at correcting social privileges or at buttressing still further the welfare arrangements that we find in every European country. Equality—social as well as economic—has been the main objective of European socialism, and although equality requires adjustments in the existing distribution of rewards, the socialists do not see it as requiring the destruction of the system by which those rewards are determined.

The most recent evidence of this accommodation is the gradual evolution of "Eurocommunism"—the effort of Europe's communist parties to separate themselves entirely from Soviet influence and from older, doctrinaire conceptions of what communism is about. The Eurocommunists claim to support not only "bourgeois" democratic liberties, but much of the market-run, private-owned structure of European economies.

Since no European communist party has yet gained power, we do not know if these declarations can be taken at full value. But certainly they reveal that the former implacable hostility of the Left toward capitalism has given way to a new, much more pragmatic and accepting attitude.

° We must be wary, however, of placing too much faith in the translation of one income —say £500—into its "equivalent"—$1,000. Too much depends on the rate of exchange, which may alter sharply. In addition, until we know the price levels, living standards, and customs of the nations we are comparing, we make such translations strictly at our own risk. But changes *within* a country, from year to year, are, of course, as meaningful in one currency as in another.

This rapprochement between socialism and capitalism owes much to the strong emphasis on welfare spending that we find in all the Common Market countries. But it is also the result of another departure for the once hide-bound capitalisms of Europe. This is their adoption of a form of economic management that use to be the exclusive property of socialism—*national economic planning.*

It is not, of course, planning of the kind that we find in the Soviet Union, into which we will look shortly. European planning limits its objects to stimulating or curbing the rate of growth, or to strengthening particular industries, or to speeding up or slowing down the growth rates of regions within nations.

Nevertheless, it is a long departure from the laissez-faire economies of the past. In France, for example, a central planning commission, working in consultation with the parliament and with representatives of industry, agriculture, labor, and other groups, sets a general plan for French growth—a plan that not only establishes a desired rate of expansion but determines whether or not, for example, the provincial cities should expand faster or slower than the nation as a whole, or where the bulk of new housing is to be located, or to what degree social services are to be increased. Once decided on, the plan is then divided into the various production targets needed for its fulfillment, and their practicality is discussed with management and labor groups in each industry concerned.

From these discussions arise two results. First, the plan is often amended to conform with the wishes or advice of those who must carry it out. Second, the general targets of the plan become part of the business expectations of the industries that have helped to formulate them. To be sure, the government has substantial investment powers that can nudge the economy along whatever path has been finally determined. But in the main, French "indicative" planning works as a *self-fulfilling prophecy*—the very act of establishing its objectives setting into motion the behavior needed to realize them.

In England, Austria, the Netherlands, and Scandinavia, we see other forms of government planning, none so elaborately worked out as the French system, but all also injecting a powerful element of public guidance into the growth and disposition of the resources of their economies.*

We must be careful not to overstate the case. Planning in Europe has been most successful in allocating resources among regions and in supervising the efforts to modernize European industry. It has not stopped inflation and it has had an uncertain impact on growth. It has brought

---

* Anyone who wishes to learn more about the important subject of European planning should read Andrew Shonfield, *Modern Capitalism* (New York: Oxford University Press, 1965).

bureaucratic problems, and an inflationary pressure from welfare expenditures, much like those of the United States.

Therefore we find a cooling of earlier enthusiasms about planning in many European nations, and a renewed emphasis on the market. *Nonetheless, there remains a commitment to the idea of a social guidance to the economy that is far more widely accepted than we find in America.*

Europe and America

How do we account for the fact that in Europe, the evolution into a guided capitalism has evidently progressed much further than in America? In part, the reason is no doubt ascribable to the problems that have racked Europe and have forced upon it a much greater degree of necessary government intervention for survival. The Common Market, for example, would never have been brought into being had Europe not suffered from the effects of economic fragmentation, and the Common Market in turn stimulated and supported the development of purely national planning efforts.

To some extent the difference may be due, as well, to the survival in Europe of those "feudal" (or at least aristocratic) attitudes that contrast so sharply with the democratic climate in America. Europeans are used to, and accept, a larger role for public authority in the economic direction of affairs; whereas Americans have traditionally tended to resist and reject such a role. Hence, the movement toward planning in Europe has not encountered the fierce ideological opposition it has met in America, where the very word still conjures up fearsome "socialistic" visions to some people. This is a matter we will discuss again in our last chapter. But we cannot put these questions into focus until we have looked into another significant drift—in the opposite direction. To see that striking development, we must now examine the rise of a totally different economic structure: the socialist economy of the Soviet Union.

PLANNING IN THE USSR

We cannot here recount in detail the history of Soviet socialism. Let us, rather, begin by noting the extraordinarily difficult problem that faced the revolutionary leaders who had secured the victory of "socialism" in Russia in 1917. In the first place, Russia was a semifeudal society in which capitalism was restricted to a small industrial and commercial sector. Second, both production and distribution were highly disorganized in the chaotic situation following the civil war.

socialism in theory

Finally, there was little guidance in the official literature of the communist movement as to how a socialist society should be run. Marx's *Das Kapital,* the seminal work of communism, was entirely devoted to a study of capital-

ism; and in those few essays in which Marx looked to the future, his gaze rarely traveled beyond the watershed of the revolutionary act itself. With the achievement of the revolution, Marx thought, a temporary regime known as "the dictatorship of the proletariat" would take over the transition from capitalism to socialism, and thereafter, a "planned socialist economy" would emerge as the first step towards a still less specified "communism." °
In the latter state—the final terminus of economic evolution, according to Marx—there were hints that the necessary but humdrum tasks of production and distribution would take place by the voluntary cooperation of all citizens and that society would turn its serious attention to matters of cultural and humanistic importance.

In reality, the revolution presented Lenin, Trotsky, and the other leaders of the new Soviet Union with problems far more complex than this utopian long-term design. Shortly after the initial success of the revolution, Lenin nationalized the banks, the major factories, the railways, and canals. In the meantime, the peasants themselves had taken over the large landed estates on which they had been tenants, and they had carved them up into individual holdings. The central authorities then attempted for several years to run the economy by requisitioning food from the farms and allocating it to factory workers, while controlling the flow of output from the factories themselves by a system of direct controls from above.

This initial attempt to run the economy was a disastrous failure. Under inept management (and often cavalier disregard of "bourgeois" concerns with factory management), industrial output declined precipitously; by 1920, it had fallen to *14 percent* of prewar levels. As goods available to the peasants became scarcer, the peasants themselves were less and less willing to acquiesce in giving up food to the cities. The result was a wild inflation, followed by a degeneration into an economy of semibarter. For a while, toward the end of 1920, the system threatened to break down completely.

the NEP   To forestall the impending collapse, in 1921 Lenin instituted a New Economic Policy, the so-called NEP. This was a return toward a market system and a partial reconstitution of actual capitalism. Retail trade, for instance, was opened again to private ownership and operation. Small-scale industry also reverted to private direction. Most important, the farms were no longer

---

° What is the difference between *socialism* and *communism?* In Marxist writing, socialism represents a stage of development in which it is still necessary to use "bourgeois" incentives in order to make the economy function; that is, people must be paid in proportion to the "value" of their work. Under communism, a new form of human society will presumably have been achieved in which these selfish incentives will no longer be needed. Then will come the time when society will be able to put into effect Karl Marx's famous description of communism: "From each according to his ability; to each according to his need."

requisitioned but operated as profit-making units. Only the "commanding heights" of industry and finance were retained in government hands.

There ensued for several years a bitter debate about the course of action to follow next. While the basic aim of the Soviet government was still to industrialize and to socialize (that is, to replace the private ownership of the means of production by state ownership), the question was how fast to move ahead—and, indeed, *how* to move ahead. The pace of industrialization hinged critically on one highly uncertain factor: the willingness of the large, private peasant sector to deliver food with which the city workers could be sustained in their tasks. To what extent, therefore, should the need for additional capital goods be sacrificed in order to turn out the consumption goods that could be used as an inducement for peasant cooperation?

the drive to total planning   The student of Russian history—or, for that matter, of economic history—will find the record of that debate an engrossing subject.[7] But the argument was never truly resolved. In 1927, Stalin moved into command, and the difficult question of how much to appease the unwilling peasant disappeared. Stalin simply made the ruthless decision to appease him not at all, but to *coerce* him by collectivizing his holdings.

The collectivization process solved in one swoop the problem of securing the essential transfer of food from the farm to the city, but it did so at a frightful social (and economic) cost. Many peasants slaughtered their livestock rather than hand it over to the new collective farms; others waged outright war or practiced sabotage. In reprisal, the authorities acted with brutal force. An estimated five million "kulaks" (rich peasants) were executed or put in labor camps, while in the cities an equally relentless policy showed itself vis-à-vis labor. Workers were summarily ordered to the tasks required by the central authorities. The right to strike was forbidden, and the trade unions were reduced to impotence. Speedups were widely applied, the living conditions were allowed to deteriorate to very low levels.

The history of this period of forced industrialization is ugly and repellent, and it has left abiding scars on Russian society. It is well for us, nonetheless, to attempt to view it with some objectivity. If the extremes to which the Stalinist authorities went were extraordinary, often unpardonable, and perhaps self-defeating, we must bear in mind that industrialization on the grand scale has always been wrenching, always accompanied by economic sacrifice, and always carried out by the more or less authoritarian use of power. We have already seen what happened in the West at the time of the Industrial Revolution, with its heavy-handed exploitation of labor; and

[7] See Alexander Erlich, *The Soviet Industrialization Debate: 1924–1928* (Cambridge, Mass.: Harvard University Press, 1960).

without "excusing" these acts, we have seen their function in paving the way for capital accumulation.

the challenge of rapid industrialization
In much the same fashion, when the Soviet leaders deliberately held down consumption, regimented and transferred their labor forces into the new raw industrial centers, and ruthlessly collected the foodstuffs to feed their capital-building workers, they were, in fact, only enforcing the basic process of industrialization. What was new about the Soviet program was that totalitarian control over the citizenry enabled the planners to carry out this transformation at a much faster tempo than would have been possible had protests been permitted. Under Stalin's iron will, the planners did not scruple to exercise their industrializing power to the hilt. In the early 1950s, writes historian Alexander Gerschenkron, "the level of real wages . . . was substantially below that of 1928, with the peasants' real income probably registering an even greater decline in comparison to 1928."[8] Thus a quarter-century of industrialization had not yet benefitted those whose efforts had brought it about.

Without seeking to justify the Russian effort, it is worth pondering one last question. Can rapid industrialization, with its inescapable price of low consumption, ever be a "popular" policy? Will poor people willingly vote for an economic transformation which will not "pay out" for twenty or forty years?[*] Does rapid and large-scale industrialization *necessitate* a large degree of authoritarian political control? We will return to these problems when we turn to underdevelopment, but we might well begin to think about them now.

the planning mechanism
A massive industrialization drive requires a determined effort to hold consumption to a minimum and to transfer resources to capital building, an effort greatly facilitated, as we have seen, by the totalitarian political apparatus. But there is still another question to be considered: How are the freed resources to find their proper destination in an integrated and workable industrial sector?

Let us remind ourselves again of how this is done under a market economy. There, the signal of profitability serves as the lure for the allocation of resources and labor. Entrepreneurs, anticipating or following de-

---

[8] A. Gerschenkron, *Economic Backwardness in Historical Perspective* (Cambridge, Mass.: Harvard University Press, 1962), p. 150.

[*] We might note in passing that universal male suffrage was not gained in England until the late 1860s and 1870s. Aneurin Bevan has written, "It is highly doubtful whether the achievements of the Industrial Revolution would have been permitted if the franchise had been universal. It is very doubtful because a great deal of the capital aggregations that we are at present enjoying are the results of the wages that our fathers went without." (From Gunnar Myrdal, *Rich Lands and Poor.* New York: Harper, 1957, p. 46.)

mand, risk private funds in the construction of the facilities that they hope the future will require. Meanwhile, as these industrial salients grow, smaller satellite industries grow along with them to cater to their needs.

The flow of materials is thus regulated in every sector by the forces of private demand, making themselves known by the signal of rising or falling prices. At every moment there emanates from the growing industries a magnetic pull of demand on secondary industries, while, in turn, the growth salients themselves are guided, spurred, or slowed down by the pressure of demand from the ultimate buying public. And all the while, counterposed to these pulls of demand, are the obduracies of supply—the cost schedules of the producers themselves. In the crossfire of demand and supply exists a marvelously sensitive social instrument for the integration of the overall economic effort of expansion.

And in the absence of a market? Clearly, the mechanism must be supplied by the direct orders of a central controlling and planning agency. *In a growing industrial economy, a planning agency must act as a substitute for the market.* Let us reflect for a moment on what this entails.

To begin with, it means that the planning agency must provide a substitute for the forward-looking operations of the great entrepreneurs in a market economy. In place of a Carnegie or a Ford building their plants in anticipation of, or response to, an insistent demand for their products, the planning body must itself set overall goals and objectives for economic growth. Not the consumer but the planners' own judgment and desires determine the force of "demand." *

Establishing the overall objectives is, however, only the first and perhaps the easiest part of the planning mechanism. It is not enough to set broad goals and then assume that they will be fulfilled by themselves. We must remember that planning in a totalitarian economy is not superimposed on a market structure in which individuals take care of the "details" of production according to the incentives of price and profit. In a totally planned economy, each and every item that goes into the final plan must also be planned. Schedules of production are needed for steel, coal, coke,

---

* In the case of the Soviet Union, the planning authority has typically set its demand goals in terms of Five-Year Plans. The first of these, from 1928 to 1932, had as its basic objective the intensification of industrialization in heavy industry, with special emphasis on electrification; the second took as its main goal the development of transportation and the beginning of agricultural planning; the third plan (1938–1942) was essentially occupied with producing the needs for a war economy; the fourth, from 1946 to 1950, was mainly a plan of reconstruction from wartime damage, with continuing emphasis on heavy industry; a fifth plan, 1951–1955, emphasized a steep increase in output, with some stress being given (for the first time) to consumer goods. A sixth plan was scrapped in midcourse; a seventh (1959–1965) aimed to increase industrial output by 80 percent and agricultural output by 70 percent, and to bring significant increases in housing (a sector long neglected in the interests of industrialization) and in consumer goods generally. We know that many of these objectives were not met, but there is no doubt of growing emphasis on consumer goods and housing in contemporary Russian planning.

lumber, on down to nails and paper clips, for there is no "automatic" device by which these items will be forthcoming without a planning directive. Supplies of labor must also be planned; or if labor is free to move where it wishes, wage rates must be planned in order to draw labor where it is wanted.

Thus, supplementing and completing the master objective of the overall plan must be a whole hierarchy of subplans, the aggregate of which must bring about the necessary final result. And here is a genuine difficulty. For an error in planning, small in itself, if it affects a strategic link in the chain of production, can seriously distort—or even render impossible—the fulfillment of the total plan.

the plan in action How is this infinitely complicated planning system carried out in the Soviet Union? It is begun by breaking down the overall, long-term plan into shorter, one-year plans. These one-year plans, specifying the output of major sectors of industry, are then transmitted to various government ministries concerned with, for example, steel production, transportation, lumbering, and so forth. In turn, the ministries refer the one-year plans further down the line to the heads of large industrial plants, to experts and advisers, and so on. At each stage, the overall plan is thus unraveled into its subsidiary components, until finally the threads have been traced as far back as feasible along the productive process—typically, to the officials in charge of actual factory operations. The factory manager of, for instance, a coking operation is given a planned objective for the next year, specifying the output needed from his plant. He confers with his production engineers, considers the condition of his machinery and the availability of his labor force, and then transmits his requirements for meeting the objective back upward along the hierarchy. In this way, just as "demand" is transmitted downward along the chain of command, the exigencies of "supply" flow back upward, culminating ultimately in the top command of the planning authority (the Gosplan) itself.[9]

From this description of the tasks of planning, it is obvious that planning is an enormously complex task. Indeed, the very complexity of the task is such that more than one economist in the first days of chaos following the Russian Revolution declared socialism—meaning by this, centralized decision making—to be "impossible."

planning and efficiency Central planning is not impossible for certain kinds of economic tasks: For "forcing" growth, in particular, it may be more effective than any other means of bringing about the needed allocation of resources. An investiga-

[9] For an excellent description of Soviet planning, see Robert W. Campbell, *Soviet Economic Power*, 2nd ed. (Boston: Houghton Mifflin, 1966).

tion into Soviet economic performance, for example, indicated that over the period 1929 to 1961, Soviet output rose between 5.2 and 7.2 percent per annum—roughly twice as fast as the United States growth over these years.[10] Part of this extraordinary record, to which must be credited Russia's passage from a peasant society to an industrial one, is certainly due to the ability of central planning to bring about tremendously high levels of investment: Measured in 1937 prices, investment was pushed from 8.4 percent of GNP in 1928 to 30.6 percent in 1961.

The trouble comes when we look to the planning system for its *efficiency* in allocating resources, rather than to its success in forcing total volumes of output. An economy may be very successful in producing larger and larger quantities of steel and electric power, but it may be very unsuccessful in producing the right kinds of steel, or in locating its electric power plants effectively, or in producing its goods at the lowest possible cost. Sooner or later, such inefficiency will interfere with the rate of growth, and that is exactly what we see in the case of the USSR. From many indications, it appears that the Soviet rate of expansion has been declining in recent years and that the economy is increasingly plagued with difficulties arising from a failure to produce the right goods at the best possible prices. The result is a system that has operated more and more unevenly and awkwardly, as first one and then another of the gears in the great machine jammed.

Back in 1962, for example, an observer reported.

The Byelorussian Tractor Factory, which has 227 suppliers, had its production line stopped 19 times . . . because of the lack of rubber parts, 18 times because of ball bearings, and 8 times because of transmission components. The pattern of breakdowns continued in 1963. During the first quarter of 1963 only about one-half of the plant's ball bearing and rubber needs were satisfied, and only half of the required batteries were available. One supplier shipped 19,000 less wheels than called for in the contract. In total, they were short of 27 items.[11]

Stories such as these still abound in any book describing the Soviet economic system. They should not be taken to mean that Russian planning is a failure, or that it is on the point of collapse. Taken as a whole, the system continues to produce at good rates. But the bottlenecks do point to deepseated troubles in running the economy smoothly, even now when industrial needs are still relatively simple and consumers are not yet highly critical. These troubles are apt to exact a higher price as the Soviet economy turns its attention to the more complex and demanding problems of a highly integrated industrial process and a much more demanding citizenry.

[10] Richard Moorsteen and Raymond P. Powell, *The Soviet Capital Stock, 1928–1962* (Homewood, Ill.: Irwin, 1966).

[11] Barry Richman, *Soviet Management* (Englewood Cliffs, N.J.: Prentice-Hall, 1965), p. 123.

the guidance of production

What is at the root of the inefficiency of central planning? *Essentially, the problem is to find a means of guiding the production of individual firms.* Do not forget that a Russian factory manager has very little leeway in what he produces or the combination of factors that he uses for production. Both his inputs and his outputs are carefully specified for him in his plan. What the manager *is* supposed to do is to beat the plan, by "overproducing" the items that have been assigned to his plant. Indeed, from 30 to 50 percent of a manager's pay will depend on bonuses tied directly to his "overfulfillment" of the plan, so that he has a very great personal incentive to exceed the output "norms" set for him.

All this seems sensible enough. Trouble arises, however, because the manager's drive to exceed his factory's quota tends to distort the productive effort from the receivers' point of view. For example, if the target for a textile factory is set in terms of yards of cloth, there is every temptation to weave the cloth as narrowly as possible, to get the maximum yardage out of a given amount of thread. Or if the plan merely calls for tonnages of output, there is every incentive to skimp on design or finish or quality, in order to concentrate on sheer weight. A cartoon in the Russian satirical magazine *Krokodil* shows a nail factory proudly displaying its record output: one gigantic nail, suspended from an immense gantry crane. (On the other hand, if a nail factory has its output specified in terms of the *numbers* of nails it produces, its incentive to overfulfill this "success indicator" is apt to result in the production of very small or thin nails.)

plans for reform

What is the way out of this kind of dilemma? A few years ago, a widely held opinion among the Russian planners was that more detailed and better integrated planning performed on a battery of computers would solve the problem. Few still cling to this belief. The demands of planning have grown far faster than the ability to meet them; indeed, one Soviet mathematician has predicted that at the current rate of growth of the planning bureaucracy, planning alone would require the services of the entire Russian population by 1980. Even with the most complete computerization, it seems a hopeless task to attempt to beat the problem of efficiency by increasing the fineness of the planning mechanism.[12]

Rather, the wind of reform in the Soviet Union is now blowing from quite another quarter. Led by economist E. G. Liberman, there is a growing demand that the misleading plan directives of weight, length, and so on be subordinated to a new "success indicator" that will, all by itself, guide the

[12] For an interesting glimpse into the Russian change of mind, see *Planning, Profit and Incentives in the U.S.S.R.*, Myron E. Sharpe, ed. (White Plains, N.Y.: International Arts and Sciences Press, 1966). And for a sharp critique of Russian "irrationality," see Aron Katsenelinboigen, *Soviet Economic Planning* (White Plains, N.Y.: M. E. Sharpe, 1978), especially Chs. 6 and 7.

manager to results that will make sense from the overall point of view. And what is that overriding indicator? It is the *profit* that a factory manager can make for his enterprise!

Note several things about this profit. To begin with, it is not envisaged that it can arise from price manipulations. Factory managers will continue to operate with the prices established by the planners; but they will now have to *sell* their output and *buy* their inputs, rather than merely deliver or accept them. This means that each factory will have to be responsive to the particular needs of its customers if it wishes to dispose of its output. In the same way, of course, its own suppliers will now have to be responsive to the factory's needs if the suppliers are to get the factory's business.

Second, the profit will belong not to the factory or its managers, but to the State. A portion of the profit will indeed be allocated for bonuses and other rewards, so that there is a direct incentive to run the plant efficiently, but the bulk of the earnings will be transferred to the State.

markets in socialism Thus, profits are to be used as an *efficiency-maximizing indicator*. Indeed, to view the change even more broadly, we can see that the reintroduction of the use of profits implies a deliberate return to the use of the *market mechanism* as a means of achieving economic efficiency. Not only profits but also interest charges—a capitalist term that would have been heresy to mention in the days of Stalin—are being introduced into the planning mechanism, to allow factory managers to determine for themselves the most efficient thing to do, both for their enterprises and for the economy as a whole.

Meanwhile, the trend toward the market has proceeded much further in a large part of Eastern Europe, and above all in Yugoslavia.* There, the market rules very nearly as supreme as it does in Western capitalist countries. Yet the Yugoslavs certainly consider themselves a socialist economy. As in the USSR, enterprise profits do not go to the "owners" of the business but are distributed as incentive bonuses or used for investment or other purposes under the overall guidance of the State. And again, as in the USSR, the market is used as a deliberate instrument of social control rather than as an institution that is above question. Thus, the main determination of investment, the direction of development of consumers' goods, the basic

---

* One of the most interesting aspects of Yugoslav socialism is its effort to introduce worker-run enterprises. At least in theory, the top authority in most enterprises is a Worker's Council, which has the right to *fire* the boss of the plant, and which also determines wage and bonus payments, plant investments, and so on. We do not yet know whether this economic democracy exists in fact as well as on paper. If it does, it may prove to be one of the important social developments of our time. See Branko Horvat, *The Yugoslav Economic System,* (White Plains, N.Y.: International Arts and Sciences Press, 1976).

distribution of income—all continue to be matters established at the center as part of a planned economy. More and more, however, this central plan is allowed to realize itself through the profit-seeking operations of highly autonomous firms, rather than through being imposed in full detail upon the economy.

How far will this drift toward the market proceed? That is a question to which we will return in our penultimate chapter. What is important to recognize at this juncture is that there has been a visible movement toward the market mechanism in every European communist nation. One ironic consequence is that we find the same ideological alarm being expressed in these nations as in the United States, as each sees itself in danger of being subverted by the introduction of some elements of the other system; indeed, one of the reasons behind the Soviet invasion of Czechoslovakia was Russia's concern that Czech economic (as well as political) liberalization had gone too far.

Before we look further into this "convergence" of systems, however, there is a last development of the market economy into which we must inquire.

10   *Key Concepts and Key Words*

1. The development of European capitalism was considerably hampered by a number of factors absent from the American scene. Among these were a *feudal heritage* that brought serious political problems, and *severe national rivalry* that prevented economic unification. As a result, productivity in Europe lagged behind that of the United States. Compounding the problem of slow growth was the *breakdown of international trade* following World War I.

National planning

2. Capitalism in Europe was seriously threatened by the rise of a *socialist opposition.* However, following World War II, conservative parties generally accepted the reformist ideas of socialism and backed large programs of *social welfare and a commitment to national economic planning.*

European Economic Community Common Market

3. Equally, or more, important was the creation of the *European Economic Community* with its *Common Market,* a successful attempt to revive European trade and production.

Indicative planning

4. Among the many European planning mechanisms, the most elaborate is the French system of *"indicative planning."* A centrally formulated plan is discussed among representatives of industry, labor, and other groups, and in the process of discussion and amendment becomes part of the general expectations of these groups. This leads to the requisite investment needed to bring the plan about. Thus the system works as a *self-fulfilling prophecy.*

Central planning

5. All the European planning systems *rely on the market mechanism.* While the commitment of the European nations to a guided economy is in most cases greater than our own, a similar drift toward planning is visible in American capitalism as well.

6. The USSR has followed a totally different course. Following the revolution of 1917, a system of *central planning* was initiated, but it early collapsed. Thereafter a semi-market system was introduced as a rescue measure.

Collec-tivization

7. Following long debates about how to secure agricultural production to feed workers engaged in industrial projects, Russia under Stalin began a *total collectivization* that used naked force to solve the food-transfer problem and the industrialization program.

Success indicators

8. The planning mechanism by which Russia carries out its industrial growth requires the formulation of *highly detailed and accurately interlocked subplans,* any one of which, if wrongly designed or unmet, can wreck the larger one. *Inefficiency* has been the plague of the central planning system, although the system did succeed in achieving its larger objectives. The problem has been that "success indicators" have led to misallocation of resources.

9. As a result, we see the *introduction of the market mechanism,* using profit as the success indicator, into European communist economics. *The market is being introduced into socialism just as planning is being introduced into capitalism.*

10	*Questions*

1. Discuss how the fragmentation of a continent can affect the gains from trade. Does the experience of Europe illustrate that the bias of nationalism constitutes the main source of international economic difficulties?

2. In what ways is communism different from socialism? Are these differences merely economic?

3. What is the difference between indicative planning, as we find it in France, and the kind of planning we find in the USSR?

4. What is a "self-fulfilling prophecy"? If you were a bank president and said in a speech that you thought your bank would fail, might that provoke behavior that would make your prediction true? Can you think of another example?

5. Imagine that you were in charge of automobile production in Russia. How would you decide how many cars to make? how expensive to make them? what materials to order? what prices to pay for various grades of labor? how to mix land, labor, and capital?

6. How is the transfer of food from country to city accomplished under capitalism? Why was the problem so acute under early Soviet rule? Do you think a program

of rapid industrialization can be managed without recourse to coercion of some sort?

7. Do you think that a profit-seeking enterprise is compatible with a planned economy? What kinds of planning could utilize such enterprises? What kinds could not?

11 The Multinational Corporation

We have looked fairly carefully into the advantages and disadvantages of the market as a means of organizing the economic activity of nations, and we shall have something more to say about it when we study the problems of the underdeveloped world. But in this chapter, we must add a new dimension, that of international economics. Everything we have heretofore learned has had to do with the internal production and distribution of goods and services. What we must now consider is a revolutionary development in international economics, having to do with the *international production* of goods and services. To understand what this means, we must learn about a new institution that has sprung up as the most important agency for international production: the multinational corporation.

the multinational corporation

What is a multinational corporation? Essentially, it is a corporation that has producing branches or subsidiaries located in more than one nation. Take PepsiCo, for example. PepsiCo does not ship its famous product around the world from bottling plants in the United States. It *produces* Pepsi Cola in more than 500 plants located in over 100 countries. When you buy a Pepsi in Mexico or the Philippines or Israel or Denmark, you are buying an American product that was manufactured in that country.

PepsiCo is a far-flung, but not a particularly large, multinational corporation: In 1977, it was only the sixty-third largest industrial corporation. More impressive by far is the Ford Motor Company, a multinational that consists of a network of sixty subsidiary corporations, forty of them foreign-based. Of the corporation's total assets of $37 billion, about one-third is invested in twenty-seven foreign nations; and of its nearly half-million employees, about the same fraction is employed outside the United States. If we studied the corporate structures of GM or IBM or the great oil companies, we would find that they, too, are *international* companies—not only because they export their goods (or import their materials), but also because they all have substantial portions of their total wealth invested in productive facilities outside the United States.

Indeed, if we broaden our view to include the top 100 American firms, we find that over sixty have such production facilities in at least six nations, as of the early 1970s. Moreover, the value of output produced overseas by the largest corporations by far exceeds the value of the goods they still export from the United States. In 1975, sales of manufacturing foreign affiliates of US firms (which means their wholly or partially owned overseas branches) came to over $458 billion.[1] In the same year, our total exports of manufactures amounted to $147 billion.

interna-tional direct investment

Another way of establishing the spectacular rise of international production is to trace the increase in the value of US foreign direct investment; that is, the value of foreign-located, US-owned plant and equipment (*not* US-owned foreign bonds and stocks). In 1950, the value of US foreign direct investment was $11 billion. In 1976, it was over $133 billion. Moreover, this figure, too, needs an upward adjustment, because it includes only the value of American dollars invested abroad and not the additional value of foreign capital that may be controlled by those dollars. For example, if a US company has invested $10 million in a foreign enterprise whose total net worth is $20 million, the US official figures for our foreign investment take note only of the $10 million of American equity (ownership), and not the $20 million of wealth that our equity actually controls. If we include the capital controlled by our foreign direct investment as a whole, the value of American overseas productive assets may be as large as $300 billion.[2] In general, something between a quarter and a half of the real assets of our biggest corporations are located abroad. Hence, it is not surprising that many top companies depend on foreign operations for a large share of their profits. In the mid-1970s, for example, Uniroyal, Gillette, Coca-Cola, and IBM all earned more than half their profits abroad. So did most of the oil companies.

the "American challenge"

The stunning expansion of American corporate production overseas, especially in Europe, has given rise to what has been called *The American Challenge*. In a 1968 book with that title, Jean-Jacques Servan-Schreiber described the "takeover" of French markets by dynamic American firms that had seized 50 percent of Europe's semiconductor market, 80 percent of its

---

[1] *Statistical Abstract*, 1977, p. 564.

[2] Based on earlier estimates by Kenneth Waltz in Brown, *World Business*, p. 219; also Louis Turner, *Invisible Empires* (New York: Harcourt, 1971), p. 71; and testimony of Judd Polk before the Subcommittee for Economic Policy of the Joint Economic Committee, July 27, 1970.

computer market, and 95 percent of its integrated-circuit production. Servan-Schreiber feared that the American Challenge portended the American-ization of Europe's fastest growing industries. "Fifteen years from now," he wrote, "it is quite possible that the world's third greatest industrial power, just after the United States and Russia, will not be Europe, but American industry in Europe." [3]

Servan-Schreiber argued that Europe must fend off this American threat by the formation of equally efficient, large pan-European corpora-tions. But he failed to see that the movement toward the internationalization of production was not a strictly American but a truly multinational phenom-enon. If the American multinationals are the most imposing (of the world's biggest 500 corporations, over 300 are American), they are closely chal-lenged by non-American multinationals. Philips Lamp Works, for example, is a huge Dutch multinational company with operations in sixty-eight coun-tries. Of its 391,000 employees, well over half work in nations other than the Netherlands "home" nation. Royal Dutch/Shell is another vast multi-national, whose "home" is somewhere between the Netherlands and the United Kingdom (it is jointly owned by nationals of both countries); Shell *in the United States* ranks among our top twenty biggest companies. Another is Nestlé Chocolate, a Swiss firm, 97 percent of whose revenues originate outside Switzerland.

Thus if we look at the world picture of production, we find that many European (and Japanese) firms have been expanding their production over-seas just as rapidly as, or even more rapidly than, American firms; and although American companies have been growing very rapidly in Europe, thereby scaring the daylights out of their European competition, non-American firms have been growing even faster in other parts of the world market, including America itself.[4] (Think, for example, of the invasion of the American automobile market within the last fifteen years by Volks-wagen, Toyota, Datsun, and a host of other foreign makes.)

the inter-national challenge   The point is that the change in international economic relations is truly worldwide. If we take the ten leading capital-exporting nations together (including the United States), we find that by 1971, their combined exports came to over $206 billion, but their combined overseas production amounted to well over $308 billion.[5] This superiority of foreign production over exports has increased since then. Judd Polk, economist for the International Cham-ber of Commerce, has estimated that total international production—U.S.

[3] J.-J. Servan-Schreiber, *The American Challenge* (New York: Atheneum, 1968), pp. 3, 13.

[4] See Robert Rowthorn and Stephen Hymer, *International Big Business* (New York: Cambridge University Press, 1971), pp. 84–85.

[5] *Multinational Corporations in World Development,* United Nations, 1973, p. 159.

production abroad, foreign production here, and foreign production in other foreign countries—may account for as much as *one-sixth* of the total value of all world output, and a much higher fraction of the world output of industrial commodities.[6]

Because we do not have complete statistics on many aspects of international production, the full extent of this new form of economic relationship is still uncertain. But a number of economists have made projections based on the continuance of the rapid growth of international production. Prof. Harold Perlmutter, for example, predicts that by 1988, most noncommunist trade will be dominated by 300 large corporations, of which 200 will be American, and that these corporations will account for roughly half of total world industrial output.[7] The late Professor Adolf Berle remarked that some corporations "can be thought of only in somewhat the way we have heretofore thought of nations." No more than a glance at Table 11–1, comparing the GNPs of various countries with the sales of selected multinational corporations, shows that Berle's statement was not just rhetoric.

Cautionary note: Corporate sales are not the equivalent of GNPs. The table vastly overstates the relative importance of corporations with respect to manpower: Portugal, for instance, has a population of nine million, whereas GM employs less than one million. On the other hand, the table understates the economic strength of corporations: GM can borrow a great deal more easily than Portugal; and it controls *all* of its receipts, whereas Portugal gets only the taxes from its GNP. Nonetheless, the table makes it clear that Berle's comparison was not a wholly fanciful one.

TABLE 11 · 1

GNP OF VARIOUS COUNTRIES, COMPARED WITH SALES OF SELECTED MULTINATIONAL CORPORATIONS

Billions of current dollars, 1976

Netherlands	$87.2	Norway	$30.2
Belgium	68.1	Texaco	26.4
Switzerland	59.5	Mobil	26.0
General Motors	47.2	Greece	23.4
Exxon	46.7	IBM	16.3
Austria	40.4	Portugal	15.8
Denmark	37.4	General Electric	15.7
Royal Dutch/Shell	36.0	Unilever	15.7
Ford	28.8	Chrysler	15.5

[6] Testimony of Judd Polk before the Subcommittee for Economic Policy of the Joint Economic Committee, July 27, 1970.

[7] Turner, *Invisible Empires,* p. 191.

Why has the multinational phenomenon arisen? The question is not alto-gether simple to answer. After all, it is cheaper to export goods or to license production abroad than to establish a branch in a faraway nation and en-counter troubles and risks, which we will look into. Why, then, has produc-tion itself leaped overseas?

The initial reason arises from a characteristic of the firm, to which we have heretofore paid only passing attention. This is the drive for expansion that we find in nearly all capitalist enterprises. In our overview of the rise of American big business, we saw the emergence of giant enterprise as a consequence of the pull of markets and the push of mass production.° Much the same logic has driven firms, from early times, to expand their markets overseas. Samuel Colt, the inventor of the first "assembly-line" revolver, opened a foreign branch in London in the mid-1850s (and promptly failed). But in those same years, American entrepreneurs were already successfully pushing a railway line to completion across the Panama isthmus, and by the 1870s, the Singer Sewing Machine Company was gain-ing half its revenues from overseas production and exports.

But what drives a firm to *produce* overseas rather than just sell overseas? One possible answer is straightforward. A firm is successful at home. Its technology and organizational skills give it an edge on foreign competition. It begins to export its product. The foreign market grows. At some point, the firm begins to calculate whether it would be more profitable to organize an overseas production operation. By doing so, it would save transportation costs. It might be able to evade a tariff by producing goods behind a tariff wall. It may be able to take advantage of lower wage rates. Finally, it ceases shipping goods abroad and instead exports capital, technology, and manage-ment—and becomes a multinational.

Or calculations may be more complex. By degree, a successful com-pany may change its point of view. First it thinks of itself as a domestic company, perhaps with a small export market. Then it builds up its exports and thinks of itself as an international company with a substantial interest in exports. Finally, its perspective changes to that of a multinational, con-sidering the world (or substantial portions of it) to be its market. In that case, it may locate plants abroad *before* the market is fully developed, in order to be firmly established abroad ahead of its competition.†

° Alfred Chandler has shown in a brilliant book, *Strategy and Structure* (Cambridge, Mass.: M.I.T. Press, 1962), that the typical domestic firm went through a series of "logical" changes in organization, growing from the single-product, single-plant firm (in which every operation was supervised personally by the founder—owner) to the multi-divisional, multiproduct enterprise in which a tiered organizational structure became necessary to superintend the strategic requirements of national geographic scope and increasing technical complexity.

† The internal dynamics that send some firms overseas, but not others, are by no means wholly understood. The internationalization of production is much more widely spread

In the multinational boom of the 1950s and 1960s, still other considerations may have played a role. For American corporations, one factor was probably our overvalued dollar, which made it possible to buy or build foreign plant and equipment cheaply. When the American dollar subsequently fell in value during the middle to late 1970s, foreign investment in the United States was correspondingly encouraged, and we heard stories about "the Arabs" who were about to buy out much American industry. (In fact they preferred to put their funds into stocks and bonds.) But unquestionably the original surge of American capital abroad was encouraged by the ability to buy foreign assets cheaply, and this impetus to American multinationalization was removed with the subsequent fall in the foreign exchange value of the dollar.

economics of multinational production

What economic changes have followed from the startling rise of international production? One clear answer is that the growth of the multinational enterprise has dramatically changed the *geographic location* and the *technological character* of international economic activity.

The shift away from exports and imports to international production has introduced two changes into the international economic scene. One change is a movement of foreign investment away from its original concentration in the underdeveloped areas of the world toward the richer markets of the developed areas. Fifty years ago, in the era of high imperialism, most of the capital leaving one country for another flowed from rich to poor lands. Thus, foreign investment in the late nineteenth and early twentieth centuries was largely associated with the creation of vast plantations, the building of railways through jungles, and the development of mineral resources.

But the growth of the multinational enterprise has coincided with a decisive shift away from investment in the underdeveloped world to investment in the industrial world. In 1897, 59 percent of American foreign direct investment was in agriculture, mining, or railways, mainly in the underdeveloped world. By the 1970s, our investment in agriculture, mining, and railways, as a proportion of our total overseas assets, had fallen to less than 20 percent; and its geographical location in the backward world came to less than one third of all our overseas direct investments. More striking, almost three-quarters of our huge rise in direct investment during the decades of the 1960s and 1970s had been in the developed world; and the vast bulk of it has been in manufacturing (and oil) rather than in planta-

---

in some industries, such as glass, than in others, such as steel. Drugs are widely produced on an international basis; machine tools are not. Perhaps the answer lies in the technological and organizational variations among industry, along the lines suggested by Chandler in *The Visible Hand* (Cambridge, Mass.: Harvard University Press, 1977). The subject has not yet been adequately explored.

TABLE 11·2

SHIFT
IN
INVESTMENT

SIZE AND DISTRIBUTION OF U.S. FOREIGN DIRECT INVESTMENT

	1929	1975
Total (millions)	$7,528	$133,168
Percent distribution, by market		
Canada	27	23
Europe	18	37
Latin America	47	12
Asia, Africa, other	8	28
Percent distribution, by industrial sector		
Manufacturing	24	42
Petroleum	15	26
Transport and Utilities	21 ⎫	N.A. ⎫
Mining	15 ⎬	8 ⎬
Trade	5 ⎬ 61	N.A. ⎬ 32
Agriculture	12 ⎬	N.A. ⎬
Other	8 ⎭	N.A. ⎭

tions, railroads, or ores.[8] *Thus, the multinational companies are investing in each other's territories rather than invading the territories of the underdeveloped world.* This is not to say that they do not wield great power in the backward regions, as we shall see, but their thrust of expansion has been in other industrial lands, not in the unindustrialized ones.

The second economic change is really implicit in the first. It is a shift away from "heavy-technology" to "high-technology" industries—away from enterprises in which often vast sums of capital were associated with large, unskilled labor forces, as in the building of railways or plantations, toward industries in which capital is perhaps less strategic than research and development, skilled technical manpower, and sophisticated management techniques typical of computer, petrochemical, and other new industries.

Table 11–2 sums up the overall shift.

Note the dramatic shift away from Latin America and away from transport, mining, and agriculture, into Europe and manufacturing, a shift that would be even more accentuated if we were not still dependent on oil as a major source of the world's energy. If nuclear power or the fuel cell displace oil within the next two decades, we can expect a still more rapid decline in investment in the backward areas (especially in the Near East), and a proportionately still larger concentration of foreign direct investment in manufacturing.

[8] See Mira Wilkins, *The Emergence of Multinational Enterprise* (Cambridge, Mass.: Harvard University Press, 1970), p. 110; also *Statistical Abstract,* 1977, p. 565.

Thus the international corporations have served as vehicles for the redirection of the world's international allocation of capital investment. But the economic effects of the multinationals are perhaps less important than their political effects, for international production has a political factor that makes international economic relationships sharply different from those of pre-multinational days.

In the main, the "classical" conception of international trade was based on the familiar model of a competitive world in which factors of production were free to move about to find their points of highest return *within* their own national territories. The result was a final equilibrium in which each nation discovered the best allocation of resources both with regard to its own resources and to the advantageous exchanges it could make with other nations. In this final equilibrium, political considerations might enter in the form of tariffs or other trade barriers, but these were always considered by economists as the product of national nearsightedness, so that in theory—and to some extent in practice—it was possible to use the notion of *an equilibrium determined entirely by economic considerations.*

Not so under the peculiar conditions of international production. For now the unit of economic activity is no longer the tiny "factor of production" subject to market forces, but a giant corporation capable of the maneuvers, tactics, and strategies characteristic of oligopolistic, rather than competitive, economic units. *Within* a given country, as we have seen, oligopolies tend to settle down to a more or less steady division of the market, usually by tacit agreement not to engage in price warfare. But this division of the market becomes rudely disturbed when a newcomer from the "outside" establishes a new production unit within the home market of another nation. Moreover, the new division of the market, between the invader and the established giants, will not be determined solely by the economic growth potentials of the various contestants. *There is an inescapable political element that will also play an important, perhaps determinative, role.*

creating pan-national enterprises This political element has two aspects. On the one hand, it depends on the ability of smaller nations, such as those we find in Europe, to relinquish their feelings of national pride sufficiently to allow the creation of big enough pan-European enterprises to challenge the (American) invader successfully. (Here is Servan-Schreiber's problem in a nutshell.) The cost of IBM's research and development, for example, is more than the entire sales earnings of its largest British competitor. To stand up against IBM, therefore, it may be necessary for British companies to merge with French or German ones, to form a competitor with the economies of scale, the ability to generate finance, the command over technical talent that will put it in a league with IBM. But that will require a *political* decision on the part of

England or France or Germany to give up exclusive national control over their biggest computer companies.

A few such genuinely international companies have come into existence. Royal Dutch/Shell and Unilever are truly bi-national enterprises, run by boards of directors that represent both Dutch and English directors; and an effort is being made to create more such genuinely "European" enterprises. Whether or not this effort will be successful, it is too early to tell. But surely, the critical element in the final division of the market among the multinationals will depend fully as much on the politics of international merger as on the economics of market tactics.

national prerogatives There is, moreover, a second political element that enters into the new multinational thrust. This is the question of the extent to which foreign governments will *permit* "foreign" corporations to operate within their borders.

This problem has its counterpart in the political decision on how much to tax (by tariffs) the goods that foreign companies sell to a given nation. But the problem of permitting the entry of a foreign-owned production unit is much more important—and much more difficult to resolve—because this may be the only way that a nation can import the *technology* and the *productivity* that the multinational invader will bring with it.

For example, in the early 1960s the French government was extremely uneasy over the virtual preemption of its high-technology computer industries by American firms. When General Electric sought to buy a 20 percent interest in Machines Bull, a leading French manufacturer of computer and desk machinery, the French government balked at the "Americanization" of the firm and forbade the transaction. Within a very few years, it became apparent that without an infusion of American technology, Machines Bull could not stand up to the competition of IBM, and the French government unhappily acquiesced in the American "takeover." But then it *was* a takeover, for GE demanded (and got) 50 percent control of Machines Bull.*

Thus, the pan-national thrust of economic activity often hinges on political decisions concerning the national independence of the economies into which the multinationals seek to move. Canadians, for example, have recently awakened to the fact that they own only *15 percent* of their own industry. All the rest is foreign-owned. Americans alone control 46 percent of Canada's manufacturing, 58 percent of its oil and gas, and almost 100 percent of its auto industry. The next biggest slice is owned by various European—mainly British—interests. Canada is thus a minority stockholder in its own economy, a situation that has led to strong sentiments to block

---

* An investment that did not work out very successfully, by the way, for GE.

further foreign ownership. But there would, of course, be a real economic price—a diminished rate of growth—for such a blockage.

host and hostage

This conflict between the jealous claims of nation-states who seek to retain national control over productive activity within their own borders and the powerful thrust of pan-national corporations for new markets in foreign territories introduces profound tensions into the political economics of multinational production. On the one hand, the multinational is in a position to win hard bargains from the "host" country into which it seeks to enter (as in the case of France and GE), because the corporation *is* the main bearer of new technologies and management techniques that every nation seeks. Therefore, if one country—say, France—refuses to give a would-be entrant the right to come in (and possibly to cause financial losses to its established firms), the multinational may well place its plants, with their precious economic cargo of productivity, in another country, leaving the recalcitrant nation the loser in the race for international growth.

On the other hand, the power is by no means entirely one-sided; for once a multinational *has* entered a foreign nation, it becomes a *hostage* of the host country. It is now bound by the laws of that country and may find itself forced to undertake activities that are "foreign." For example, in Japan it is an unwritten law that workers engaged by giant corporations are *never* fired, but become permanent employees. Japan has been extremely reluctant to allow foreign capital to establish manufacturing operations on Japanese soil, to the great annoyance of foreign companies. But if, as now seems likely, Japan is opened to American and European capital, we can be sure that American and European corporations will be expected to behave in the Japanese way with their employees. This will not be an easy course to follow, since these corporations are not likely to receive the special support that the Japanese government gives to its own big firms.

Or take the problem of a multinational that is forced by a fall in demand to cut back the volume of its output. A decision made along strictly economic lines would lead it to close its least profitable plant. But this may bring very serious economic repercussions in the nation in which that plant is located—so serious that the government will threaten to take "action" if the plant is closed. What dictates shall the multinational then follow: those of standard business accounting or those of political accounting?

Or consider the multinational seeking to expand or to alter its operations in an underdevolped country. This, too, may lead to friction, for as former Undersecretary of State George Ball has candidly asked, "How can a national government make an economic plan with any confidence if a board of directors meeting 5,000 miles away can, by altering its pattern of purchasing and production, affect in a major way the country's economic life?" [9]

[9] Brown, *World Business*, p. 334.

As we have seen in Peru, Bolivia, and Libya, this incompatibility of aims may become so great that the underdeveloped country eventually seizes and nationalizes the assets of the multinational.

multi-
nationals
and world
order

Is there an "answer" to this conflict between the business rationality of the multinational corporation and the political priorities of the nation-state? At this stage in the development of both institutions, none is in sight. The very idea of pan-national production is itself so new that we lack even a conceptual model of how to deal with its problems, much less a set of practical rules and regulations to follow. Take something so simple—but so important—as the location of the head office of the corporation, to which a nation would make representations if the action of an international corporation were contrary to national interest. From one nation to another, the legal definition of the *head office* differs: In the United States and the United Kingdom, it is the place where the company is formally incorporated; in Morocco, it is the location of the "registered" home office; in France, Germany, and Belgium, it is the main center of management; in Italy and Egypt, it is the place of principal business activity. Which of these will respond when a country in search of legal redress calls out, "Will the real head office please stand up?"

Or take the question of the patriotic accountability of the multinational enterprise. Suppose a company wishes to move its profits from country A to country B, but that country A has balance-of-payments difficulties. Is the company bound to obey the wishes of A? Suppose the government in B also has balance-of-payments difficulties and desires the company to import capital? What should the corporation do? In 1966, for example, the United States government asked corporations not to export capital, lest our precarious balance of payments be worsened. But the Ford Motor Company decided that its long-term interests required the purchase of British Ford, so, despite objections of the U.S. government, Ford exported $600 million of capital to make the purchase. Was Ford "unpatriotic" if its actions were in the long-term interests of the company? Was it similarly "unpatriotic" (from a British point of view) for a group of English investors to export British capital to finance the building of the Pan Am skyscraper in New York?

Again, in the late 1970s the US dollar was under sharp attack. The consequent fall in the value of the dollar was a serious problem for America. What was the "duty" of the treasurer of a US multinational that held perhaps $10 millions in dollars in a German account? Should the treasurer keep his eye only on his company's balance sheet and sell the dollars, hoping to make money; or should he put his loyalty to his country above that to his company, and hang onto the dollars to help relieve the pressure on the dollar? Most—perhaps all—treasurers took the first course, arguing that by themselves they could not stem the tide, and that they had to maximize profits to stay in business. In so doing, however, the MNCs were major contributors to the international financial panic. What, if anything, should be done about that?

Or suppose a multinational company, in one of its foreign plants, undertakes work that is integral to the defense of that nation; and that the foreign policy of the nation in question brings its military strength to bear against another country in which the multinational is also located? Is the company supposed to take sides?

unresolved questions

There are no answers to such questions, only speculations.[10] Here are some of them:

Speculation 1. Will the conglomerate serve as a means of mediating between the demands of business production efficiency and political "national" control? For example, why didn't Ford build the Pan Am building, and why didn't the British investors put their pounds into autos? Both sides would have told you (back in the 1960s) that they weren't "in the business" of real estate or cars, as the case may be. But the rise of the conglomerates opens new possibilities in this direction. If, in the future, the controlling center of Ford becomes (as IT&T has already become) a capital-allocation office rather than the headquarters of an auto firm, it is possible that Ford *will* build buildings and that British realtors *will* build automobiles. In that case, the big corporation may surrender some of its multi-nationality in exchange for multi-industrial coverage.

Speculation 2. Will the multinationals, if they continue their growth, constitute the skeleton of a new form of world order? Some economists and businessmen see the rise of a pan-national system of oligopolies controlled by boards of directors that represent many nations (rather than mainly one, as is now the case), whose operations will pave the way for a much more pragmatic, down-to-earth, effective system of world production and distribution than the present competition of hostile, suspicious, and dangerous nation-states. Such an international rationalization of production, they believe, could bring a "businessman's peace," in which the big companies serve to accelerate world growth, to introduce efficiency into the backward areas, and to assert the logic of economic performance over the outmoded rivalries of jealous nation-states.

Speculation 3. Will the multinationals, on the contrary, serve to heighten the tension of a world that, for better or worse, must continue to use the powerful appeal of nationhood? How can giant corporations, necessarily dedicated to profit making, adjust their operations to the often

[10] For a searching commentary, see Detlev F. Vagts, "The Multinational Enterprise: A New Challenge for Transnational Law," *Harvard Law Review*, February 1970.

unprofitable needs of national development? How can corporations, jockeying for market position, provide the basis for a stable world economic system? The opponents of the multinationals see in them not a force for progress but only a means of imposing a calculus of profits on a world whose needs at the moment often demand an entirely different set of fundamental values.

*an
unwritten
ending*

It is much too early to determine which of these arguments will eventually be proven correct. Perhaps the safest guess is that all will be, at least in our lifetime. The big corporations are likely to continue to go in both multinational and conglomerate directions. To some extent, they will be the international carriers of efficiency and development, especially in the high-technology areas for which they seem to be the most effective form of organization. But if the power of the nation-state will be challenged by these international production units, it is not likely to be humbled by them. There are many things a nation can do that a corporation cannot, including, above all, the creation of the spirit of sacrifice necessary both for good purposes such as development and for evil ones such as war.

Perhaps all we can say at this stage of human development is that both nation-states and huge corporations are necessary, in that they seem to be the only ways in which we can organize people to perform the arduous and sustained labor without which humanity itself would rapidly perish. Perhaps after the long age of capital accumulation has finally come to an end and sufficient capital is available to all peoples, we may be able to think seriously about dismantling the giant enterprise and the nation-state, both of which overpower the individual with their massive organized strength. However desirable that ultimate goal may be, in our time both state and corporation promise to be with us, and the tension between them will be part of the evolutionary drama of our period of history.

11	*Key Concepts and Key Words*

**Multinational
corporations**

1. The basic conception of international trade has entered a new stage marked by *international production carried on by the multinational corporation.*

2. The natural impetus of the drive for growth has pushed most large US corporations into multinational operations. As a result, our exports of manufactures are today only about a third as large as our overseas production of manufactured commodities. In fact *overseas production is now about one-quarter as large as total GNP.*

Foreign
direct
investment

3. As a result of the thrust of the multinationals, US foreign direct investment has risen to approximately $133 billion of foreign direct American investment and may be much larger than that if the value of foreign capital controlled by American equity is included.

4. The rise of the American multinational in Europe has been very rapid and has led to a European fear of an "American challenge." However justified in Europe, this fear masks the fact that *European (and Japanese) foreign investment is rising as rapidly as American—and much of it in America.*

International-
ization of
production

5. *The prospect is for a genuine internationalization of production within the next few decades.* A few hundred large firms, of which the majority will probably be American, are apt to control a very large fraction of the production of industrial commodities on a worldwide basis.

6. *The rise of multinational production has resulted in striking shifts in the geographic location and technological character of international investment.* The trend has been away from investment in underdeveloped nations to investment in the markets of high-consumption countries; and away from low-skilled labor-intensive or capital-intensive industries to high-skill-intensive industries.

7. The *incursion of the multinationals across national boundaries has raised sharp new problems of political economics.* An equilibrium in international production will depend on political decisions as well as economic forces. These are:
   - The ability of smaller nations to abandon national prerogatives in order to form effective international corporations to challenge American or other companies.
   - The willingness of countries to allow foreign companies to dominate industries that they may consider vital to their national interests.

High
technology

   - The ability of most nations to import new high technology if they deny entry to the multinationals.

8. Equally perplexing problems are posed for the multinationals themselves. *If they are often in a position to drive hard bargains before entrance, once they*

Hostage

have committed themselves, they are "hostages." To which of the many countries where they may be located do they owe allegiance if the interests of those countries clash? To what extent should the dictates of profit determine their international allocations of manpower and capital? To what extent can a multi-

Host

national defy, and to what extent must it bow before, the demands of a host country?

9. There are no answers to the questions above. *We still have no established rules or procedures or laws to cover this new mode of organizing the world's production.* Nor do we know if the growth of multinational enterprise will serve as a force for order and rationality or for friction and tension.

1. How many products produced in America can you identify as "foreign"? (You might start with the detergents and soaps produced by Lever Brothers, the office machinery produced by Olivetti-Underwood, the gas and oil refined by Shell.)

2. Can you suggest a hypothesis that might be testable as to why certain industries seem to go overseas more rapidly than others? Why autos and tractors, but not washing machines? Why plate glass, but not sheet steel? (Little is known about this, so you might become famous if you come up with an idea that tests out.)

3. Do you think a nation is right to exclude a foreign company from producing in certain areas? Would you wish to exclude from the United States Japanese production of, say, high-speed computers *if this were the only way we could get high-speed computers?*

4. What do you think is the duty of a company that is active in nations A, B, and C, when all have balance-of-payments problems and request domestic corporations not to make unnecessary international payments? Suppose the headquarters of the company is in A and the stockholders want the profits from B and C repatriated?

5. Can you draw up a plan for a company that would be privately owned and managed but not officially headquartered in any one nation? From whom would it receive its charter? Under what laws will it operate so far as the top management is concerned?

6. Do you think that the rise of multinational production opens the way for a more rational world, or a more divided one?

12 · *The Underdeveloped World*

We must begin this very important chapter with a sobering realization. It is that our account of the long sweep of Western economic advance has largely ignored the economic existence of four out of five human beings on earth. Mere parochialism was not, however, the reason for this concentration on Western progress. Rather, it was the shocking fact that, taken in the large, *there was no economic progress in the rest of the world.*

This is not to say that tides of fortune and misfortune did not mark these areas, that great cultural heights were not achieved, and that the political or social histories of these regions do not warrant interest and study. Yet the fact remains that the mounting tide of *economic* advance that has engaged our attention was a phenomenon limited to the West. It is no doubt something of an oversimplification, but it is basically true to claim that in Asia, Africa, South America, or the Near East, economic existence was not materially improved for the average inhabitant from the twelfth— and, in some cases, the second—to the beginning of the twentieth century. Indeed, for many of them it was worsened. A long graph of non-Western material well-being would depict irregular rises and falls but an almost total absence of cumulative betterment.

The near end of such a graph would show the standard of living of three-quarters of the human race who inhabit the so-called underdeveloped areas today. Most of this mass of humanity exists in conditions of poverty that are difficult for a Westerner to comprehend. When we sum up the plight of the underdeveloped nations by saying that a billion human beings have a standard of living of "less than $100 a year," and that another, more fortunate, billion people enjoy in a year one-quarter to one-half the income a typical American family spends in a single *month*, we give only a pale statistical meaning to a reality that we can scarcely grasp.*

* In Iraq, for instance, in years of famine, the children of the poor examine the droppings of horses to extract morsels of undigested oats. In Calcutta, 250,000 people have no home whatsoever and live in the streets. In Hong Kong, large numbers of families of four or more live in one bed-space in a squalid dormitory. In Cali, Colombia, when the river

Why are the underdeveloped nations so pitiably poor? Only a half-century
ago, it was common to attribute their backwardness to geographic or cli-
matic causes. The underdeveloped nations were poor, it was thought, either
because the climate was too debilitating or because natural resources were
lacking. Sometimes it was said that the natives were just too childlike or
racially too inferior to improve their lot.

Bad climates may have had adverse effects. Yet, many hot areas have
shown a capacity for sustained economic growth (for example, the Queens-
land areas of Australia), and we have come to recognize that a number of
underdeveloped areas, such as Argentina and Korea, have completely tem-
perate climates. So, too, we now regard the lack of resources in many areas
more as a *symptom* of underdevelopment than a cause—which is to say that
in many underdeveloped areas, resources have not yet been *looked for*.
Libya, for instance, which used to be written off as a totally barren nation,
has been discovered to be a large reservoir of oil. Finally, little is heard
today about native childishness or inherent inferiority. (Perhaps we remember how the wealthy classes similarly characterized the poor in Europe not
too many centuries ago.) Climate and geography and cultural unprepared-
ness unquestionably constitute obstacles to rapid economic growth—and in
some areas of the globe, very serious obstacles—but there are few economists who would look to these disadvantages as the main causes of economic backwardness.

Why then are these societies so poor?

The answer takes us back to an early chapter of our book. These are
poor societies because they are *traditional* societies—that is, societies that
have failed to develop mechanisms either of command or of the market by
which they might launch into a sustained process of economic growth.
Indeed, as we examine them further, we will have the feeling that we are
encountering in the present the anachronistic counterparts of the static
societies of antiquity.

Why did they remain traditional societies? Why, for instance, did
Byzantium, which was economically so advanced in contrast with the Crusaders' Europe, fall into decline? Why did China, with so many natural
advantages, not develop into a dynamic economic society? There are no
simple, or even fully satisfactory, answers. Perhaps the absence of economic progress elsewhere on the globe forces us to look upon our Western
experience not as the paradigm and standard for historic development, but
as a very special case in which various activating factors met in an environment peculiarly favorable for the emergence of a new economic style in
history. The problem is one into which we cannot go more deeply in this

---

rises, the city's sewers run through the homes of the poor. In Hyderabad, Pakistan,
child labor employed in sealing the ends of bangles over a kerosene flame is paid eight
cents per *gross* of bangles.

book. At any rate, it is today an academic question. The dominant reality of our times is that the backward areas are now striving desperately to enter the mainstream of economic progress of the West. Let us examine further their chances for doing so.

conditions of back-wardness

There is a rough sequence to the order of demands in human society; and every people, to exist, must first feed itself. But to go beyond existence, it must achieve a certain level of efficiency in agriculture, so that its efforts can be turned in other directions. What is tragically characteristic of the underdeveloped areas is that this first corner of economic progress has not yet been turned.

Consider the situation only a few years ago in that all-important crop of the East, rice. Table 12–1 shows the difference between the productivity of rice fields in the main underdeveloped Asiatic countries and those of the United States, Australia, and Japan, as of 1975.

What is true of rice can be duplicated in most other crops.° It is a disconcerting fact that the backward peasant nations that depend desperately on their capacity to grow food cannot even compete in these main products with the advanced countries: US Louisiana rice undersells Philippine rice, California oranges are not only better but cheaper than Indonesian oranges.

mini-agriculture

Why is agriculture so unproductive? One apparent reason is that the typical unit of agricultural production in the underdeveloped lands is far too small to permit efficient farming. What has been called "postage-stamp cultiva-

TABLE 12·1

RICE PRODUC-TION, 1975

	100 kilograms per hectare
U.S.	51.0
Australia	51.2
Japan	61.9
Thailand	17.1
India	18.3
Indonesia	26.9
Philippines	32.4

° Table 12–1 shows only the productive differentials of equal *areas* of land. When we consider that a single American farmer tends up to a hundred times as large an acreage as a peasant in an underdeveloped area, the difference in output *per man* would be much more striking. The "Green Revolution" has improved the situation, but we do not yet have the data we need to determine outputs for the new rice strains. Despite the improvement, a vast gulf still separates U.S. agricultural productivity from that of the underdeveloped nations.

tion" marks the pattern of farming throughout most of Asia and a good deal of Africa and South America. John Gunther, reporting the situation in India forty years ago, described it vividly. It has not changed since that time.

There is no primogeniture in India as a rule, and when the peasant dies his land is subdivided among all his sons with the result that most holdings are infinitesimally small. In one district in the Punjab, following fragmentation through generations, 584 owners cultivate no less than 16,000 fields; in another, 12,800 acres are split into actually 63,000 holdings. Three-quarters of the holdings in India as a whole are under ten acres. In many parts of India the average holding is less than an acre.[1]

In part, this terrible situation is the result of the divisive inheritance practices Gunther mentions; in part, it is due to landlord systems in which peasants cannot legally own or accumulate their own land; in part, to the pressure of too many people on too little soil. There are many causes, with one result: Agriculture suffers from a devastatingly low productivity brought about by grotesque man/land ratios.

lack of capital   These are, however, only the first links in a chain of causes for low agricultural productivity. Another consequence of these tiny plots is an inability to apply sufficient capital to the land. Mechanical binders and reapers, tractors and trucks are not only impossible to use efficiently in such tiny spaces, but they are costly beyond the reach of the subsistence farmer. Even fertilizer is too expensive; in much of Asia, animal dung is used to provide "free" fuel, rather than returned to the soil to enrich it.

This paralyzing lack of capital is by no means confined to agriculture. It pervades the entire range of an underdeveloped economy. The whole industrial landscape of a Western economy is missing: No factories, no power lines, no machines, no paved roads meet the eye for mile upon mile as one travels through an underdeveloped continent. Indeed, to a pitiable extent, an underdeveloped land is one in which human and animal muscle power provide the energy with which production is carried on. In India in 1953, for instance, 65 percent of the total amount of productive energy in the nation was the product of straining man and beast.[2] The amount of usable electrical power generated in that year in all of India would not have sufficed to light up New York City.

social inertia   A lack of agricultural and industrial capital is not the only reason for low productivity. As we would expect in traditional societies, an endemic cause

[1] *Inside Asia* (New York: Harper, 1939), p. 385.
[2] Daniel Wit and Alfred B. Clubok, "Atomic Power Development in India," *Social Research*, Autumn 1958, p. 290.

of low per capita output lies in prevailing social attitudes. Typically, the people of an underdeveloped economy have not *learned* the "economic" attitudes that foster rapid industrialization. Instead of technology-conscious farmers, they are tradition-bound peasants. Instead of disciplined workers, they are reluctant and untrained laborers. Instead of production-minded businessmen, they are trading-oriented merchants.

For example, Alvin Hansen has reported from his observations in India:

Agricultural practices are controlled by custom and tradition. A villager is fearful of science. For many villagers, insecticide is taboo because all life is sacred. A new and improved seed is suspect. To try it is a gamble. Fertilizers, for example, are indeed a risk. . . . To adopt these untried methods might be to risk failure. And failure could mean starvation.[3]

In similar vein, a UNESCO report tells us:

In the least developed areas, the worker's attitude toward labour may entirely lack time perspective, let alone the concept of productive investment. For example, the day labourer in a rural area on his way to work, who finds a fish in the net he placed in the river the night before, is observed to return home, his needs being met. . . .[4]

An equally crippling attitude is evinced by the upper classes, who look with scorn or disdain upon business- or production-oriented careers. More than a decade ago, UNESCO reported that of the many students from the underdeveloped lands studying in the United States—the majority of whom come from the more privileged classes—only 4 percent were studying a problem fundamental to all their nations: agriculture.[5] This has not changed over time.

All these attitudes give rise to a *social inertia* that poses a tremendous hurdle to economic development. A suspicious peasantry, fearful of change that might jeopardize the slim margin yielding them life, a work force unresponsive to monetary incentive, a privileged class not interested in production—all these are part of the obdurate handicaps to be overcome by an underdeveloped nation.

further problems: population growth

Many of these problems, as we anticipated, remind us of the pre-market economies of antiquity. But in addition, the underdeveloped lands face an obstacle with which the economies of antiquity did *not* have to cope: A crushing rate of population increase threatens to nullify their efforts to emerge from backward conditions.

[3] *Economic Issues of the 1960s* (New York: McGraw-Hill, 1960), pp. 157–58.
[4] *Report on the World Social Situation*, UNESCO, March 9, 1961, p. 79.
[5] UNESCO, March 9, 1961, p. 81.

Only a few figures are needed to make the point. Let us begin with our southern neighbor, Mexico. Today, Mexico has a population equal to that of New York State, Pennsylvania, New Jersey, and Connecticut. Thirty years from now, if Mexico's present rate of population increase continues, it will have as many people as the present population of these four states *plus* the rest of New England, *plus* the entire South Atlantic seaboard, *plus* the entire West Coast, *plus* Ohio, Indiana, Illinois, Michigan, and Wisconsin. Or take the Caribbean and Central American area. In some thirty years, at present growth rates, its population will outnumber the entire population of the United States today. South America, now 5 percent less populous than we, will be 200 percent larger than our present population. India will then very likely number a billion souls. The world will hold at least 6 billion inhabitants—and will still threaten to double in size by the end of another thirty years.

We have already seen one result of the relentless proliferation of people in the fragmentation of landholdings. But the problem goes beyond mere fragmentation. Eugene Black, formerly president of the International Bank for Reconstruction and Development (the World Bank), tells us that in India, a population equivalent to that of all Great Britain has been squeezed out of any landholding whatsoever—even though it still dwells in rural areas.[6] Consequently, population pressure generates massive and widespread rural poverty, pushing inhabitants from the countryside into the already overcrowded cities. Five hundred families a day move into Jakarta from the surrounding Javanese countryside where population has reached the fantastic figure of 1,100 per square mile.

Even these tragic repercussions of population growth are but side effects. The main problem is that population growth adds more mouths almost as fast as the underdeveloped nations manage to add more food. They cancel out much economic progress by literally eating up the small surpluses that might serve as a springboard for faster future growth.

Ironically, this population explosion in the underdeveloped countries is a fairly recent phenomenon, attributable largely to the incursion of Western medicine and public health into the low-income areas. Prior to World War II, the poorer countries held their population growth in check because death rates were nearly as high as birthrates. With DDT and penicillin, death rates have plunged dramatically. In Sri Lanka, for example, death rates dropped 40 percent in one year following the adoption of malaria control and other health measures. As death rates dropped in the underdeveloped areas, birthrates, for many reasons, continued high, despite efforts to introduce birth control. In the backward lands, children are not only a source of prestige and of household labor for the peasant family, but also

[6] Eugene R. Black, *The Diplomacy of Economic Development* (Cambridge, Mass.: Harvard University Press, 1960), p. 9.

the only possible source of "social security" for old age. The childless older couple could very well starve; as parents or grandparents, they are at least assured of a roof over their heads.

Is there a solution to this problem? The mood of demographers has swung between black despair and cautious hope over the past decades. Recently the mood has been brighter. After many years of disappointment, the world population situation seems finally to have taken a turn for the better. The reason is that birth rates—already very low in the developed nations—have finally begun to fall in the underdeveloped nations. Behind that important change lies the adoption of birth control on a widening basis, spearheaded by a very successful Chinese program aimed at cutting population growth.

It is too early to celebrate a victory not yet obtained. Hundreds of thousands will die and millions or tens of millions will be undernourished for lack of proteins or calories in the next decades, especially in some very poor areas, such as sub-Saharan Africa. Nonetheless, the pendulum seems finally to be swinging. *The decade 1970–1975 was the first time in modern history that the rate of population growth slowed down.* There is reason to hope that the population problem will diminish in urgency over the decades ahead.

nineteenth-century imperialism

This gives us a brief introduction to underdevelopment as it exists today. Before we turn to the problem of how this condition can be remedied, we must inquire into one more question. Why did not the market society, with all its economic dynamism, spread into the backward areas?

The answer is that the active economies of the European and American worlds *did* make contact with the underdeveloped regions, beginning with the great exploratory and commercial voyages of the fifteenth and sixteenth centuries. Until the nineteenth century, unfortunately, that contact was little more than mere adventure and plunder. And then, starting in the first half of that century and gaining momentum until World War I, came that scramble for territory we call the Age of Imperialism.

What was this imperialism? It was, in retrospect, a compound of many things: militarism, jingoism, a search for markets and for sources of cheap raw materials to feed growing industrial enterprises. Insofar as the colonial areas were concerned, however, the first impact of imperialism was not solely that of exploitation. On the contrary, the incursion of Western empires into the backward areas brought some advantages. It injected the first heavy dose of industrial capital: rail lines, mines, plantation equipment. It brought law and order, often into areas in which the most despotic personal rule had previously been the order of the day. It introduced the ideas of the West, including, most important, the idea of freedom, which was eventually to rouse the backward nations against the invading West itself.

Yet if capitalist imperialism brought these positive and stimulating influences, it also exerted a peculiarly deforming impulse to the under-developed—indeed, then, totally undeveloped—economies of the East and South. In the eyes of the imperialist nations, the colonies were viewed not as areas to be brought along in balanced development, but essentially as immense supply dumps to be attached to the mother countries' industrial economies. Malaya became a vast tin mine; Indonesia, a huge tea and rubber plantation; Arabia, an oil field. In other words, economic develop-ment was steadily pushed in the direction that most benefited the imperial owner, not the colonial peoples themselves.

The result today is that the typical underdeveloped nation has a badly lopsided economy, unable to supply itself with a wide variety of goods. It is thereby thrust into the international market with its one basic commodity. For instance, in South America we find that Venezuela is dependent on oil for some 90 percent of its exports; Colombia, on coffee for three-quarters of its exports; Chile, on copper for two-thirds of its foreign earnings; Hondu-ras, on bananas for half its foreign earnings. On the surface, this looks like a healthy specialization of trade. We shall shortly see why it is not.

Economic lopsidedness was one unhappy consequence of imperialism. No less important for the future course of development in the colonial areas was a second decisive influence of the West: its failure to achieve political and psychological relationships of mutual respect with its colonial peoples. In part, this was no doubt traceable to an often frankly exploitative eco-nomic attitude, in which the colonials were relegated to second-class jobs with third-class pay, while a handful of Western whites formed an insulated and highly paid managerial clique. But it ran deeper than that. A terrible color line, a callous indifference to colonial aspirations, a patronizing and sometimes contemptuous view of "the natives" runs all through the history of imperialism. It has left as a bitter heritage not only an identification of capitalism with its worst practices, but a political and social wariness toward the West that deeply affects the general orientation of the developing areas.

imperialism today

What about imperialism today? Certainly it has changed. The naked power grabs are in the past, when imperialism often meant only the acquisition of territory that would look good on a map. In the past, also, are the seizures of raw materials on the unfair terms characteristic of mineral empires built in the late nineteenth century. Less prominent, too, are attitudes of racial "superiority" so infuriating to peoples whose culture was often of far greater delicacy and discrimination than that of the West. Thus, the nature of imperialism is now changing, partly under the pressures exerted by a restive Third World, partly as a result of developments within the advanced nations themselves. The rise of the multinational corporation, for example, puts the problem of the economic relationship of advanced and backward countries in a new light. The backward nations are extremely wary of the power inherent in a giant US or European corporation. Yet they also want some of the things the multinationals offer. Big multinationals pay higher wages, keep more honest books, provide better working conditions and fancier career opportunities, and bring in more technological expertise than do the domestic enterprises of the "host" nation.

The result is that the problem of imperialism in our day, at least so far as the United States is concerned, has taken an unexpected turn. On the economic side of the question, *the danger now is that the big companies will bypass the backward nations as much as that they will dominate them.*

Meanwhile, the political element of imperialism seems to be diminishing. The erstwhile capitalist empires of Germany, Belgium, the Netherlands, and England have (with a few exceptions) disappeared. What is left is a strong effort on the part of the United States to preserve its ideological and political influence; with what long-term success we do not know.

THE ENGINEERING OF DEVELOPMENT

Up to this point, we have concentrated our attention mainly on the background of underdevelopment. Now we must ask a more forward-looking, more technically "economic" question: How can an underdeveloped nation emerge from its poverty?

From what we have learned, we know the basic answer to this question. The prerequisite for economic progress for the underdeveloped countries today is not essentially different from what it was in Great Britain at the time of the Industrial Revolution, or what it was in Russia in 1917. To grow, an underdeveloped economy must build capital.

How is a starving country able to build capital? When 80 percent of a country is scrabbling on the land for a bare subsistence, how can it divert its energies to building dams and roads, ditches and houses, railroad embankments and factories, which, however indispensable for progress tomorrow, cannot be eaten today? If our postage-stamp farmers were to halt work on their tiny unproductive plots and go to work on a great project like, say, the Aswan Dam, who would feed them? Whence would come the necessary food to sustain these capital workers?

At first sight, the problem looks insuperable. If an underdeveloped country is to amass capital, it will have to swing labor from agricultural tasks to capital-building tasks. But when a country can barely feed itself, how can it make this switch?

At second look, however, the prospect is not quite so bleak. These economies *do* have unemployed factors, and a large number of peasants who till the fields are *not* feeding themselves. They are, also, in a sense, taking food from one another's mouths.

As we have seen, the crowding of peasants on the land in these areas has resulted in a diminution of agricultural productivity far below that of the advanced countries. Hence, the abundance of peasants working in the fields obscures the fact that *a smaller number of peasants, with little more equipment—perhaps even with no more equipment—could raise a total output just as large.* Twenty years ago an observer wrote: "An experiment carried out near Cairo by the American College seems to suggest that the present output, or something closely approaching it, could be produced by about half the present rural population of Egypt." [7] Here is an extreme case, but it still applies, to some degree, to nearly every underdeveloped land.

the hidden labor surplus

Now we begin to see an answer to the predicament of the underdeveloped societies. In nearly all these societies, there exists a disguised and hidden surplus of labor that, if it were taken off the land, could be used to build capital. Most emphatically, this does not mean that the rural population should be literally moved, en masse, to the cities where there is already a hideous lump of indigestible unemployment. It means, rather, that the inefficient scale of agriculture conceals a reservoir of both labor and the food to feed that labor if it were elsewhere employed. By raising the productivity of the tillers of the soil, a work force can be made available for the building of roads and dams, while this "transfer" to capital building need not result in a diminution of agricultural output.

This rationalization of agriculture is not the only requirement for growth. When agricultural productivity is enhanced by the creation of larger farms (or by improved techniques on existing farms), *part of the ensuing larger output per man must be saved.* In other words, the peasant who remains on the soil cannot enjoy his enhanced productivity by raising his standard of living and eating up all his larger crop. Instead, the gain in output per cultivator must be siphoned off the farm. It must be "saved" by the peasant cultivator and shared with his formerly unproductive cousins, nephews, sons, and daughters who are now at work on capital-building projects. We do not expect a hungry peasant to do this voluntarily. Rather, by taxation or exaction, the government of an underdeveloped land must arrange for this indispensable transfer. Thus, in the early stages of a *successful* development program, there is apt to be no visible rise in the individual peasant's food *consumption,* although there must be a rise in his food *production.* What is apt to be visible is a more or less efficient—and sometimes harsh—mechanism for assuring that some portion of this newly added productivity is not consumed on the farm but is made available to support

[7] Ragnar Nurkse, *Problems of Capital Formation in the Underdeveloped Countries* (New York: Oxford University Press, 1958), p. 35, fn. 2.

the capital-building worker. We see here the problem that caused the Russian planners such trouble in the early days of Soviet industrialization.

What we have just outlined is not, let us repeat, a formula for immediate action. In many underdeveloped lands, as we have seen, the countryside already crawls with unemployment, and to create, overnight, a large and efficient farming operation would create an intolerable social situation. We should think of the process we have just outlined as a long-term blueprint that covers the course of development over many years. It shows us— as did our earlier model—that the process of development takes the form of a huge internal migration from agricultural pursuits, where labor is wasted, to industrial and other pursuits, where it can yield a net contribution to the nation's progress.

problem of capital equipment

Our model also showed us that capital building is not just a matter of freeing hands and food. Peasant labor may construct roads, but it cannot, with its bare hands, build the trucks to run over them. It may throw up dams, but it cannot fashion the generators and power lines through which a dam can produce energy. In other words, what is needed to engineer the great ascent is not just a pool of labor. It is also a vast array of industrial equipment.*

How is this equipment obtained? In our model, by expanding the machine-tool—that is, the capital-equipment-building—subsector. But an underdeveloped economy does not have a capital-equipment-building sector. Consequently, *in the first stages of industrialization, before the nucleus of a self-contained industrial sector has been laid down, a backward nation must obtain its equipment from abroad.*

This is can do in one of three ways: (1) It can buy the equipment from an industrialized nation by the normal process of *foreign trade*. Libya, for example, can sell its oil and use the foreign currency it receives to purchase abroad the tractors, lathes, and industrial equipment it needs. (2) It can receive the equipment by *foreign investment* when a corporation in an advanced nation chooses to build in a backward area. This is the route by which the United States got much of its capital from Britain during the

---

* An allied problem of no less importance arises from the lack of technical training on which industrialization critically depends. At the lowest level, this is evidenced by appalling rates of illiteracy (up to 80 or 90 percent), which make it impossible, for instance, to print instructions on a machine or a product and expect them to be followed. And at a more advanced level, the lack of expert training becomes an even more pinching bottleneck. Before its catastrophic civil war, United Nations economists figured that Nigeria alone would need some 20,000 top-level administrators, executives, technicians, etc., over the next ten years and twice as many subordinates. On a worldwide scale, this implies a need for at least 700,000 top-level personnel and 1,400,000 second-level assistants. Not 1 percent of these skilled personnel exists today, and to "produce" them will be a task of staggering difficulty. Yet, without them it is often impossible to translate development plans into actuality.

nineteenth century, and it is the means by which the underdeveloped nations themselves received capital during their colonial days. (3) It may receive the foreign exchange needed to buy industrial equipment as a result of a grant or a loan from another nation or from a United Nations agency such as the World Bank. That is, it can buy industrial equipment with *foreign aid.*

trade
problems

Of these three avenues of industrialization, by far the most important is foreign trade. In 1974, the underdeveloped nations earned over $100 billion a year from their exports. Not all of this, by any manner of means, however, was available for *new* industrial capital. A lion's share of export earnings, unfortunately, must go to pay for indispensable imports—replacements of old equipment, or even food—or to pay interest on loans contracted with the industrialized world. In fact only $30 billion was available for *all* manufactures, from pharmaceuticals to jet aircrafts, Mercedes Benzes to tractors.

In addition, another problem plagues the underdeveloped nations in foreign trade. We have seen how international trade is the means by which a great international division of labor can be achieved—that is, by which productivity can be enhanced in all trading countries, by enabling each to concentrate on those products in which it is most efficient. With the underdeveloped nations, however, this international division of labor has worked badly.

First, as we have seen, their structural backwardness has prevented them from developing their productivities even in their main occupational tasks. Second, most of them suffer from another problem. As sellers of raw commodities—usually only one raw commodity—typically, they face a highly inelastic demand for their goods. Like the American farmer, when they produce a bumper crop, prices tend to fall precipitously, and demand does not rise proportionately. At the same time, the industrial materials they buy in exchange tend to be firm or to rise in price over the years. Thus the "terms of trade"—the actual *quid pro quo* of goods received against goods offered—are likely to move against the poorer nations, which must give more and more, say, coffee for the same amount of machinery.* In 1957 and 1958, when commodity prices took a particularly bad tumble, the poor nations actually lost more in purchasing power than the total amount of all foreign aid they received. In effect, they subsidized the advanced nations! As another example, it has been estimated that falling prices have

---

* It should be noted that not everyone agrees with this argument, which was first advanced by Dr. Raul Prebisch, a famous Chilean economist. The argument on the other side claims that the quality of machinery and industrial products is constantly improving, whereas the quality of raw commodities is not, so that the higher prices of indusrial goods are offset by their greater productivity when put to use.

cost the African nations more, in the two decades since World War II, than all foreign funds given, loaned, or invested there.[8]

the great oil crisis

To this tale of difficulty and disappointment must be added a startling new development—one whose final outcome we do not yet know. This is the banding together of the oil-producing nations into a cartel called OPEC (Organization of Petroleum Exporting Countries) in 1959. For many years, OPEC was relatively powerless. But with the outbreak of the Arab-Israeli War in the fall of 1973, the Arab producers imposed a boycott on sales to the West, and overnight the price of oil rose from $3 per barrel to $12.

The oil-consuming nations were caught in a terrible squeeze. Despite efforts to conserve oil, they had no choice but to continue to buy huge quantities at the new, higher price levels. As a result, enormous sums of foreign exchange flowed into the hands of the OPEC nations, particularly those of the Middle East. In the years 1973 and 1974 the world's oil exporters increased their earnings from $40 to $120 billion, probably the largest single bonanza in history including even the Spanish discovery of gold in America in the sixteenth century. In a single year (1974), the Arab states built up half the foreign investment accumulated by the United States in a century! And there was no end to this process in sight.

It is not surprising that the Western nations regarded the advent of the OPEC cartel with undisguised trepidation. "A landslide of immense proportions is rumbling downhill," wrote the prestigious London *Economist,* "a landslide capable of breaking the financial system and the economies of several major nations." The International Monetary Fund similarly expressed its alarm over a threatened piling up of dollar earnings that were estimated to reach $300 billion or even more.

The fear was twofold. First, there was concern that the much higher price of oil would deal a severe blow to the economies of the West (and also to the underdeveloped countries) by bringing to an end the era of cheap energy on which (it was suddenly clear) the industrial system had been built. Second, financial experts worried that the dollar earnings of the oil exporters would not find their way back into circulation in the West, thereby causing an eventual breakdown in the world trading system itself.

recycling oil dollars

But five years after the OPEC crisis, it appears that these fears have been exaggerated. The high price of oil did indeed deal a blow (it was called "oil shock") to many nations, helping to cause the worldwide recession of 1975. That recession, however, brought about a let-up in the expanding

[8] Reginald H. Green and Ann Seidman, *Unity or Poverty* (Baltimore: Penguin, 1968), p. 400.

demand for oil. Thus the high price of oil itself served to diminish the growth in the demand for oil, and in so doing, cut down some of the expected flow of dollars and European currencies into OPEC hands.

Second, the OPEC nations lost no time spending their oil dollars on ambitious development projects, or simply on higher imports. For OPEC countries as a whole, imports increased by a huge two-thirds, first in 1974 and then again in 1975. In fact, so great was the oil exporters' demand for Western goods, that within a short time many of the OPEC countries had turned from net dollar earners, to net spenders. All this, of course, also speeded the recycling of Western currencies.

Third, the high price of oil sparked an intensified search both for new oil sources and for oil substitutes. The vast Alaskan oil slope and the enormous Mexican oil fields have helped (or are expected in the future to relieve) pressure on OPEC oil sources. Meanwhile, there has been a slow but steady shift away from oil toward competitive fuels and toward energy-conserving technologies. All the major oil companies are now assuming that energy use will rise at a much slower rate than GNP during the 1980s; we have been forced to learn energy-saving ways.

the effect of OPEC   As a consequence of all these factors, the export surplus of the OPEC nations has fallen from $50 billion to about $20 billion in 1978 and it may fall further during the 1980s.[9] This is not to say that the OPEC cartel has had no effect. Energy prices are now permanently higher, slowing down economic growth in all nations. The effect of higher energy prices on many poor countries has brought a serious blow to their development plans—more serious than to the prospects for the rich countries.

Meanwhile, a number of nations has suddenly been given tremendous claims on the world's wealth. The oil sheikdoms of the Middle East are among these, but so are Nigeria, Venezuela, and Mexico, and even Norway (which is not a member of the OPEC cartel, but which benefits from OPEC-determined prices). Thus the effect of the cartel has been to bring about an unprecedented redistribution of wealth in the world, comparable perhaps to the discovery of gold in the New World. Some poor nations have become rich, but other poor nations have become even more poor.

the longer run   Will the cartel itself last, or will the producers fall out with one another, and begin to undercut prices? That has been the fate of cartels over much of history, and it may yet become the fate of the OPEC group, whose members have divergent short- and long-term objectives.

[9] See Bruce K. MacLaury, "OPEC's Billions," Brookings *Bulletin* Vol. 15, No. 2, Fall 1978. For an appraisal of OPEC's future see Charles Issawi, "The 1973 Oil Crisis and After," *Journal of Post-Keynesian Economics*, Winter, 1978–79.

We simply do not know what the short-term result will be. But it is well to recall from Chapter 9 that we are steadily increasing the global use of oil, and moving toward a level of demand that will exceed the quantities of oil that are now offered for sale at the cartel's price. When that "cross-over" point is reached, the price of oil will be pulled up by the demand of consumers, not propped up by the collective action of producers. Thus even if the cartel breaks, it is likely that oil prices will again rise by the late 1980s or early 1990s, once again directing dollars and other hard currencies into the hands of oil producers, many of which are underdeveloped countries.

other cartels?
What is more difficult to predict is whether other nations who produce raw materials will also succeed in concerting their economic strength to obtain the benefits of a monopoly price. In a world that may be pressing hard against its conventional sources of supply, this becomes a possibility to be reckoned with. Coffee, phosphate, bauxite, bananas, tin, and copper are among the commodities whose producers are openly eying the OPEC cartel with envy. If the OPEC pattern is in fact duplicated elsewhere, it would funnel large sums into other areas of the underdeveloped world.

But we cannot count on such dramatic changes. The chances are still great that the underdeveloped countries will continue to suffer from inadequate markets for their products, and will continue to feel aggrieved in their trade relations with the developed world. One major point of conflict lies in the difficulty experienced by the backward nations in developing *noncommodity* exports, such as handicrafts, light manufactures, and the like. The difficulty is that these exports may compete with the domestic industry of the advanced nations; witness the problems of the American textile industry in the face of textile shipments from Hong Kong. No doubt a large source of potential earnings lies along this path, but it is unlikely to rise rapidly as long as the advanced nations refuse to allow the backward countries equal access to their own markets.

limitations on private foreign investment
A second main avenue of capital accumulation for the backward nations is foreign investment. Indeed, before World War II, this was *the* source of their industrial wealth. Today, however, it is a much diminished avenue of assistance, for reasons we have learned in our exploration of the multinational corporation. The former capital-exporting nations are no longer eager to invest private funds in areas over which they have lost control and in which they fear to lose any new investments they might make. For reasons that we have discussed, many of the poorer nations view Western capitalism with ambivalence. They need capital, technology, and expertise; but the arrival of a branch of a powerful corporation run by faraway "head-

quarters" looks to them like another form of the domination they have just escaped. As a result, foreign investment is often hampered by restrictive legislation in the underdeveloped nations, even though it is badly needed. Consequently, not much more than $3 billion to $4 billion a year from all the advanced nations goes overseas as foreign investment into the under-developed world.

Another difficulty is that Western corporations partially offset the growth-producing effects of their investments by draining profits out of the country. In the period 1950–1965, for example, the flow of income remitted from Latin America to the United States was $11.3 billion, three times larger than the flow of new capital into Latin America. In 1975, income of $4.1 billion was transmitted to the United States, and only $1.9 billion was sent back to Latin America. This pattern of economic flows should not be mis-interpreted as implying that foreign investment is a "negative" influence; the plant and equipment that the West has sent abroad remains in the underdeveloped world, where it continues to enhance the productivity of labor, or perhaps to generate exports. But the *earnings* on this capital are not typically plowed back into still more capital goods, so that their poten-tial growth-producing effect is far from realized.

the avenue of foreign aid   These considerations enable us to understand the special importance that attaches to the third channel of capital accumulation: foreign aid. Surpris-ingly, perhaps, in the light of the attention it attracts, foreign aid is not a very large figure. International assistance, from *all* individual nations and from the UN and its agencies, ran at a rate of about $6 billion to $7 billion per year through the 1960s and rose to $14 billion only after the OPEC nations devoted considerable sums from their oil earnings to development purposes.

Even $14 billion is an insignificant contribution to the gross output of the noncommunist underdeveloped world. It is, however, a substantial fraction—perhaps as much as 15 percent—of the *gross investment* of South Asia or Africa. Thus, foreign aid makes possible the accumulation of indus-trial capital much faster than could be accomplished solely as a result of the backward lands' export efforts or their ability to attract foreign private capital.* To be sure, an increase in foreign earnings or in private capital imports would have equally powerful effects on growth. But we have seen the difficulties in the way of rapidly increasing the receipts from these sources. For the near future, foreign aid represents the most effective channel for *quickly* raising the amount of industrial capital that the under-developed nations must obtain.

* Note "makes possible." There is some disturbing evidence that foreign aid may displace domestic saving, so that an underdeveloped country receiving aid may relax its own efforts to generate capital. Much depends on the political will of the recipient country.

Foreign aid, particularly from UN sources, is also an extremely important source of *technical assistance* that enables the backward regions to overcome the handicaps imposed by their lack of skilled and trained personnel. For the near term, this may be even more important than the acquisition of the industrial capital itself in promoting growth.

economic possibilities for growth

Against these handicaps, can the underdeveloped nations grow? Can the terrible conditions of poverty be relegated to the past? Economic analysis allows us to ask these questions systematically, for growth depends on the interplay of three variables:

1. *Rate of investment that an underdeveloped nation can generate.*

As we know, this depends on the proportion of current effort that it can devote to capital-creating activity. In turn, the rate of saving, the success in attracting foreign capital, the volume of foreign aid—all add to this critical fraction of effort on which growth hinges.

2. *Productivity of the new capital.*

The saving that goes into new capital eventually results in higher output. But not all capital boosts output by an equal amount. A million-dollar steel mill, for example, will have an impact on GNP very different from that of a million-dollar investment in schools. In the short run, the mill may yield a higher return of output per unit of capital investment; in the long run, the school may have the edge. But in any event, the effect on output will depend not merely on the amount of investment, but on the marginal capital-to-output ratio of the particular form of investment chosen.

3. *Population growth.*

Here, as we know, is the negative factor. If growth is to be achieved, output must rise faster than population. Otherwise, per capita output will be falling or static, despite seemingly large rates of overall growth.

the critical balance

With these basic variables, is growth a possibility for the backward lands? We can see that if investment were 10 percent of GNP and if each dollar of new investment gave rise to a third of a dollar of additional output,* a 10 percent rate of capital formation would yield a 3.3 percent rate of growth (10 percent × one-third). This is about equal to population growth rates in the nations with the highest rates of population income.

---

* This seems to be *roughly* what the marginal capital–output ratio of new investment in the underdeveloped areas may be.

The trouble is that most of the backward nations (except the oil producers) have investment rates that are closer to 5 than to 10 percent of GNP. In that case, even with a marginal capital–output ratio of one-half, growth rates would not be enough to begin a sustained climb against a population growth of 2.5 percent (5 percent $\times \frac{1}{2} = 2.5$ percent). And this gloomy calculation is made gloomier still when we confront the fact that the labor force is rising faster than the population as a whole, as vast numbers of children become vast numbers of workers. In 1976 the International Labor Office estimated that 40 percent of the populations of Asia, Africa, and Latin America were either unemployed or underemployed— working less than a 40-hour week, or working at less than subsistence wages.

economic prospects: the Green Revolution

Nobody can confront these economic realities and make optimistic forecasts for the developing countries. Yet the situation is not hopeless. Commodity cartels, although bad for the industrial world, may speed the needed accumulation of capital in the non-industrial world. For many nations, an increase in their capital formation rates of 50 or 100 percent—a difficult but by no means impossible task, especially if they become beneficiaries of a resource squeeze—should bring them to the point of cumulative growth. What is then needed is a program of encouragement to small industry, to absorb the flood of unemployed while the essential industrial core is being built, and an all-out effort to bring about manageable rates of population growth. These are also difficult but, again, not impossible undertakings.

Meanwhile, a vitally important breakthrough has been scored on the agricultural front with the development of new crops that can literally double and triple yields. This so-called *Green Revolution*, in effect in parts of India, is a main hope in preventing the mass famine that haunts the food officials of the world as they look ahead to the 1980s. But the Green Revolution will require vast amounts of fertilizer, huge irrigation projects, and much administration. It is far from a simple "solution" to the development problem, but it may offer vital time for a critical effort to stop the juggernaut of population growth and to institute an all-out developmental effort.

social and political problems

Thus it is possible, not only in theory but in actuality, to foresee a long, slow developmental climb. But this is not the end of our analysis, for it is impossible to think of development only in terms of economics. As we have seen in the case of Western growth, *economic development is nothing less than the modernization of an entire society.* When we talk of building capital or redirecting agriculture, we must not imagine that this entails only the addition of machines and farm equipment to a peasant society. It entails the conversion of a peasant society into another kind of society. It means a change in the whole tenor of life, in the expectations and motivations, the environment of daily existence itself.

We have already noted some of the changes that economic development imposes on a society. Illiterate peasants must be made into literate farmers. Dispirited urban slumdwellers must be made into disciplined factory workers. Old and powerful social classes, which have for generations derived their wealth from feudal land tenure, must be deprived of their vested rights. New managerial attitudes must be implanted in new elites. Above all, the profligate generation of life, conceived in dark huts as the only solace available to a crushed humanity, must give way to a responsible and deliberate creation of children as the chosen heirs to a better future.

These changes will *in time* be facilitated by the realization of development itself. A growing industrial environment breeds industrial ways. The gradual realization of economic improvement brings about attitudes that will themselves accelerate economic growth. A slowly rising standard of living is likely to quicken the spread of birth control, as it did in the West.

All these changes, as we have said, may take place in time. But it is time itself that is so critically lacking. The changes must begin to take place now—today—so that the process of development can gain an initial momentum. Given the momentum of population growth, the transition from a backward, tradition-bound way of life to a modern and dynamic one cannot be allowed to mature at its own slow pace. Only an enormous effort can inaugurate, much less shorten, the transition from the past into the future.

collectivism and under-development

These sobering realities converge in one main direction. They alert us to the fact that *in the great transformation of the underveloped areas, the market mechanism is apt to play a much smaller role than in the comparable transformation of the West during the Industrial Revolution.*

We will recall how lengthy and arduous was the period of apprenticeship through which the West had to pass in order for the ideas and attitudes, the social institutions and legal prerequisites of the market system to be hammered out. When the Industrial Revolution came into being, it exploded within a historic situation in which market institutions, actions, customs had already become the dominant form of economic organization.

None of this is true in the underdeveloped nations today. Rather than having their transition to a market society behind them, many of these nations must leap overnight from essentially tradition-bound and archaic relationships to commercialized and industrialized ones. Many of them are not even fully monetized economies. None of them have the network of institutions—and behind that, the network of "economic" motivations—on which a market society is built.

Hence, it is not difficult to foresee that the guiding force of development is apt to be tilted in the direction of central planning. Regardless of the importance of private enterprise in carrying out the individual projects of development, the driving and organizing force of economic growth will have to be principally lodged with the government.

political
implications

But the outlook indicates more than a growth of economic command. Implicit also in the harsh demands of industrialization is the need for strong political leadership, not only to initiate and guide the course of development, but to *make it stick*. For it is not only wrong, but dangerously wrong, to picture economic development as a long, invigorating climb from achievement to achievement. On the contrary, it is better imagined as a gigantic social and political earthquake. Eugene Black, ex-president of the World Bank, has pointed out that we delude ourselves with buoyant phrases such as "the revolution of rising expectations" when we describe the process—rather than the prospect—of development.[10] To many of the people involved in the bewildering transformations of development, the revolution is apt to be marked by a loss of traditional expectations, by a new awareness of deprivation, a new experience of frustration. For decades, perhaps generations, a developing nation must plow back its surplus into the ugly and unenjoyable shapes of lathes and drills, conveyor belts and factory smokestacks. Some change toward betterment is not ruled out, particularly in health, basic diet, and education; but beyond this first great step, material improvement in everyday living will not—cannot—materialize quickly.

As a consequence, many of the policies and programs required for development, rather than being eagerly accepted by all levels of society, are apt to be resisted. Tax reform, land reform, the curtailment of luxury consumption are virtually certain to be opposed by the old order. In addition, as the long march begins, latent resentments of the poorer classes are likely to become mobilized; the underdog wakens to his lowly position. Even if his lot improves, he may well feel a new fury if his *relative* well-being is impaired.

social
stresses

These considerations enable us to understand how social tensions and economic standards can rise at the same time. And this prospect, in turn, enables us to appreciate the fearful demands on political leadership, which must provide impetus, inspiration, and, if necessary, discipline to keep the great ascent in motion. The strains of the early Industrial Revolution in England, with its widening chasm between the proletariat and capitalist, are not to be forgotten when we project the probable course of affairs in the developing nations.

In the politically immature and labile areas of the underdeveloped

---

[10] *The Diplomacy of Economic Development*, p. 9.

world, this exercise of leadership typically assumes the form of "strong-man" government. In large part, this is only the perpetuation of age-old tendencies in these areas; but in the special environment of development, a new source of encouragement for dictatorial government arises from the exigencies of the economic process itself. Powerful, even ruthless, government may be needed, not only to begin the development process, but to cope with the strains of a *successful* development program.

It is not surprising, then, that the political map reveals the presence of authoritarian governments in many developing nations today. The communist areas aside, we find more or less authoritarian rule in Egypt, Pakistan, Burma, South Korea, Indonesia, and the succession of South American junta governments. From country to country, the severity and ideological coloring of these governments varies. Yet in most of them we find that the problems of economic development provide a large rationale for the tightening of political control. At least in the arduous early stages of growth, some form of political command seems as integral to economic development as the accumulation of capital itself.

the ecological problem To this endless list of problems, one last one must now be added. It is the fact that the sheer resources of the earth may be insufficient, at least with our present technology, to make possible a "Western" standard of living for all the peoples of the world. Paul and Anne Ehrlich, of Stanford University, write:

> To raise all the 3.6 billion people of the world of 1970 to the American standard of living would require the extraction of almost 30-billion tons of iron, more than 500-million tons of copper and lead, more than 300-million tons of zinc, about 50-million tons of tin, as well as enormous quantities of other minerals. That means the extraction of some 75 times as much iron as is now extracted annually, 100 times as much copper, 200 times as much lead, 75 times as much zinc and 250 times as much tin. The needed iron is theoretically available, and might be extracted by tremendous efforts over long periods of time, but . . . needed quantities of the other materials far exceed *all* known or inferred reserves. Of course, to raise the standard of living of the projected world population of the year 2000 would require doubling all of the above figures.[11]

The solution to this problem reinforces the political argument above. For it is clear that the free play of market forces, *insofar as these are permitted to develop along the lines of traditional capitalism*, would lead rapidly to an ecological impasse. Instead, the development of the backward nations, once an initial momentum has been attained, will have to be planned to economize on materials and production to a degree unknown in the West. The absurd waste of resources involved in providing transporta-

11 *Population, Resources, Environment* (San Francisco: Freeman, 1970), pp. 61–62.

tion through the proliferation of private automobiles instead of public conveyances; the encouragement of individual ownership of washing machines and television sets and domestic conveniences—the very center of the Western ideal of a "high standard of living"—will be impossible to duplicate on a global scale.

What will be required in their place is a new pattern of *public consumption,* new ideals of stable rather than ever-rising standards of material achievement, perhaps even a wholly new conception of what is meant by an advanced society. All this will be required not as a matter of ideological preference, but as one of long-run necessity. The ecological barriers of resource availability and the absorption capacity of the earth thus pose truly staggering problems for the underdeveloped nations, once they manage to escape from the stagnation that still characterizes most of them. No one knows how these obdurate limitations of nature will be translated into the realities of social life, but it is doubtful that the relatively laissez-faire attitudes of Western capitalism will be adequate to the task.

12	*Key Concepts and Key Words*

Underdevelopment
1. *Underdevelopment* constitutes the economic environment for the vast majority of mankind. It is ascribable in part, perhaps, to bad climates or inadequate resources, but in the main it springs from the inability of traditional societies to mount sustained programs of investment and change.

Population explosion
2. The main attributes of underdevelopment are *very low levels of productivity,* especially in agriculture when man/land ratios often impose highly inefficient scales of production. No less important, and more difficult to correct, are deep-seated *attitudes of inertia* on the part of the population. And constituting a main obstacle to a development effort are very high rates of *population growth.* (Here, the new birth-control techniques now offer some hope for the future.)

Industrialization
3. The development effort requires a *shift from consumption* to *investment activity.* This necessitates a prior increase in agricultural productivity, accompanied by measures that will transfer the food surplus from the peasant cultivator to workers on capital projects. This is an exceedingly difficult task to carry out.

4. In addition to shifting resources from agriculture to capital-building tasks, a nucleus of *industrial equipment* must be brought in. This can be done by *international trade,* by *foreign investment,* or by *foreign aid.*

Imperialism and lopsided economies
5. The channel of international trade is a difficult one for many backward nations, as a consequence of *imperialism.* Many underdeveloped nations have "lopsided" *economies* that sell one raw commodity in markets where demand is

typically inelastic. The OPEC cartel has brought vast wealth to its members, but has imposed still new difficulties for poor nations that must import their oil. Meanwhile, foreign investment has not produced much capital for the backward nations, partly because of their own suspicions of Western nations, partly because the West has not reinvested its earnings there. *Foreign aid* thus becomes a small but crucial avenue for the transfer of funds and skills. It should be noted that skill is often essential to acquire before funds can be absorbed.

Foreign investment and foreign aid

Rate of investment

6. Development hinges on three economic variables: the *rate of investment*, the *capital—output ratio* (the size of additional output yielded by net investment), and the *rate of population growth*. With a 10 percent net investment rate and a one-third capital–output ratio, it should be possible to begin growth even against a 3 percent population increase.

Marginal capital–output ratio

7. The problem is that the economic effort is not detachable from the whole array of *social and political problems*. To mount a developmental program requires that many traditional institutions and ways be discarded for new and untried ones. This process of change occurred over several centuries in the West, but the exigencies of the population crisis make it necessary to compress it within a few generations today.

Ecological constraints

Cartels

8. Constraints imposed by resource limitations have a double effect. On the one hand, they make possible cartels that will amass capital for some underdeveloped nations. On the other hand, they impose ceilings on the material attainments open to the underdeveloped nations. At least in the long run, these nations will be forced to develop resource allocation patterns very different from ours. *Planned economies* are not a matter of choice, but necessity, for their futures.

---

12   *Questions*

1. In what ways do you think underdeveloped countries are different from the American colonies in the mid-1600s? Think of literacy, attitudes toward work and thrift, and other such factors. What about the relationship to more advanced nations in each case?

2. Why do you think it is so difficult to change social attitudes at the lowest levels of society? at the upper levels? Are there different reasons for social inertia at different stations in society?

3. Does the United States have a population problem? Will population growth here affect economic or social aspects of life more? Do you think we should adopt an American population-control policy? If so, what sort of policy?

4. Many economists have suggested that all advanced nations should give about

1 percent of their GNP for foreign aid. In the United States, that would mean a foreign-aid appropriation of $25 billion. Actually, we appropriate about $2 billion. Do you think it would be practicable to suggest a 1 percent levy? How would Americans feel about such a program?

5. What are the main variables in determining whether or not growth will be self-sustaining? If net investment were 8 percent of GNP and the capital–output ratio were 1:4, could a nation grow if its rate of population increase were 2.25 percent? What changes could initiate growth?

6. What do you think is the likelihood of the appearance of strong-arm governments and collectivist economies in the underdeveloped world? the appearance of effective democratic governments? capitalist economies? socialist ones? Is it possible to make predictions or judgments in these matters that do not accord with your personal preferences?

7. If you had to plan the 50-year development of a nation like India, and if you knew that it would be essential to economize on the production and consumption of minerals, how would you suggest that patterns of consumption be changed to effect major resource savings? To what extent would such changes impose further changes in the pattern of social life?

The Trajectory
of Economic Society

STAGES OF ECONOMIC DEVELOPMENT

Our journey through history has brought us into the present. It is time to take stock of the array of economic systems that marks our times.

It is, at first glance, an extraordinary assortment: We find, in this last quarter of the twentieth century, a spectrum of economic organization that represents virtually every stage in economic history from the earliest and most primitive. But at second look, a significant pattern can be seen within this seemingly disordered assemblage. The few remaining wholly traditional economies, such as those of New Guinea or tribal Africa, have not yet begun to move into the mainstream of economic development. A much larger group of underdeveloped nations, in which institutions of economic command are now rising amid a still traditional environment, have just commenced their development efforts and are now coping with the initial problems preparatory to eventual all-out industrialization. Going yet further along, we find the economies of iron command, such as China and, to a much lesser extent, Russia; here we find national communities that are (or recently were) wrestling with the gigantic task of rapid massive modernization. Finally, we pass to the market economies of the West, to encounter societies with their developmental days behind them, now concerned with the operation of high-consumption economic systems.*

The categorization suggests a very important general conclusion. *The economic structures of nations today bear an integral relation with their stage of economic development.* Acts of foreign intervention aside, the choice of command or market systems is not just the outcome of political considerations, or ideologies and preferences. It is also, and perhaps primarily, the result of functional requirements that are very different at different levels of economic achievement.

* A map on pp. 262–263 is keyed to these economic differences. Needless to say, the map gives no more than a subjective interpretation of the extent of Tradition, Command, and Market in the various countries of the world.

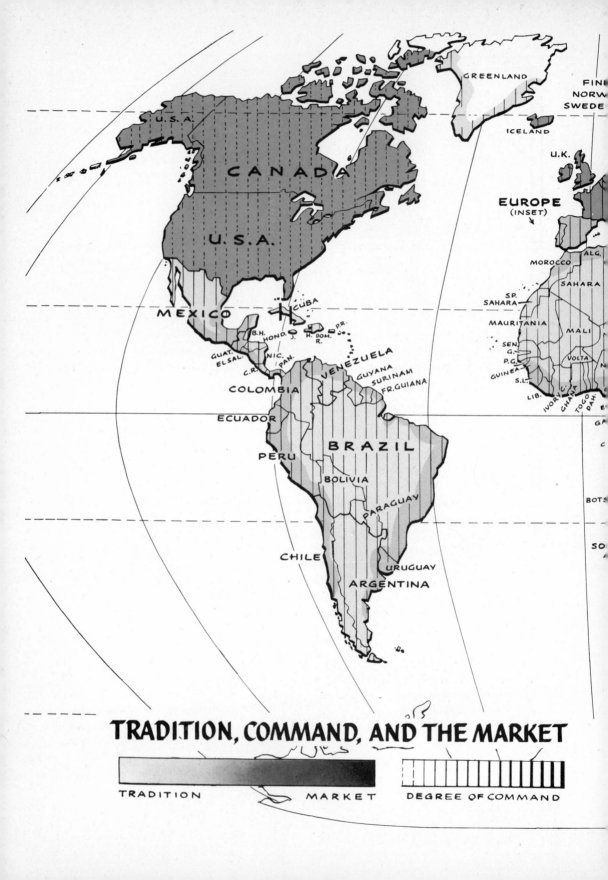

GREENLAND

FIN
NORW
SWEDE

ICELAND

U.S.A.

U.K.

CANADA

EUROPE
(INSET)

U.S.A.

ALG.

MOROCCO

SAHARA

SP.
SAHARA

MEXICO

CUBA

MAURITANIA

MALI

B.H.

HOND.

J.

P.R.

GUAT.

H.

DOM.

SEN.

ELSAL.

NIC.

R.

G.

VOLTA

C.R.

PAN.

VENEZUELA

P.G.

GUINEA

COLOMBIA

GUYANA

S.L.

SURINAM

LIB.

IVORY

GHANA

TOGO

DAH.

FR.GUIANA

ECUADOR

GA

BRAZIL

PERU

BOLIVIA

PARAGUAY

BOTS

CHILE

URUGUAY

SO

ARGENTINA

TRADITION, COMMAND, AND THE MARKET

TRADITION   MARKET   DEGREE OF COMMAND

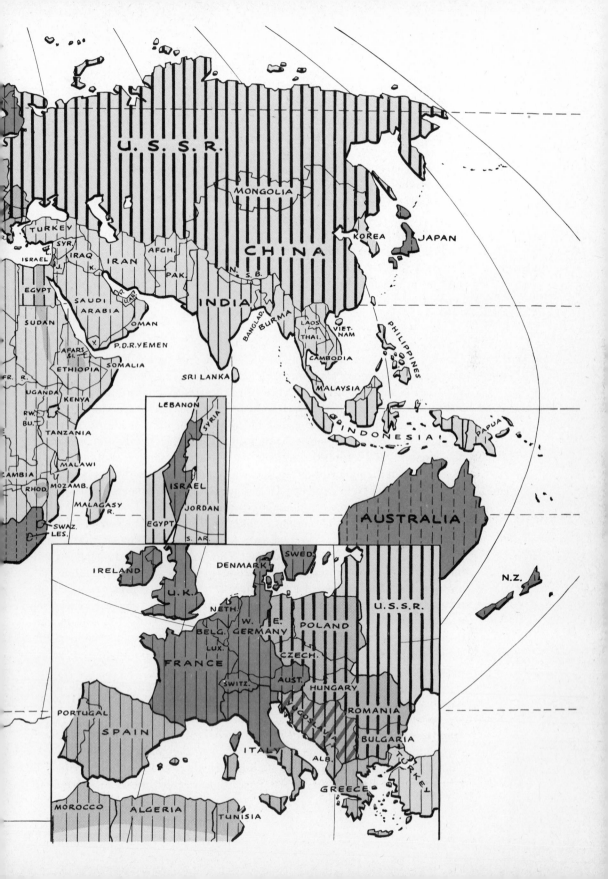

We have already noted this connection in our discussion of the under-developed areas. Now, however, we can place what we have learned into a wider frame of reference. For if we compare the trend of events in the underdeveloped economies with the "equivalent" stage of development in Western history, we see a significant point of resemblance between the two. The emergence of command in the development-minded countries today has a parallel in the mercantile era, when the Western nations also received a powerful impetus toward industrialization under the organizing influence of the "industry-minded" governments of that period.

Thereafter, to be sure, the resemblance ceases. In the West, following the first push of mercantilism, it was the market mechanism that provided the main directive force for growth; in the underdeveloped lands, as we have seen, this influence is likely to be preempted to a much larger extent by political and economic command.

Three main reasons lie behind this divergence of paths. First, *the under-developed areas today start from a lower level of preparedness* than did the West in the seventeenth and eighteenth centuries. Not only have the actual institutions of the market not yet appeared in many backward lands, but the whole process of acculturation has failed to duplicate that of the West. In many ways—not all of them economic—the West was "ready" for economic development, as Chapter 3 sought to make clear. A similar readiness is not in evidence in the majority of the backward lands today, with the result that development, far from evincing itself as a spontaneous process, comes about as the result of enforced and imposed change.

Second, *the West was able to mount its development effort in leisurely tempo.* This is not to say that its rate of growth was slow or that strong pressures did not weigh upon many Western countries, arousing within them feelings of dissatisfaction with their progress. Yet the situation was unlike that of the backward areas today. Here immense pressures, both of population growth and of political impatience, create an overwhelming need and desire for speed. As a result, the process of growth is not allowed to mature quietly in the background of history, as it did for much of the West, but has been placed at the very center of political and social attention.

Finally, the underdeveloped countries, which suffer from so many handicaps in comparison with the developmental days of the West, enjoy one not inconsiderable advantage. Because they are in the rear guard rather than the vanguard of history, they know where they are going. *In a manner denied to the West, they can see ahead of them the goal they seek to reach.* They do not wish to reach this goal, however, by retreading the painful and laborious path marked out by the West. Rather, they intend to shortcut it, to move directly to their destination by utilizing the mechanisms of command to bring about the great alterations that must be made.

Can economic command significantly compress and accelerate the growth process? The remarkable performance of the Soviet Union suggests that it can. In 1920, Russia was but a minor figure in the economic councils of the world. Today, it is a country whose economic achievements bear comparison with those of the United States. If Soviet production continues to gain on American production at the rate of the last ten years, in little more than another generation its total industrial output (although not its per capita output) will be larger than our own.

The case of China is less clear-cut. Until the famine disaster of 1959–1960, Chinese economic growth was double or triple that of India; since then, perhaps because of the convulsions of the Cultural Revolution, its record is less easy to appraise. It may possibly have grown less rapidly than India in *quantitative terms;* but by the reports of all observers, its *qualitative* improvements in health, education, and welfare are strikingly better than those of India.

It is no doubt wise not to exaggerate the advantages of a command system. If it holds the potential for an all-out attack on backwardness, it also contains the possibilities of substantial failure, as in the disappointments of the planned Cuban economy. The mere existence of a will to plan is no guarantee that the plans will be well drawn or well carried out or reasonably well obeyed. Nonetheless, these caveats must be set against the dismal record of economies that continue to wallow in the doldrums of tradition or that undertake the arduous transition into modernity under the inadequate stimulus of halfhearted regimes and half-formed market systems. In this regard, we should note that underdeveloped economies such as Taiwan or South Korea or Hong Kong, which have shown potent developmental thrusts and which have a pronounced capitalist, market flavor, also rely on strong government supports and guides for growth. They are combinations of command and market systems.

economies in mid-development Once the development process is well under way, however, the relative functional merits of the market and the command mechanisms begin to change. After planning has done its massive tasks—enforcing economic and social change, creating an industrial sector, rationalizing agriculture—another problem begins to assume ever more importance. This is the problem of efficiency, of dovetailing the innumerable productive efforts of society into a single coherent and smoothly functioning whole.

In the flush period of mid-development, the market mechanism easily outperforms the command apparatus as a means of carrying out this complex coordinating task. Every profit-seeking entrepreneur, every industrial salesman, every cost-conscious purchasing agent becomes in effect part of a gigantic and continuously alert planning system within the market economy. Command systems do not easily duplicate their efforts. Bottlenecks, unusable output, shortages, waste, and a cumbersome hierarchy of bureaucratic forms and officials typically interfere with the maximum efficiency of the planned economy in midgrowth.

plan vs. market What we see here is not just a passing problem, easily ironed out. One of the critical lessons of the twentieth century is that the word *planning* is exceedingly easy to pronounce and exceedingly difficult to execute. When targets are still relatively simple, and the priorities of action beyond dispute—as in the case of a nation wrenching itself from the stagnation of an ineffective regime—planning can produce miracles. But when the economy reaches a certain degree of complexity, in which the coordination of ten activities gives way to the coordination of ten thousand, innumerable problems arise, because *planned economies enjoy no "natural" congruence between private action and public necessity.*

Here is where the market comes into its own. In a market system, each firm must combine its factors of production with one eye on their relative costs and the other on their respective productivities, finally bringing about a mix in which each factor is used as effectively as possible, given its cost. Thus, in seeking only to maximize their own profits, the units in a market system inadvertently tend also to maximize the efficiency of the system as a whole.

Even more remarkable, one operating rule alone suffices to bring about this extraordinary conjunction of private aims and public goals. *That single rule is to maximize profits.* By concentrating on that one criterion of success, and not by trying to maximize output in physical terms or trying to live by a complicated book of regulations, entrepreneurs in a competitive environment do in fact bring the system to a peak of operating efficiency. In other words, *profits are not only a source of privileged income, but also an enormously versatile and useful "success indicator" for a system that is trying to squeeze as much output as possible from its given inputs.*

the invisible hand Furthermore, the market mechanism solves the economic problem *with a minimum of social and political controls.* Impelled by the drives inherent in a market society, the individual marketer fulfills his public economic function without constant attention from the authorities. In contradistinction to his counterpart in a centralized command society, who is often prodded, cajoled, or even threatened to act in ways that do not appeal to his self-interest, the classical marketer obeys the peremptory demands of the market as a voluntary exercise of his own economic "freedom."

Thus, it is not surprising that we find many of the motivating principles of the market being introduced into command societies. For as these societies settle into more or less established routines, they too can utilize the pressure of want and the pull of pecuniary desire to facilitate the fulfillment of their basic plans.

Economic freedom, as we know it in the West, is not yet a reality, or even an official objective, in any of these countries. The right to strike, for example, is not recognized, and nothing like the fluid, consumer-responsive market system is allowed to exert its unimpeded influence on the general direction of economic development. But the introduction of more and more discretion at the factory level argues strongly that the principles of the market society are apt to find their place in planned societies at an appropriate stage of economic development.

problems of high- consump- tion economies

Thus our survey of successive stages of development brings us to a consideration of Western economic society—that is, to the advanced economies that have progressed beyond the need for forced industrialization and now enter the stage of high consumption.

From our foregoing discussion, it is clear that the market mechanism finds its most natural application in this fortunate period of economic evolution. Insofar as the advanced Western societies have reached a stage in which the consumer is not only permitted but encouraged to impose his wants on the direction of economic activity, there is little doubt that the market mechanism fulfills the prevailing social purpose more effectively than any other.

1. *Public goods.*

Nonetheless, the market is not without its own grave problems, even in this regard. For one thing, *it is an inefficient instrument for provisioning societies—even rich societies—with those goods and services for which no "price tag" exists,* such as education or local government services or public-health facilities.

A market society "buys" such public goods by allocating a certain amount of taxes for these purposes. Its citizens, however, tend to regard these taxes as an exaction, in contrast with what they pay for the items they voluntarily buy. Typically, therefore, a market society underallocates resources to education, city government, public health, or recreation, since it has no means of "bidding" funds into these areas, in competition with the powerful means of bidding them into autos or clothes or personal insurance.

2. *Moral blindness.*

A second and perhaps even deeper-seated failing of the market system is its application of a strictly economic calculus to the satisfaction of human wants and needs. As we said before, the market is an assiduous servant of the wealthy, but an indifferent servant of the poor. Thus it presents us with the anomaly of a surplus of luxury housing existing side by side with a shortage of inexpensive housing, although the social need for the latter is incontestably greater than that for the former. Or it pours energy and resources into the multiplication of luxuries for which the wealthier classes offer a market, while allowing more basic needs of the poor to go unheeded and unmet.

3. Social costs.

Finally, these shortcomings are aggravated by *the inability of the market system to cope with certain social costs that the private sector thrusts on the public. Pollution, traffic congestion, and oil spills are familiar examples of such "externalities."* In one form or another, all indicate a central weakness of the market mechanism: *its inability to formulate effective stimuli or restraints other than those that arise from the marketplace itself.*

So long as the public need roughly coincides with the sum of the private interests to which the market automatically attends, this failing of the market system is a minor one. But in an advanced economic society, it tends to become ever more important. As primary wants become satisfied, the public aim turns toward stability and security, objectives not attainable without a degree of public control. As technological organization becomes more complex and massive, again a public need arises to contain the new agglomerations of economic power. So, too, as wealth increases, pressure for education, urban improvement, welfare, and the like comes to the fore, not only as an indication of the public conscience, but as a functioning requirement of a mature society. And finally, the public management of growth takes on increased political urgency as the ecological problems of industrial societies multiply.

We have already paid much attention to the rise of planning in the advanced market societies as a corrective force to deal with just such problems. Now we can go so far as to generalize the economic meaning of this trend. *Planning arises in the advanced market societies to offset their inherent goal-setting weaknesses, just as the market mechanism arises in advanced command societies to offset their inherent motivational weaknesses.* In other words, planning and market mechanisms, in those societies that have begun to enter the stage of high consumption, are not mutually incompatible. On the contrary, they powerfully supplement and support one another.

convergence of mechanisms What seems to impend at the moment, then, is a *convergence of economic mechanisms* for the more advanced societies. In the planned economies, the market is being introduced to facilitate the smoother achievement of established objectives, while in the market economies, a degree of planning is increasingly relied upon to give order, stability, and social direction to the outcome of private activity.

This does not imply that the two major systems today are about to become indistinguishable. The convergence of economic mechanisms may blur but not obliterate the basic distinctions between them. Nor does the convergence of mechanism in itself portend profound changes in the larger social structures of socialism and capitalism. A gradual rapprochement of the economic mechanisms should not lead us to hasty conclusions about the rebirth of "capitalism" in the Soviet Union or the advent of "socialism" in the United States. This is a matter into which we will look more deeply in our last chapter.

common problems   There is another way in which the phenomenon of convergence reveals itself, in addition to that of a coming together of economic mechanisms. *It is the appearance of similar problems in advanced industrial societies.* When we examine capitalism and socialism, we will pay special attention to the problems that separate and distinguish these two kinds of societies. Here it is important to realize that they are also bound together by certain common difficulties.

What is the nature of these overarching problems? As we would expect, they stem from the very technical capability and social organization that bring similar economic mechanisms into being. Three problems in particular seem of major importance:

1. *The control over technology.*

One of the most important attributes of modern history is lodged in a striking difference between two kinds of knowledge: the knowledge we acquire in physics, chemistry, engineering, and other sciences, and that which we gain in the sphere of social or political or moral activity. The difference is that knowledge in some sciences is cumulative and builds on itself, whereas knowledge in the social sphere does not. The merest beginner in biology soon knows more than the greatest biologists of a century ago. By way of contrast, the veteran student (or practitioner) of government, of social relations, of moral philosophy is aware of his modest stature in comparison with the great social and moral philosophers of the past.

The result is that all modern societies tend to find that their technological capabilities are constantly increasing, while the social and political and moral institutions by which those capabilities are controlled cannot match the challenges with which they are faced. Television, for example, is an immense force for cultural homogenization; medical technology changes the composition of society by altering its age groups and life expectancy; rapid transportation vastly increases mobility and social horizons; and the obliterative power of nuclear arms casts a pervasive anxiety over all of life. All these technologically rooted developments fundamentally alter the conditions and problems of life, but we do not know what social, political, and moral responses are appropriate to them. *As a result, all modern societies—socialistic and capitalistic—experience the feeling of being at the mercy of a technological and scientific impetus that shapes the lives of their citizens in ways that cannot be accurately foreseen or adequately controlled.*

2. *The problem of participation.*

The second problem derives from the first. Because advanced societies are characterized by high levels of technology, they are necessarily marked by a high degree of organization. The technology of our era depends on the cooperation of vast masses of men, some at the levels of production, some at the levels of administration. The common undergirding of all advanced industrial or "postindustrial" societies lies not alone in their gigantic instrumentalities of production, but in their equally essential and vast instrumentalities of administration, whether these be called corporations, production ministries, or government agencies.

The problem is then how the citizen is to find a place for his individuality in the midst of so much organization; how he is to express his voice in the direction of affairs, when so much bureaucratic management is inescapable; how he is to "participate" in a world whose technological structure calls for even more order and coordination. This is a matter that, like the sweeping imperative of technology, affects both capitalism and socialism. In both kinds of societies, individuals feel overwhelmed by the impersonality of the work process, impotent before the power of huge enterprises—above all, the state itself—and frustrated at an inability to participate in decisions that seem more and more beyond any possibility of personal influence.

No doubt, much can be done to increase the feeling of individual participation in the making of the future, especially in those nations that still deny elementary political freedoms. *But there remains a recalcitrant problem of how the quest for increased individual decision making and participation can be reconciled with the organizational demands imposed by the technology on which all advanced societies depend.* This is a problem that is likely to trouble societies—capitalist or socialist—as long as technology itself rests on integrated processes of production and requires centralized organs of administration and control.

3. *The problem of the environment.*

As we saw in Chapter 9, all industrial nations face an era in which exponential growth is beginning to absorb resources at rates faster than we may be able to provide them with new technologies; and all industrialized societies—indeed, the whole world—may soon be entering an era in which environmental limitations will impose a slowdown on rates of growth.

Moreover, we stand at a period in history when underdeveloped nations are belatedly making their own bid for a share in the rising output per capita that has until now mainly been confined to advanced nation-states.

In this period of long-run economic stringency, industrial socialist and capitalist nations again seem likely to share common problems—not alone in bringing about a controlled slowdown in output, but in achieving social harmony under conditions that no longer allow their citizens to look forward to ever-higher standards of material consumption. Here, too, similar social and political problems may override differences in economic institutions and ideologies.

convergence and history   In a larger sense, then, "convergence" brings us beyond economics to the common human adventure in which economic systems are only alternate routes conducting humanity toward much the same general direction and destination. Perhaps it is well that we end our survey of economic history with the recognition that the long trajectory of the market system does not bring us to a terminus of social history, but only to a state in which some kinds of problems—the pitifully simple problems of producing and distributing goods—begin to be solved, only to reveal vastly larger problems in the very technology and organization that prepared the means for solving them.

But those are problems for the future. Meanwhile, it is the present that absorbs us, for it is in the present that we have our personal encounter with history. And so we cannot end our study of economics until we have considered a question to which we have often glancingly referred but that we are only now ready to confront. This is the question of America today, and more specifically, of American capitalism today. What are its prospects, its portents?

| 13 | *Key Concepts and Key Words* |

Stages of development   1. The spectrum of economic systems in the world corresponds generally to their *stages of economic development.*

Mercantilism   2. The inception of growth seems to require a political stimulus. In the West, this was provided by *mercantilism*, after which the market took over the task of growth. The West was favored over the present underdeveloped areas by its ability to mount a *leisurely development*, and by its *vanguard position* vis-à-vis the rest of the world.

Command
economies

3. Today, *command economies* are attempting to push their societies off dead center and to initiate the process of growth. For these tasks, command seems a more appropriate system than the market.

Mid-
development

4. *Economies in mid-development,* such as the Soviet Union, are characterized by mixtures of command and market systems. Command is best suited for massive economic and social reallocations, but not for the problems of running a smoothly integrated high-output economy. Bureaucratic inefficiency, and the absence of a congruence between private interest and public requirement, introduce many difficulties into the planning mechanism. Here the market begins to achieve a new relevance.

High-
consumption
economies
Market and
goals

5. *High-consumption economies* are naturally suited to market guidance. However, these economies now suffer from the inability of the market to formulate public needs. *Thus, planning arises in market systems to offset their inherent goal-setting weaknesses, just as the market arises in command systems to offset their inherent motivational weaknesses.*

Convergence

6. Thus we see a *convergence of systems* in the more advanced nations. However, a convergence of economic systems does not mean that "capitalism" and "socialism" are becoming indistinguishable.

Cumulative vs.
noncumulative

Participation

Ecology

7. Convergence seems to mean, also, that all advanced industrial societies share certain overarching problems: (1) a noncumulative social or political or moral understanding trying to control the effects of a cumulative technology; (2) finding a place for the individual who wants to participate in a system that demands large-scale, coordinated processes of production and administration; and (3) coping with the problems of a threatened environment. These problems manifest themselves differently in capitalism and socialism, but in neither does a solution seem to be in sight.

---

13   *Questions*

1. How do you account for the simultaneous existence in the world of such radically different economic systems?

2. In what ways was the early growth experience of the West unlike the present growth prospects of the backward world? Do you think these differences will have a substantial effect on the choice of economic systems for the underdeveloped countries?

3. Discuss the difference in social goals and priorities between a nation that is just beginning its development and one in mid-development; between one in mid-development and one at a stage of high mass consumption. What is the relevance of planning techniques for each of these stages of development? Would you expect the techniques of planning to be similar in all stages? What differences would you look for?

4. What is meant by the congruence of self-interest and public requirement in a market system? How can this congruence be reconciled with the fact that the market has no means of establishing public priorities?

5. What are the advantages of the market system for economic freedom? Do you think the market system is also productive of political freedom? Draw a scatter diagram showing on one axis the degree of planning and on the other axis your estimate of relative political freedoms for the following nations: Sweden, England, the United States, France, South Africa. Is there much, if any, relationship between the two variables?

6. Do you think there can be a convergence of economic systems without a convergence of social and political systems?

7. What specific technological processes seem to defy social control? How about the effect of television? urbanization? the arms race? Can you think of others?

8. Why do you think that knowledge accumulates more easily in science than it does in the areas of morality or politics or social activities?

9. Do you think that bureaucracy is an avoidable aspect of industrial society? If so, how? If not, what problems does it pose?

14   Is Capitalism the Problem?

We have reached the final stage in our inquiry; and now, as in our introductory pages, let me again speak in the first person, because what I have to say should not be given the authority that, rightly or wrongly, seems to adhere to statements made in the impersonal third person of textbook prose. What follows is no more than the fruit of personal reflection, offered not to settle matters, but only to make explicit my own convictions and to give student and instructor an opportunity to discuss the most important social issue with which economics is ultimately concerned. As the title of this chapter indicates, the ultimate problem is capitalism itself, and the extent to which it must be held responsible for the troubles of our country.

what is capitalism? We had better begin with definitions. If we are now to ask whether America's troubles are due to capitalism, we should know what we mean by that crucial word.

It is surprisingly difficult to find a succinct definition of capitalism.[1] But I think that all shades of opinion, from right to left, would agree that its essential characteristics are these:

1. *The legal right to private ownership of the forces of production.*

Under capitalism, the productive forces of society are all owned privately, and owners are entitled to withhold the services of these forces unless they are adequately paid. This applies not only to capitalists, who own society's capital equipment, and to landlords who own its land, but to workers who own their own skills and energy. (Recall that a slave does not have the right to *sell* his labor power.) This is what is really meant by "pri-

---

[1] One of the few clear-cut definitions is in Max Weber's *General Economic History* (New York: The Free Press, 1950), Chapters 22 and 30. The Marxian definition is more diffuse, referring at different times to an *economic system,* to the *bourgeois society* built on that system, and occasionally to a *stage of Western civilization*. See George Lichtheim, *Marxism* (New York: Praeger, 1961), p. 164, note 4.

vate property." It is not just ordinary goods and services that are privately owned under capitalism, but *productive property*. Legally, the ownership of labor by a worker places the working person on exactly the same footing as the ownership of a factory by a capitalist. In fact, of course, the capital ownership relation becomes the crucial one for the dynamic momentum of the system, for capitalists use their ownership to guide production toward profit.

2. The market determination of distribution.

Capitalism relies primarily on the market system, not only to allocate its resources among various uses, but also to establish the levels of income (such as wages, rents, profits) of different social classes.

what is socialism? What is the corresponding definition of socialism? As we might expect, it is something of a mirror image of capitalism. "In its primary usage," writes Paul M. Sweezy, a leading socialist theoretician, "the term 'socialism' means a social system which is differentiated from other social systems by the character of its property relations. . . . Capitalism recognizes a relatively unrestricted right of private ownership in the means of production, while socialism denies this right and reserves such ownership to public bodies." [2]

Thus, Sweezy, like most socialists, makes the crucial distinction between capitalism and socialism the question of *property ownership*. We should note that he stresses the private ownership of capital (and land), but not the private ownership of labor. It is the latter, of course, that provides the legal basis for the right to strike in a capitalist society, and that may undermine it in a socialist one. Most socialists would also add that socialism, unlike capitalism, depends primarily on *planning*, rather than on the market, both for its overall allocation of resources and for its distribution of income.

ideal types vs. real cases These definitions are what the sociologist Max Weber called "ideal types." They are meant to summarize and abstract out of the enormous variety of actual institutions and historical experiences those essential elements that make up a pure model of the institution or activity in which we are interested. We dealt with such an ideal type when we studied the operation of a "market" under pure competition, knowing full well that no market was in fact ever free of all imperfections. In the same fashion, the emphasis on public vs. private property, and on market vs. planned distribution, serves to sharpen our conception of the irreducible elements of capitalism and socialism that are to be discovered behind their many variations in actual history.

[2] Paul M. Sweezy, *Socialism* (New York: McGraw-Hill, 1948), p. 3.

But no sooner do we create these ideal types than we find ourselves in something of a quandary. For the question then arises as to what practical function these models of capitalism and socialism serve. For example, if one asks a dedicated humanitarian socialist if "socialism" is better than "capitalism," he will unhesitatingly tell you that it is, basing his reply on the superiority of public over private ownership and on the preference to be accorded to planning over the market. But the same humanitarian socialist recoils in horror at the repressiveness of Russia and looks with approval on the humaneness of (capitalist) Denmark. How does he reconcile this contradiction? By telling you that Russia is not "really" socialist, but only a grim travesty of socialism; and that Denmark is not "really" capitalist but a modified socialist version of capitalism. Yet, unquestionably, the Soviet Union has public ownership of productive property and a thoroughgoing system of planning, and Denmark has private ownership of productive property and a general market determination of incomes and outputs.

The point of this disconcerting confrontation is clear. It is that the elements that all agree are decisive in defining capitalism and socialism as "ideal types" do not tell us very much about the societies that display those characteristic elements. As a matter of fact, thinking about the differences among capitalist nations—compare Sweden and the Union of South Africa —or among socialist countries—contrast Russia and China—we begin to wonder if the words *capitalism* and *socialism* mean anything at all.

capitalism and socialism as economic systems

I think the answer is that the terms *do* mean something, although perhaps less than we often assume. As we shall see, there are crucial areas of life to which they add little if any understanding. But there are other areas where they add a good deal, and it is to these that we now direct our attention.

The first such area should be obvious. It is that of economics proper. *Capitalism and socialism as ideal types identify for us a series of economic problems that we find among all members of each type.*

What are these problems? For capitalism, the answer lies in a series of problems with which much of formal economics is concerned: instability evidenced by recessions or inflations, misallocation of resources, and inequality of incomes. For these are results of the economic process in *every* society in which there is private ownership of property and a market determination of prices. Whether we look to Japan or Sweden, the Union of South Africa or the United States, we see similar tendencies toward too much or too little growth, inflation or unemployment, a struggle between the private and the public sector, and a highly uneven division of incomes between the property-owning and the working classes. These are problems as specific to capitalism as the problems of guild life were specific to feudalism.

Can we apply the same general finding to socialism? Ta certain extent, our comparison is muddied by the fact that so many socialist systems are still in (or only very recently out of) a period of forced economic growth. Hence, we do not really have "mature" socialisms to compare with mature capitalisms.

Nonetheless, there seems to be a set of common economic problems that is built into socialism in much the same fashion as the problems that are intrinsically part of the capitalist mechanism. As we would expect, these are problems of public ownership and planning—in particular, the problem of controlling unwieldy state bureaucracies and avoiding inefficient production and distribution directives. Indeed, one of the most brilliant socialist economic theoreticians, the late Oskar Lange, wrote presciently in 1938, *"The real danger of socialism is that of the bureaucratization of economic life. . . ."* [3]

capitalism and socialism as political systems

We shall return to a consideration of what these deep-rooted problems imply for capitalism and socialism.[*] But first let us ask if we find a parallel to the economic attributes of the two systems in their political characteristics. Some eminent political economists, Milton Friedman prominent among them, believe that we do. Friedman believes that the *existence of a market mechanism separate from the state provides the necessary basis for a free political life.* He does not insist that every capitalist society is therefore a free one—indeed, he specifically singles out Fascist Italy and Nazi Germany and Spain and Tsarist Russia as societies in which capitalist economic structures did *not* provide political freedom. But he is firm in his conviction that the existence of capitalism is a *necessary,* even if not a sufficient, condition for political freedom.

Friedman spells out his argument forcefully:

One feature of a free society is surely the freedom of individuals to advocate and propagandize openly for a radical change in the structure of society. . . . It is a mark of the political freedom of a capitalist society that men can openly advocate and work for socialism. . . . How could the freedom to advocate capitalism be preserved and protected in a socialist society?

In order for men to advocate anything, they must in the first place be able to earn a living. This already raises a problem in a socialist society, since all jobs are under the direct control of political authorities. It would take an act of self-denial whose difficulty is underlined by experience in the United States after World War II with the problem of "security" among Federal employees, for a socialist government to permit its employees to advocate policies directly contrary to official doctrine.

[3] Oskar Lange and Fred M. Taylor, *On the Economic Theory of Socialism* (New York: McGraw-Hill, 1956), p. 109.

[*] It is equally obvious that the phenomenon of convergence in the economic mechanisms of the two systems tends to bring the problems of one system into the other.

But let us suppose this act of self-denial to be achieved. For advocacy of capitalism to mean anything, the proponents must be able to finance their cause—to hold public meetings, publish pamphlets, buy radio time, issue newspapers and magazines and so on. How could they raise the funds?[4]

Does Friedman's logic establish a second fundamental dividing line between capitalism and socialism? It may. There *is* a certain refuge for the dissident individual in the free-for-all of the market that may be missing in socialism for the very reasons that Friedman suggests. Indeed, as M. A. Adelman has written, one main objection to socialist society is that it too much resembles the company town under capitalism, in which one employer has power over everyone within his jurisdiction.[5]

Yet I do not think that the issue has the clarity of the economic differences between capitalist and socialist societies. Certainly it weakens Friedman's position that among capitalist societies—that is, in the spectrum of systems relying on private property and the market system—*there seems to be no correlation whatsoever between the degree of political freedom and the use of "socialistic" limitations of property rights or the market mechanism.* Indeed, the most "socialistic" capitalisms, such as the Scandinavian bloc, England, and New Zealand, are probably the world's freest political societies.

Second, it should be pointed out that in the provision of a *guaranteed income* to all citizens, there is available a protection against the very kind of political vulnerability Friedman warns us about. As we have seen, the United States seems to be moving slowly toward such a system, and there is no reason why a socialist system could not adopt one very easily. A guaranteed income under socialism would free the dissident citizen from political pressure, just as private employment offers him this freedom under capitalism.

To be sure, such a system also requires that a socialist state value political liberty so highly that it would not cut off the income of an agitator for capitalism. Certainly, no socialist state today displays any such easy tolerance—just as very few capitalist states allow complete liberty for agitators against capitalism. In all societies, there is a natural defensive reaction against hostile ideas, and there is no reason to suppose that socialist authorities will be more tolerant of dissent than are capitalist ones. Indeed, in the present stage of historical development, it is doubtful that socialist governments in general can be expected to be as politically tolerant as capitalist ones, partly because many socialist economies are in the throes of forced growth, and partly because most socialist governments feel insecure in a world in which capitalist power is still dominant.

[4] *Capitalism and Freedom,* pp. 10, 16–18.
[5] Cited in *The Business Establishment,* ed. Earl Cheit (New York: Wiley, 1964), p. 217, note 17.

Whether socialism will continue to be less politically free than the most liberal capitalism is a question about which little can be said at present. As we have seen, it is possible to guard against the company-town aspect of socialism by means of a guaranteed income. But that is not to say that even a wealthy and self-assured socialist society will *wish* to put political liberty, with all its risks, high on its agenda.

values and life-styles under capitalism and socialism   This complex relationship between economic structures and political liberty brings us deeper into the question of how "capitalism" as an ideal type differs from "socialism." Specifically, it leads to the question of whether we can discover a basis for *social* difference between the two systems—differences in values or life-styles that might find their origins in the economic systems characteristic of each.

At first glimpse, there seems no relationship whatsoever between the two. Indeed, if we were to compare "socialist" Yugoslavia with "capitalist" Italy, we would probably find many *more* similarities of social tone, cultural life, and general atmosphere than if we compared "socialist" Yugoslavia with "socialist" China. And in the same way, "capitalist" West Germany probably more closely resembles "socialist" East Germany in general life-style than it does "capitalist" Australia. *National* differences in culture and tradition seem so overwhelmingly important that any common social traits traceable to capitalism or socialism recede far into the background, if indeed they are discoverable at all.*

This emphasis on national differences is, I believe, of the greatest importance, and we will return to it in full measure when we inquire further into the problems of American capitalism. Yet at this stage of our inquiry, while we are still seeking to divide all capitalisms from all socialisms, perhaps one distinctive element should be noted. It is the presence within all socialist countries of an ideal not to be found in any capitalist country. This is the ideal of Socialist Man—of man transformed from the competitive, acquisitive being that he is (and that he is *encouraged* to be) under all property-dominated, market-oriented systems, into the cooperative human being who finds fulfillment in unselfishness and who presumably can develop only in the benign environment of a propertyless, nonmarket social system.

It need hardly be said that this ideal of Socialist Man remains an

---

* Merely as one indication of this diversity, let us look into the much discussed matter of suicide rates. Does "welfare capitalism" bring a high suicide rate, as President Eisenhower once suggested? The evidence does not show it. Suicides per 100,000 population are higher (18.5 per 100,000) in Sweden than in the U.S. (10.4 per 100,000), but they are higher here than in Norway (7.9) or the Netherlands (6.6 per 100,000). Denmark, on the other hand, has an even higher rate—20.3 per 100,000—but it suffered from this rate *before* it became a welfare state. See Alan Gruchy, *Comparative Economic Systems* (Boston: Houghton Mifflin, 1966), p. 436.

unrealized goal in any socialist society, and may perhaps even be an un-realizable goal, comparable to the ideal of a truly religious community vainly pursued by centuries of Christianity. Yet, however distant, however vulgar-ized in practice, however abused as a mere slogan for social manipulation, the conception of Socialist Man provides a spiritual basis for an ideology that is powerfully persuasive. Capitalist nations may be efficient, humane, democratic, permissive, creative, but they do not have a "vision" built on the elements of property ownership and the market—a vision comparable to that which is founded on the ideal of common ownership and sharing.

This absence of a capitalist ideal may strike some as a fact little to be regretted, in view of the human suffering that so many official ideals have brought in the past. But if we suspend our judgments and merely ask whether there is an ultimate difference between the worlds of socialist and capitalist values and goals, I think the answer must be "Yes," that socialism has a sense of high human mission—perhaps even redemption—that cap-italism, even at its best, cannot quite match.*

*problems
and
solutions*

Our discussion suggests that the ideal types of "capitalism" and "socialism" *are* useful because they indicate different kinds of problems that the two systems tend to generate. But we have not yet inquired into an extremely important question that our findings pose. Granted that capitalism and socialism have common problems, *does this mean that they all find similar solutions to these problems?*

To ask the question is to answer it. Obviously, different capitalisms respond to their economic and social and political problems in very different ways, as do different socialisms. Take capitalism as an example. Two well-known Marxist critics of capitalism have written that genuine planning or resolute action to provide housing would be impossible in America because "such planning and such action . . . will never be undertaken by a govern-ment run by and for the rich, as every capitalist government is and must be." [6] They have obviously concentrated on the lack of an effective social sector in the United States, and overlooked the planning and housing un-dertaken by Norway, Sweden, Denmark, New Zealand, the Netherlands, and other governments presumably run by and for the rich, since they are

---

* I think we should also face the other side of the coin. The very moral commitment implicit in a desire to create Socialist Man may ill accord with the attitude of tolerance required for political liberty. Tolerance is partly an expression of a lofty ideal. It may also be, at least in part, the expression of an indifference to the risk of "immoral" ideas. Bourgeois societies, I suspect, feel less defensive about their beliefs (and therefore more easygoing in permitting dissent) simply because capitalism is a system justified mainly by expediency and success, not by appeal to a semi-religious vision.

[6] Paul Sweezy and Paul Baran, *Monopoly Capital* (New York: Monthly Review Press, 1966), p. 300.

certainly countries in which private ownership of the means of production prevails.

In the same way, because all capitalist systems do suffer from macro-instabilities, it does not follow that all therefore suffer from the same degree of unemployment. As we have previously seen, during the 1960s when unemployment here and in Canada reached levels over 5 percent, in West Germany unemployment never rose over 1 percent of the labor force, and in New Zealand it was considerably less than that.

This same variety of responses can be found in socialist economies. Oskar Lange's diagnosis of bureaucracy has proved all too true within all socialisms, but some have responded with a reliance on market socialism (Yugoslavia or pre-invasion Czechoslovakia); others, with efforts to solve the problem with better computer planning (USSR); and still others, with a search for "moral incentives" (Cuba or Mao's China).

THE OUTLOOK FOR AMERICAN CAPITALISM

All this has an obvious relevance to the central issue with which we began this chapter. For we can see now that whereas many of the problems that beset America undoubtedly have their roots in our capitalist institutions, the fact that we have coped with them so inadequately is not a matter that can be blamed on capitalism as such.

Take, for example, the question of social neglect that is so dismaying an aspect of American life. If we compare the United States with, say, Norway in terms of various indicators of social well-being, there is no doubt that we show up poorly. Infant mortality in the United States is a full 50 percent higher than it is in Norway. Norway spends a higher proportion of its GNP on education than we do, even though Norway has a much smaller per capita GNP. Norway has more hospital beds per thousand population than we do. It allocates a larger proportion of its GNP to social-security expenditures than does the United States. Its cities are essentially free of all slums. Although Norwegian citizens have a much lower GNP than American citizens, "poverty" as a relative condition—or poverty as a human condition of neglect by society—has been virtually eliminated there.

If we are willing to grant on the basis of these and other indicators that Norway has a record of social welfare superior to that of the United States, we would expect large differences in the economic structures of the two countries; for instance, in their income distributions. Yet, as Table 14–1 shows, there are not!

What the table shows is that the pre-tax distribution of income—that is, the relative shares of rich and poor as determined by the market mechanism—is much the same in both nations. But this surprising result is totally altered if we now take into account the distribution of income *after* taxes and subsidies. In contrast to the generally nonprogressive structure of

TABLE 14·1

PRE-TAX
INCOME
DISTRIBU-
TION:
UNITED
STATES
AND
NORWAY

	Percentage of income going to percentile groups, recent years *	
	Norway	U.S.
Lowest 20%	4.5	5.4
Second 20%	12.1	11.8
Third 20%	18.5	17.6
Fourth 20%	24.4	24.1
Top 20%	41.5	41.1

* Norway, 1963; U.S. 1976: latest available figures. Note that the years are not identical, but in view of the extreme slowness of movements in income distribution, this is not a serious consideration.

US taxes, the Norwegian tax structure is one of the most progressive in the world, and this progressive tax incidence is further emphasized by a system of subsidies to low-income groups, which greatly lightens their net tax burden. The point is clear: *The original capitalist dispositions of the marketplace do not leave an irretrievable mark on their societies, but can be radically modified by taxes and transfers.*[7]

capitalism, or American capitalism?

All this has a sobering, as well as an encouraging, implication. It is that much of what troubles America seems to be related to factors that, however much exacerbated by our economic system, cannot be uniquely attributed to capitalism as such. The low level of social services in America, the enormous role played by the military, the "rat-race" tempo of American life, the extent of our slums, the callous treatment of criminals, and many other unlovely aspects of our social system are not predominant in many other *capitalist* systems.

The problem, in other words, resides in those elements of our society that are *American* than in those that are capitalist. To put it differently, the significant question for us is to understand why capitalism here has not achieved the possibilities realized by capitalism elsewhere, rather than to compare the deficiencies of life in America with the presumed advantages that "socialism" might bring. For unless we understand and correct the failures of American capitalism, the likelihood is that a change of economic systems in this country would produce only an American socialism that would manifest many of the very same failings.

Can we identify the elements in America that have brought about the failure of capitalism here to match the social achievements of similar sys-

[7] See Gruchy, *Comparative Economic Systems*, p. 338. See also his discussion of Swedish tax incidence, p. 402.

tems abroad? Here we move from the reasonably firm grounds of empirical evidence to the quicksand regions of social conjecture. There are, perhaps, no "right" or "wrong" answers to this crucial question—only answers that are more or less useful in helping us think about an immensely complex and elusive problem. But with all the difficulties, let me try to suggest some possible explanations for the failures of our system.

two hypotheses that fail: size and homo- geneity

We might start by asking what the most striking difference is between the United States and the more socially responsive capitalisms we have referred to. One such difference that immediately suggests itself is sheer *size*. Is the greater social neglect of American capitalism simply the result of the scale of our continental country? Are we too big to create a genuine sense of community?

It is certainly plausible that a large country, with its variations in regions and interests, is less apt to feel a sense of shared responsibility than a small one. And yet, at best, the explanation of size can be only a partial one. Canada, which is geographically larger than the United States, has a considerably more highly developed social-welfare program and "point of view" than we do. Australia is another example of a large, regionally variegated nation with a high level of social services. Perhaps more to the point, our density of population (which is the way that "size" becomes translated into human experience) is 25 percent *greater* than Sweden and double that of New Zealand, so that our continental expanse does not physically separate man from man to a degree that might explain the lack of our "communal feelings."

A second hypothesis seems more convincing. It would explain the failures of American capitalism by the extreme diversity of our population —the many ethnic and cultural groups that have obstructed the formation of a socially minded single community, comparable to the Danes or the Swedes.

Yet this hypothesis also loses some of its persuasiveness under scrutiny. Switzerland, for example, has three different language and nationality groups and yet maintains a very high level of communal concern. Canada, despite the political friction of its French- and English-speaking regions, has a well-developed social-welfare system. Perhaps even more telling is a great deal of social neglect in certain areas of the United States where there *are* strong ethnic, regional, and racial bonds—the rich whites of Appalachia have paid little attention to the decline of their poor white kinsmen.

the race problem

Yet, if our social heterogeneity does not provide a fully adequate reason for our inadequate social performance, it does point in one direction that sharply differentiates American capitalism from capitalism in other nations.*

---

* With the exception of the Union of South Africa, which significantly also displays many of the same symptoms of social neglect that we do—and for the same reasons.

This is the fact that America is burdened with a *race problem* that is closely entwined with many areas of its laggard social performance.

There is no need at this point to cite the statistics of Negro poverty and neglect. Instead, it is necessary to link our deep-seated prejudice against the Negro with our national disregard of the (largely black) slums, our national neglect of the prisons (disproportionately filled with blacks), the low level of welfare provision (roughly half of which goes to Negroes). To a substantial degree, this burden of race prejudice also falls on Hispanics and American Indians. To put it bluntly, one very likely reason for the continued failure of American society to clean up its ghettos, improve its prisons, and liberalize antipoverty programs is the unwillingness of many white Americans to allow their hardearned dollars to be taxed and spent in ways that will tend to benefit dark Americans more than light ones.

the tradition of democratic individualism   The race issue, so central a part of our history, reaches deep into the core of American social neglect, but it does not account for every aspect of our problems. Racism does not explain our reluctance to deal generously with white poverty through higher Social Security levels, nor our militarism, nor our failure to cope effectively with the deterioration of the environment. To what special factors in American experience might we attribute these weaknesses of American capitalism?

The first answer I will suggest may be a surprising one. It is America's tradition of *democratic individualism*—a tradition born and nurtured on our frontiers, and perpetuated in the image of the town meeting as the ideal, democratic mode of government.

This is surely an odd suggestion, in that it is precisely this tradition that is one of the proudest claims of American society—indeed, the genuinely democratic quality of American life continues to impress visitors even from the most socially advanced European nations.

Yet, there is a price to be paid for this heritage. It is the lack of a tradition of strong central government and *noblesse oblige*, the duty of the benevolet ruler to provide for his less fortunate subjects. Both these traditions are woven into the cultural traditions of most European nations and have helped them create *welfare* capitalisms.

Alexis de Tocqueville, the great nineteenth-century French sociologist, wrote perceptively about the difference in traditions when he visited America in the 1830s:

Aristocracy [he wrote] links everybody, from peasant to king, in one long chain. Democracy breaks the chain and frees each link. As social equality spreads, there are more and more people who, though neither rich nor powerful enough to have much hold over others, have gained or kept enough wealth and enough understanding to look after their own needs. Such folk owe no man anything and hardly expect anything from anybody. They form the habit of thinking of themselves in isolation and imagining that their whole destiny is in their own hands. Thus, not only does democracy make men forget their ancestors, it also clouds their view of their descendants, and isolates them from their contemporaries. Each man is forever thrown back on himself alone, and there is a danger that he may be shut up in the solitude of his heart.[8]

This is not to claim that European aristocracies were in fact more solicitous of their peoples in the nineteenth century than was democratic America. On the contrary, as the direction of immigration showed, quite the opposite was the case. Nonetheless, with eloquence and perception, Tocqueville points to a deep difference between democratically based and aristocratically based social systems. It is the presence, within the older governments of Europe, of a *legitimacy of authority* that, in the changed conditions of the twentieth century, made possible a much more vigorous and direct governmental attack on social problems than was possible in the American democratic-individualist environment.

But it is not only our tradition of small-scale local government that has handicapped us in dealing with large-scale, national problems. What Tocqueville alerts us to is an inhibition in the *feeling of social responsibility* of a democratic society, compared with one of more aristocratic lineage. This suggests that one of the reasons that Americans have not developed an effective attack on social problems is that there is no popular support for the idea that government should help the needy. The result has not only been an anaesthetizing of the American social conscience, but a paralysis of the mechanism by which that conscience might have been best expressed.*

lack of a social democratic heritage

To this possibly heretical suggestion, let me now add a second, which applies to America at the other end of the sociopolitical scale. It is that American capitalism, unlike its European counterparts, never developed much of a tradition of *democratic socialism as a reformist force.*

Many observers have commented on the failure of the socialist ideal to implant itself in America, a failure due in part to our economic success and in part to our political (if not economic) stress on equality, at least for whites. "On reefs of roast beef and apple pie," as the economic historian

---

[8] Alexis de Tocqueville, *Democracy in America* (New York: Harper, 1966), p. 478.

* Sociologist Seymour Martin Lipset gives a telling illustration of the difference in national attitude between our highly individualist tradition and that of a more aristocratic society. Both the United States and Canada have created national folk heros connected with the frontier that was so important for both societies. How suggestive that America should have chosen the free-wheeling cowboy and that Canada should have picked the scarlet-clad Canadian mounted police, representative of central authority and law and order! See Lipset, *The First New Nation* (New York: Basic Books, 1963), p. 251.

Werner Sombart put it, "socialistic utopias of every sort [were] sent to their doom." [9]

It has been customary for Americans to congratulate themselves on the absence of a native socialist movement, for socialism has certainly brought sharp conflicts and severe social tensions within many nations. Yet it has also brought an impetus for social change and a widened agenda for discussion that has been missing from America. In Sweden, Norway, Denmark, England, the Netherlands, New Zealand—and in short, virtually everywhere that capitalism has achieved a high level of social welfare—the driving force for change has been a democratic socialist party, pushing against the limits of conservative capitalism. In America, with the important exception of the early New Deal, no such "socialistic" enlargement of the conception of what a society might achieve has ever significantly enlarged the conception of what "capitalism" meant. Hence, measures such as the nationalization of industry where that might be useful, or the massive redistribution of income—both measures used by a number of capitalist nations—are avoided in America because they smack of "socialism." [*]

the problem of military power

There remains, however, one vast problem to which neither of the preceding suggestions directly applies. It is the question of the relationship of capitalism to the rise of an American military state.

Is militarism itself a specifically capitalist phenomenon? The evidence of history would hardly indicate as much. There have been pacific capitalisms (Sweden, Switzerland) and aggressive ones (prewar Germany, postwar United States); and the actions of the Soviet Union and China are enough to indicate that capitalism has no monopoly on international violence.

There is no doubt that American capitalism during the 1950s and 1960s felt impelled to police the world. In those decades the United States intervened in Lebanon, the Dominican Republic, Cuba, South Vietnam, Cambodia, and Laos; clandestinely overthrew at least one government (Guatemala), and probably another (Iran), and contributed to the demise of a third (Chile); actively supported repressive right-wing regimes in

---

[9] Quoted in Daniel Bell, *Marxian Socialism in the United States* (Princeton, N.J.: Princeton University Press, 1967), p. 4.

[*] The political scientist Robert A. Dahl has written that Americans are "half colorblind" when they think about such problems as how to control giant corporations. "An important reason," he writes, "is that our history has left us without a socialist tradition. . . . The consequence, I think, is a serious limit to our capacity for clearheaded consideration of how economic enterprises should be governed. Because we have no socialist tradition, our debates about economic institutions nearly always leave some major alternatives— chiefly 'socialist' alternatives—unexplored." (*After the Revolution?* New Haven: Yale University Press, 1970, p. 119).

Greece and Brazil; entered into a worldwide system of secret military arrangements; and "showed the flag" on a total of at least fifty occasions.

Whence derived this military commitment? The answer is not easy to give. In part, it lay in a genuine fear of postwar Soviet intentions, hardly reassured by Russia's general truculence, by its walling off of East Berlin, and by its anticapitalist rhetoric. Yet, compared with the reaction of many European nations, the American response to these threats was exaggerated —indeed, so exaggerated that it undoubtedly helped to provoke the very Soviet (and later Chinese) belligerence by which Americans could then justify their uncompromising stand.

The sources of this American response were many: clergymen who equated the rise of communism with the anti-Christ and who stirred the fears of fundamentalist religious groups; labor unions whose anticommunist feelings reached such irrational levels that longshoremen refused to unload Polish merchandise at the very time that Poland was trying to break away from the Soviet bloc; veterans' organizations to whom patriotism meant an uncritical support of American "might"; congressmen who subscribed to the belief that America must defend "freedom" everywhere, except perhaps for selected members of their own constituencies; military leaders who gradually enlarged the conception of American "defense" to the ability to wage two major wars and one minor war *simultaneously;* industrial circles for whom the arms economy provided a seemingly inexhaustible source of revenue; high government officials who saw America as the world's bulwark against "international communism," even after international communism had dissolved into mutually hostile nation-states; intellectuals and professors who applied the cool logic of "maximizing" national security but never questioned the premises on which security might be based.

In this multiplicity of causes, each of which has played its part in the American anticommunist stance, the role of "capitalism" is both central and elusive. Certainly, capitalism all over the world has felt itself menaced by the rise of powerful socialist governments in Russia and China and the prospect of revolutionary socialism in the underdeveloped areas, much as the Catholic Church once felt menaced by the rise of Protestantism, or the British aristocracy by the rise of democracy in France. Yet, as we know, Catholicism made its peace with Protestantism—differently, to be sure, in different countries—and the aristocracies made their peace with democracy —also differently in different countries. That private property and the market mechanism can also make peace with public property and planning seems equally evident—but that, too, will take place differently in different countries.

In many capitalist nations, that process of peacemaking seems now far advanced. Various capitalist nations have long carried on trade freely with Russia, have learned to invest in communist nations, and, while maintaining a healthy skepticism toward the national policies of these nations, have felt no need to mount an anticommunist crusade against them. Now, after the disastrous Indochinese War that was the price America paid for its blind anticommunism, the opportunity is open to us, too, to find a pragmatic mode of co-existence, and to become once again a citizen, and not the policeman, of the world.

WHAT SHOULD BE DONE?

If our discussion points to any conclusion, it is that we must seek to change many aspects of American capitalism in the direction that capitalism in other nations has indicated. This does not mean, of course, that America could or should set out to "copy" the achievements of other lands. Institutions, like good wines, do not always travel easily. We shall have to find our own ways of coping with the problems of health and the cities and national planning and the arts and pollution and education—ways that may take inspiration from foreign accomplishments, but that must in the end reflect our own ways of doing things.

the great disillusion As we enter the decade of the 1980s, the national mood does not seem propitious for attempts at social improvement. Disillusioned with two decades of trying to create a Great Society (in Lyndon Johnson's phrase), Americans are dismayed at the failure of crime to disappear, at the refusal of slums to go away, at the evidence of widespread welfare cheating, and the ubiquitous presence of government bureaucracy. They are equally irked at the payment of onerous taxes for purposes that seem to defy money expenditure—fed up with "throwing money at problems," as the saying goes.

Therefore the stage seems set for a period of relative inactivity on the social welfare front, a period of hiatus in the movement into a welfare state that has been our principal direction of change for at least half a century. Perhaps this pause will last a considerable period.

But I am inclined to think that the movement will resume once again, after a time. It is entirely possible, heretical though it may sound, that our failure to remedy social evils partly reflects the failure to throw *enough* money at them. A figure or two may give us thought in this regard. Over the decade 1965–1975 the federal government spent approximately $600 billion on armaments and $6 billion on public housing. Does anyone doubt that our cityscapes would look differently if we had spent as much on housing as on arms? Another example: in the mid-1970s we spent $10 billion a year for travel abroad and about $3.5 billion a year for "correctional facilities"—prisons. Can it be doubted that the condition of prisoners would have been significantly better had those two sums been reversed?

This is not to say, of course, that money carelessly spent will clear slums or that we know how to eradicate criminal tendencies in offenders. But at least it suggests that our present impatience with our "failures" in social improvement may arise from our doing too little rather than too much; and it further suggests that even a heavier level of taxation might be felt as less onerous than the present one, *if it were perceived as bringing useful and desirable social results.*

Figure 14–1 showing US tax collections as a percentage of GNP, compared with other nations of the world, makes us realize that we are a relatively "undersocialized" economy, and asks us to consider whether we may not eventually have to move toward a greater degree of social support.

I cannot predict whether the present skeptical and negative mood regarding government and social well-being will give way to a more positive attitude. Moreover, textbooks are not proper places for the expression of political sentiment. They are not improper places, however, in which to give vent to moral sentiments, provided these are properly identified. Hence, let me end our long discussion of the origins and character and problems and promise of our society by saying that I believe that American capitalism stands at the threshold of a crucial decade. For almost a generation, our society has been identified in the eyes of much of the world as a nation that is rich but indifferent; peace-loving in rhetoric but aggressive in behavior; boastful of its economic strength, blind to the misuse of that strength. Now the years are at hand in which that image—and the realities

Total Tax Revenues Expressed as a Percentage of Gross Domestic Product

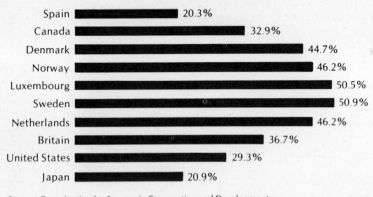

Spain	20.3%
Canada	32.9%
Denmark	44.7%
Norway	46.2%
Luxembourg	50.5%
Sweden	50.9%
Netherlands	46.2%
Britain	36.7%
United States	29.3%
Japan	20.9%

Source: Organization for Economic Cooperation and Development

FIGURE 14 · 1   TAXES AROUND THE WORLD, 1976

that are uncomfortably close to the image—can be changed. We will continue to be a rich nation; we must cease to be in so many ways a poor one. We will continue to be a powerful nation; we must learn the limits of our power. We will continue to be an economic colossus, but our economic system must now become the undergirding for a good society.

In view of our heritage, our traditions, our deeply rooted failings, this will not be an easy transformation for America to make. It may even prove to be an impossible one, although I strongly believe that this is not the case. But in any event, the all-important thing is to make the effort. The challenge is to change America today into a different and much better America tomorrow. In my view, this will be the most searching test of its character that American society has ever faced.

14	*A Last Word*

All the previous chapters offered summaries at the end—key words to be learned and concepts that an instructor is likely to hold you responsible for. Not this chapter. This is not so much a chapter to be "studied" as it is to be thought about. This time you must pose your own questions.

Index